PPP Design
and
Debugging

PPP Design and Debugging

James Carlson

ADDISON–WESLEY

An Imprint of Addison Wesley Longman, Inc.
Reading, Massachusetts • Harlow, England • Menlo Park, California
Berkeley, California • Don Mills, Ontario • Sydney
Bonn • Amsterdam • Tokyo • Mexico City

Many of the designations used by manufacturers and sellers to distinguish their products are claimed as trademarks. Where those designations appear in this book, and Addison Wesley was aware of a trademark claim, the designations have been printed in initial capital letters or all capital letters.

The author and publisher have taken care in preparation of this book, but make no expressed or implied warranty of any kind and assume no responsibility for errors or omissions. No liability is assumed for incidental or consequential damages in connection with or arising out of the use of the information or programs contained herein.

The publisher offers discounts on this book when ordered in quantity for special sales. For more information, please contact:

Corporate & Professional Publishing Group
Addison–Wesley Publishing Company
One Jacob Way
Reading, Massachusetts 01867

Library of Congress Cataloging-in-Publication Data

Carlson, James D.
      PPP design and debugging / James D. Carlson.
         p.   cm.
      Includes bibliographical references and index.
      ISBN 0-201-18539-3
      1. PPP (computer network protocol) I. Title.
TK5105.582C37 1997
004.6'2--dc21   97-41553
                                        CIP

ISBN 0-201-18539-3
Text printed on acid-free paper

1 2 3 4 5 6 7 8 9—MA—0100999897
First printing, December 1997

For

Beth and Madeline

Contents

Acknowledgments

Although this book has only one name on the cover, many people have contributed time, effort, and material toward its publication. First and foremost, I thank my wife, Beth, and our daughter, Madeline, for their patience and understanding during the months it has taken and for the lost hours every night and weekend.

Many reviewers and contributors made this book more readable, more complete, and more accurate than I ever expected. Thanks are due to Fred Baker, Paolo Bevilacqua, Miguel Cruz, Craig Estey, Gary Greenberg, Terrance Hodgins, J. S. Jensen, Frank Kastenholz, Patrick Klos, Al Longyear, Bill Melohn, John Nagle, Marc C. Poulin, Scott Reeve, Craig Richards, William Allen Simpson, Mike Taillon, and Andrew Valencia. A special thank-you goes to Vernon Schryver, who has gone above and beyond the call of duty as a reviewer to take the time to explain patiently many of the more esoteric ideas.

Special thanks are also due to the good folks at Addison–Wesley who have seen this project through: my editor, Mary Harrington; and executive editors Karen Gettman and Carol Long; and all of the artists, publicists, marketers, and other folks behind the scenes who get the job done.

Finally, thanks to Richard Stallman for all the tools and to Bay Networks for access to FrameMaker.

This book was written on AIX 4.1.4 using emacs-19.30 and xfig-3.1 for drawings, then composed in FrameMaker version 5 on SunOS 4.1.4. No PCs were harmed during the production of this work.

Chapter

1

Introduction

I hate quotations. Tell me what you know.

—Ralph Waldo Emerson

IN THIS CHAPTER

When most users today think of Point-to-Point Protocol (PPP), they probably think of personal computers (PCs), modems, and surfing the Internet. PPP, though, is a much broader protocol that is used to transfer data among diverse kinds of computers and computing systems, such as routers, satellites, and mainframes. This one protocol has the ability to span from the lowest to the highest data rates in use and is compatible with almost every networking technology ever developed.

This book covers PPP from the bits and bytes transmitted up through the connections to other networking software. Along the way, it gives guidance in the often confusing array of standards documents and tips for debugging PPP connections and implementations.

It does not give specific details on particular interfaces, such as modem drivers, since these are both quite numerous and also well covered in other books. Nor does it pretend to replace the "Request For Comments" documents (RFCs), as these are both easily available and very detailed. Instead, this book works as a companion alongside the operating system reference works of your choosing and the public documents.

There have been several waves of advancement in computing techniques, though these advances have hardly been linear. In fact, the pattern for most of these advances is quite regular, and repeats often. The first advancements are often made by the mainframe computer users. Then these are either rediscovered or borrowed by minicomputer users and, finally, by microcomputer users. Each generation leaves its own mark on the technology, but the pattern remains the same.

The history of machine-to-machine communication is similar to the development of computing in general. Mainframe communications (primarily the International Standards Organization's (ISO's) X.25 and International Business

Machine's (IBM's) Systems Network Architecture (SNA)) developed many of the concepts important to networking in general, such as routing and layering, in the 1960s. This technology was reinvented by the minicomputer users in the 1970s as TCP/IP (Transmission Control Protocol/Internet Protocol) and XNS (Xerox Network Systems), and once more in the 1980s by the microcomputer users as IPX (Internet Packet Exchange; actually just a copy of XNS) and AppleTalk. Of course, not all of these developments are equal, and both X.25, which is limited to a few media types, and IPX, which is used with only a minority of operating systems, are falling from favor as TCP/IP and the global Internet gain ground.

For most Unix computers, this communication began with a series of protocols called UUCP (Unix-to-Unix Copy), which eventually developed into a robust and widespread automatic file and electronic mail (email) transfer protocol. Much of what people now refer to as "the Internet," including the bulletin board–like news groups known as "usenet" and email, was actually developed using this automated file transfer protocol.

For small computers, communication began with file transfer protocols, like Ward Christiansen's X Modem. This simple protocol allowed two computers to exchange a single file at a time using a simplex protocol. Later innovations, like Chuck Forsberg's Z Modem, extended this idea for higher speed by omitting the positive acknowledgments used in a traditional simplex protocol and reporting only negative acknowledgments, at the expense of protocol resilience in the face of congestion and buffering.

At the same time, others were developing protocols for both the new PCs and larger computers, like Kermit and BLAST (Blocked Asynchronous Transmission), that borrowed the networking concept of *windowing*. Windowing permits a set number of acknowledgments to remain outstanding at a given time, thus mitigating the effects of transmission buffering, latency, and occasional data corruption. Notably among these, Columbia University's Kermit also permitted remote execution of commands via extensions to the file transfer protocol.

All of these file transfer protocols are asymmetric. One side, usually called a *client*, requests actions, such as the transferring of a file, and the other side, called a *server*, performs the requested actions. This design is therefore known as *client/server*.

Meanwhile, in the Unix world, TCP/IP began gaining ground against the file transfer protocols faster than the supporting telecommunications technologies developed. Although 3MB and then 10MB Ethernets were available for local networks, the primary means of communicating over distance was through the use of primitive modems. To make use of these, a simple protocol called SLIP (Serial Line Internet Protocol) was developed at the University of California at Berkeley. This protocol is easily described by saying that a raw IP datagram is first expanded by replacing any byte equal to hexadecimal C0 with the sequence DB DC and any byte equal to DB with DB DD; then it is transmitted with C0 at either end as framing.

This process is easily reversed at the other end of the link, and if the data are ever corrupted, synchronization can always be achieved by looking for the next C0, since this will never occur in the user's data. RFC 1055, which documents SLIP, is only six pages long. Also note that this protocol requires a hardware link that can transmit arbitrary 8-bit bytes without modification.

SLIP's architecture is fundamentally different from the file transfer protocols developed on microcomputers and others in use on minicomputers running Unix. First, notice that it is not at all obvious from the description given how one would send email over it, or even transfer a file between two computers, even though the description given is complete. With SLIP, all that you are given is a means to transmit packets from one computer to another over a serial line.

In the networking world, this difference is called *layering*. In the old file transfer programs, the definitions of the protocols included such things as detecting the start of the data, detecting errors, and signaling the file name to the receiver all in the same protocol. With networking, there are instead application programs (such as file transfer) that use the services of transport protocols (such as TCP), which in turn run on network protocols (such as IP), and finally on top of link-level protocols (such as SLIP). Each of these protocols is separate and is described in a separate document.

There are many advantages to this technique, including the ability to use old applications on the latest network devices and the ability to develop and migrate between networking protocols and applications without disturbing the link layer. This means that the design and development of each part of the system can continue independently, unlike with more primitive file transfer protocols, which required a complete rewrite to support enhanced error-control algorithms or new media types.

Notice also that unlike the client/server file transfer protocols, SLIP is inherently symmetric. Neither side is defined to be the client or the server. Such protocols, are termed *peer-to-peer*, since both sides of the link are equal parties to the conversation and both may request and perform actions.

PPP owes much to SLIP, although it also uses transmission techniques developed for mainframes. The marketplace for dial-up Internet connectivity, which has driven much of the development work on PPP, would not exist if it were not for SLIP, and many of the important algorithms in use with PPP were first developed for SLIP.

Unlike many of the other so-called standards of the microcomputer and minicomputer world, including SLIP, PPP was developed by a standards body. The Internet Engineering Task Force (IETF), which has guided PPP development, is made up of representatives from industry, telecommunications, academia, and user groups. It is an open group; anyone with an interest in setting the standards is free to participate.

The rules of the IETF are a little different from other standards bodies, such as the International Telecommunications Union (ITU) and the International Standards Organization (ISO). The IETF has fostered a culture in which it is far more important to produce a working protocol than it is to produce documents with which all participants agree. Unlike the other standards bodies, IETF participants commonly discuss their prototype implementations and experimental results at the same time the protocols are being written.

This environment produces specifications that are usually rather brief but very dense in subject matter and documentation that is scattered among a large number of documents that do not necessarily refer to each other. It also occasionally produces experiments that turn out to be dead ends. One of the aims of this book is to tie all of these documents together for PPP and illustrate some of the important but unwritten concepts.

PPP, like all other network protocols, exists as a layer between two other layers of the protocol stack. Below it is the hardware interface, which must be some kind of bidirectional data stream, and above it are the network-layer protocols, such as IP and IPX. These are illustrated diagrammatically in Figure 1.1.

PPP borrows part of high-level data link control (HDLC) from the telecommunications world for its low-level interface, though it restricts the feature set usable in a conforming implementation, and it extends the protocol to run over asynchronous serial lines. In running over serial lines, it borrows SLIP's "escape" mechanism, which is also common in the old file transfer programs like Z Modem and Kermit, and allows it to run on hardware that cannot properly deal with certain byte sequences. It does not, though, go so far as to define sequences that would allow it to be run on hardware that cannot transfer full 8-bit bytes, as do Kermit and Z Modem.

Thus, on the hardware interface, we have this set of features and limitations for synchronous lines:

- Can be used with standard HDLC controllers.

- Defined only for point-to-point links; any kind of multidrop usage is a proprietary extension due to address restrictions.

- Can coexist with other HDLC-based protocols on the same link only if the other protocols are restricted in address usage.

For asynchronous lines, we have this set of features and limitations:

- Can be run on lines that use software flow control and are unable to transfer some binary values.

- Cannot be run on lines that do not support full 8-bit bytes without proprietary extensions.

- Defines error-detection mechanisms that are as strong as those used by HDLC.

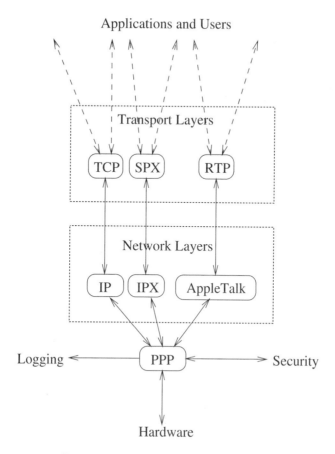

Figure 1.1: NETWORK LAYERING WITH PPP

For the network-layer protocols, PPP presents a packet-oriented interface, and it can provide sequencing and reliability if needed.

PPP also connects to the world through relationships with certain applications that provide services for PPP in an implementation-dependent manner. For instance, a dial-up communications server may need to use RADIUS (Remote Authentication Dial-In User Service), TACACS (Terminal Access Controller Access Control System), or ACP (Access Control Protocol) to verify the dial-up peer's identity or obtain network addresses for negotiation. It also may have relationships with logging devices, to track errors, and with encryption key servers, for secure communications.

Throughout this book, data values are given in hexadecimal unless otherwise noted. Equivalences for these values in decimal and octal are given in Appendix D.

2

PPP Communication Basics

IN THIS CHAPTER

This chapter provides all of the background necessary to read the rest of this book. In it, we will cover the link-level details for transmission and reception of PPP data, some system design issues, and the general model for PPP operation. Subsequent chapters go into detail on each protocol within PPP and on variant forms of transmission. Remember that all values are in hexadecimal unless otherwise noted.

How PPP Fits In

Figure 2.1 shows how a PPP implementation might be connected in a system using TCP/IP. PPP works at the network interface level and is similar to Ethernet in capabilities. Note that since PPP is not a broadcast interface, Address Resolution Protocol (ARP) does not run over it. Some implementations, though, emulate an Ethernet via PPP and require special tests to generate fake ARP replies.

Media

PPP runs on virtually all media that are full duplex in nature and can be modified to run on some that are half duplex.

The two principal means of communication on serial lines are *synchronous* and *asynchronous*. Asynchronous line hardware, usually called a UART (Universal Asynchronous Receiver/Transmitter), can send and receive one character at a time.

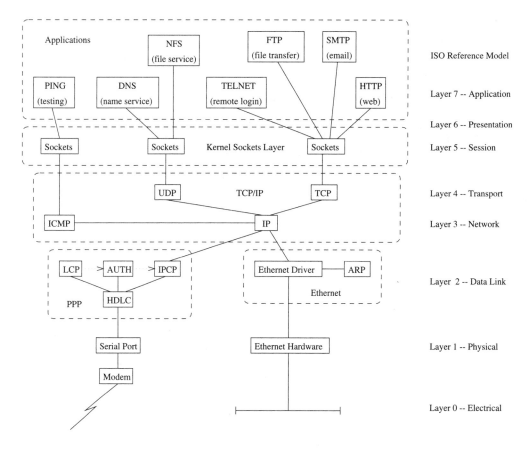

Figure 2.1: PPP IN A COMPLETE SYSTEM

Synchronous line hardware, sometimes called a USART or framer, can send or receive a variable-length block of bytes at one time. These two techniques are used over a wide variety of electrical interfaces. A few of these (all full duplex) are:

- EIA RS-232, an electrical and cabling standard that has little to say about the bit-level protocols run on it. It uses the familiar D-shaped 25-pin connectors (or sometimes the 9-pin variant found on PCs). Traditionally, RS-232 is used to carry asynchronous serial traffic, like the connection from a PC to a modem. On some equipment, RS-232 is used for synchronous data. The standard allows for data rates through 9600bps, but common implementations run as fast as 230.4Kbps for short runs.

- RS-422, a lower-voltage and higher-speed cabling standard similar in many respects to RS-232.

- RS-485, a multidrop version of RS-422. PPP requires proprietary, although obvious and simple, modifications to run point-to-point in a multidrop system.

- V.35, a common interface used for synchronous lines over short distances from 9600bps (DS0-B) up through 2Mbps (E1).

- BRI S/T, one of the ISDN (Integrated Services Digital Network) interfaces. It is a four-wire interface and is usually used with RJ-45 connectors (which are similar to but wider than the RJ-11 modular jacks used with standard household telephone wiring) and runs two synchronous channels at 64Kbps each plus a third at 16Kbps.

- T1/E1, standard telecommunications interfaces. Both are synchronous and are implemented using many different types of electrical and optical interfaces. T1 (used in the U.S., Canada, Japan, Hong Kong, and Taiwan) runs at 1.544Mbps with at most 1.536Mbps available for user data. E1 (used in most of the rest of the world) runs at 2.048Mbps with 1.984Mbps available.

- OC-3, an optical telecommunications standard that runs at 155.52Mbps with 149.76Mbps available to PPP.

- Frame Relay, X.25, AAL-5, FUNI, all telecommunications software interfaces. In the case of PPP over Frame Relay (RFC 1973), little more than a modification of the standard PPP address and control fields is necessary. The others, like RFC 1598 PPP in X.25, are a bit more complex since they offer more services, but all share the same basic design and use hex CF as a frame type (Network Layer Protocol ID [NLPID]) to identify PPP.

A wide variety of other standards may come into play when working with PPP, depending on the hardware in use. For instance, modern modems implement V.42bis for data compression, V.42 for error correction, V.34 for the actual modulation, and V.8 for negotiation. On some hosts, there are also interface standards that must be followed. For instance, on PCs running Microsoft software, a standard known as *plug and play* is used for communicating with hardware, such as modems. (See Chapter 8 for references to other books that may be helpful in understanding these other standards.)

Some serial hardware is notoriously deficient. For instance, the DIN connector serial port on old Macintosh computers does not carry Data Carrier Detect (DCD). This means that PPP implementations on these machines must go to great lengths to detect lost connections by other means, such as using Link Control Protocol (LCP) Echo-Requests. This book does describe these mechanisms but does not give a comprehensive list of all such broken hardware or all possible work-arounds. These are issues that particular implementations may have to deal with.

HDLC

PPP is built atop a restricted subset of the standard HDLC protocol, so a description of that protocol's features will be helpful. HDLC operates conceptually in two stages, frame formation followed by medium-dependent frame transmission, although typical implementations mix these two together for efficiency.

Taking frame formation first, an HDLC frame consists of three variable-length fields and one fixed-length field (Figure 2.2). The fixed-length check value is usually a standard cyclic redundancy check (CRC) over the preceding three fields and occupies the last two or four octets. Putting this value last allows optimized generation of the CRC in most implementations, as we will see later. Oddly, though, this number is transmitted least significant octet first, also known as *little-endian*, even though all other networking values are normally *big-endian*.

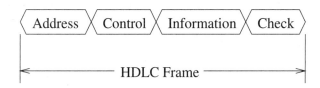

Figure 2.2: HDLC FRAME

The address and control fields are each single integers of variable length. The HDLC protocol reserves the least significant bit (LSB) as a flag (called *Poll/Final*) to indicate whether more octets follow; a zero bit means that more octets follow, and a one bit indicates the last octet. For example, the decimal value 533 (hex 215) would be sent as an HDLC-encoded integer as the sequence 08 2B, formed as shown in Figure 2.3. Of course, all sequences of the form 00 . . . 00 08 2B are equivalent, since leading zeroes do not change the value of the number. In practice, though, these zeroes are usually not sent.

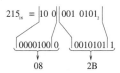

Figure 2.3: HDLC INTEGER

The address field is intended for multidrop links, so the devices on the link need only examine the first N octets, up to the first with an LSB of one, in order to identify frames intended for that device. Decimal address 127 (encoded as FF) is reserved to mean "all-stations" or "broadcast." The control field specifies a type of message. Its primary purpose is to distinguish frames used for error and flow control when using higher-level protocols such as Link Access Procedure–Balanced (LAP-B).

The HDLC information field consists simply of all octets following the control field and preceding the check value. Its contents depend on the application used but are generally filled with user data.

Since PPP uses standard HDLC medium-dependent frame transmission, this will be discussed after the following section on PPP's use of HDLC. (For more information on HDLC itself, see ISO 3309 and 4335.)

HDLC and PPP

PPP restricts its use of the general HDLC protocol in the following ways, as described in RFC 1662:

- HDLC address field is fixed to the octet FF (all stations).
- HDLC control field is fixed to the octet 03 (unnumbered-information).
- The receiver must be prepared to accept an HDLC information field of 1502 octets.

A device using PPP may accept the variable-length HDLC integer fields, but any interoperable implementation must default to transmitting only the values above. (These values will vary, however, if RFC 1663 "reliable transmission," also known as "numbered mode," is used. See Chapter 3.)

PPP also adds a third variable-length HDLC-like integer at the start of the HDLC information field (immediately following the control value). However, to cause all values that follow to fall on four-octet (32-bit) boundaries, this value is constrained to a two-octet representation by default, including a zero-octet pad if necessary. (Occasionally, some system architectures permit faster operation if data are kept on even boundaries. This is why alignment is always considered when protocol headers are designed.)

Although this protocol field very much resembles the other HDLC integer values, the PPP specification avoids describing the encoding and decoding process by simply declaring and using all values in their encoded form. Thus, for example, you will read of HEX protocol 00 21 (IP) for PPP, instead of protocol (decimal) 16, as you might for other HDLC protocols. The lack of this encoding description is a hazard for the unwary designer who does not read section 2 of RFC 1661 carefully when assigning new protocol numbers. (In fact, such an error was made during the design of the Shiva Password Authentication Protocol (SPAP) security protocol, and the protocol number had to be reassigned after the implementation was in the field. Such errors are very difficult to correct.)

PPP's information field, as defined by RFC 1661, follows this PPP protocol field. From now on we will refer only to PPP's information field, and not the HDLC information field, which also includes the PPP protocol field. The final structure is shown in Figure 2.4.

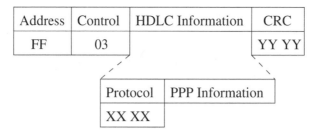

Figure 2.4: PPP FRAME FORMAT

Framing

PPP declares three standard framing techniques for use with various media. These are all documented in RFC 1662 and are referred to as asynchronous HDLC (AHDLC), bit-synchronous HDLC, and octet-synchronous HDLC.

AHDLC

AHDLC is used for all asynchronous lines, such as modems used on ordinary PCs. PPP's AHDLC makes use of two special octet values, which are 7E and 7D in hexadecimal. These are similar in PPP's usage to the C0 and DB values used in SLIP and are never found in any of the transmitted user data. The 7E value is a frame delimiter, which marks the end of a frame and the beginning of another. The 7D value is an escape character, to be interpreted by the receiver as a signal to form the next actual decoded octet value in the HDLC frame as an exclusive-OR between the next transmitted octet and the fixed value 20. For example, the value 7E in the user data would be sent as 7D 5E.

Since 7D is the only character-escape mechanism defined and no value below 80 can be transformed into a value over 80 by an exclusive-OR with the value 20, this implies that asynchronous PPP cannot run on any link that does not transfer 8-bit values. For instance, an asynchronous line set to 7 bits with even parity (a standard setting on old Unix systems) will destroy the value of the most significant bit. PPP cannot recover from this kind of configuration error, though many implementations can detect the problem and report it to an administrator.

By default, all values between 00 and 1F (inclusive) plus the values 7D and 7E are escaped by the transmitter when sending the PPP frame. The transmitter may also escape 7F, FF, and 80 through 9F at its option.

As transmitted, an example PPP frame that looks like Figure 2.5 (ignore the information field contents for the moment) will look like this on the serial link:

```
7E FF 7D 23 C0 21 7D 21 7D 21 7D 20 7D 2E 7D 22 7D 26 7D 20
7D 20 7D 20 7D 20 7D 27 7D 22 7D 28 7D 22 70 34 7E
```

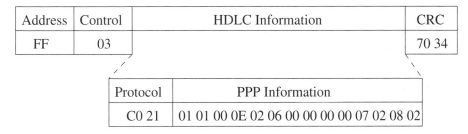

Figure 2.5: EXAMPLE PPP FRAME

Several things should be noted here. First the data transmitted waste a significant amount of time sending escape codes. Second, the CRC is performed on the original data, not the escape codes, and is itself escaped if necessary.

The initial 7E is optional here, but decent implementations will send it if the previous frame is not immediately back-to-back with this frame. This technique improves reliability with naturally bursty network traffic on links with random errors by discarding what is likely to be just interframe noise, rather than treating it as part of the next transmitted packet.

A possible output routine for PPP frames could do the two octet-oriented operations, escaping and CRC generation, at once in a procedure like the following. (This example, as well as the other coding examples in the text of this book, is intended only to illustrate the main ideas. It is not written in any particular machine-readable language. There are C code examples of these same routines in Appendix A.)

```
send initial 7E                              (mark frame start)
while (frames in output queue) do

  get next frame to send from queue

  set CRCvalue to FFFF
  while (octets left in current frame) do    (send frame)
    get next octet as "value"
    recalculate CRCvalue based on value
    if value less than 20 or value is 7D or value is 7E then
        send 7D
        set value to value XOR 20
    endif
    send value
  enddo ; go do next octet

  set value to low-order octet of CRCvalue   (send CRC)
  if value less than 20 or value is 7D or value is 7E then
```

```
    send 7D
    set value to value XOR 20
  endif
  send value

  set value to high-order octet of CRCvalue  (send CRC)
  if value less than 20 or value is 7D or value is 7E then
    send 7D
    set value to value XOR 20
  endif
  send value

  send 7E                                   (mark frame end)

enddo ; go do next frame
```

See RFC 1661 for the standard CRC-16 procedure used in PPP.

This description of AHDLC escaping is incomplete. See Chapter 3 for the Asynchronous Control Character Map (ACCM) parameter, that allows this escaping to be mostly disabled on links that can safely handle some or all of the values in the range 00 to 1F.

On input, this data stream can be decoded with a rather simple state machine, which looks something like this:

```
set escaped to FALSE
set datapointer to start of receive buffer
set CRCvalue to FFFF
set octetcount to 0
while (link is attached) do
 get next input octet as "value"        (get input)
 if value less than 20 then
   discard value
   continue with next octet
 endif
 if escaped then                        (handle escaping)
   set escaped to FALSE
   if value is 7E then
     ; silently discard (RFC 1134)
     set datapointer to start of receive buffer
     set CRCvalue to FFFF
     set octetcount to 0
```

```
            continue with next octet
        endif
        set value to value XOR 20
    else if value is 7E then                    (handle frame end)
        if CRCvalue is F0B8 then
            remove last two octets in buffer (CRC)
            deliver HDLC frame in buffer
        else if octetcount greater than 3 then
            signal receive CRC error
        endif
        set datapointer to start of receive buffer
        set CRCvalue to FFFF
        set octetcount to 0
        continue with next octet
    else if value is 7D then
        set escaped to TRUE
        continue with next octet
    endif
    if octetcount greater than or equal to buffer size then
        signal receive error
        set datapointer to start of receive buffer
        set CRCvalue to FFFF
        set octetcount to 0
    else                                        (store received data)
        recalculate CRCvalue based on value
        store value at datapointer
        advance datapointer
        increment octetcount
    endif
enddo
```

Again, this description is somewhat incomplete. See the ACCM discussion for modifications to this procedure for different transparency modes and Appendix A for a C language implementation.

Although the PPP specification and the examples above describe escaping only the so-called ASCII control characters, 00 to 1F, and the framing characters 7D and 7E, any source character may be escaped other than 5E and any other character already being escaped XOR 20, since the result of escaping these would be 7D followed by an illegal value. For example, escaping 5E would give 7D 7E, which should be interpreted as a "discard-frame" signal, and escaping 21 would give 7D 01, which is itself normally escaped before transmission.

For another example, to run PPP over rlogin, which cannot pass 8-bit data cleanly due to the "window size change" sequence[1], an implementation of PPP may legally elect to escape additionally FF as 7D DF. All conforming PPP clients must be able to decode correctly any escaped characters received at any time, regardless of the negotiated ACCM. The sender need not inform the recipient which values will be escaped.

Escaping of characters outside the range 00 to 1F is not negotiated by the standard PPP protocol. Doing this typically requires administrator controls to set the list of escaped characters, such as with the "escape" keyword in the freely available "pppd" implementation.

AHDLC and Flow Control

AHDLC links often employ flow control, either in-band (XON/XOFF, typically 11 [ASCII DC1] and 13 [ASCII DC3]) or out-of-band (RTS/CTS, or, in rare cases, DTR/DSR). For in-band flow control, the flow control characters appear at arbitrary locations in the data stream. The receiver must discard these characters after modifying the flow control state (stopping or starting its own transmit process) and must not include them in any part of the received data or CRC calculation, and the transmitter must always escape the characters also used for flow control if they appear in the transmitted HDLC frame.

Often the removal of these characters from the input data stream and the handling of flow control happens automatically in a low-level serial driver. PPP's handling of escaping integrates well with almost any in-band flow control implementation, since removal or insertion of these escaped characters is ignored by PPP.

For users monitoring the data, this situation adds the complication that they must ignore these values when they are present in the data stream. They are not part of the PPP data. Negotiation of the ACCM, though, will alter this situation, and users must follow these negotiations to know which characters are ignored and which are data.

Out-of-band flow control uses separate hardware signals, such as Request to Send (RTS) and Clear to Send (CTS) in RS-232, to signal when transmit and receive are possible. For most systems, this action is transparent for PPP and presents no additional complications, though it does require two more wires than in-band flow control and some hardware support logic.

---

1. BSD rlogin protocol defines a special character sequence (FF FF 73 73) indicating that the terminal window size is being changed by the user and that the new size in binary follows in the data stream. This sequence was chosen as "unlikely" to be typed by a human user. Of course, PPP is not a human user and may accidentally trigger this feature, causing packet loss or even connection failure. Escaping FF when running PPP over rlogin avoids this problem.

Bit-Synchronous HDLC

Bit-synchronous HDLC is used on most telecommunications interfaces for PPP, such as "switched 56," T1, and most ISDN links. Unlike AHDLC, it is commonly implemented in hardware devices that do the framing and CRC work, there are no escape characters used, and there is no flow control. Instead, all of the work is done at the bit level. Using the same PPP message as in the AHDLC example (Figure 2.5), we have the following data in binary format (note that HDLC transmits LSB first, so all of the octets appear to be written backward):

```
11111111 11000000 00000011 10000100 10000000 10000000 00000000
01110000 01000000 01100000 00000000 00000000 00000000 00000000
11100000 01000000 00010000 01000000 00001110 00101100
```

HDLC will frame these data for transmission by inserting a zero bit after any run of five consecutive data bits set to one. This distinguishes the user data from the HDLC end-of-frame mark, which is 01111110 in binary, or a run of six ones, which cannot by definition be part of the encoded user data. After framing and this "bit stuffing," the above data become:

```
01111110 11111S11 111S0000 00000000 11100001 00100000 00100000
00000000 00011100 00010000 00011000 00000000 00000000 00000000
00000000 00111000 00010000 00000100 00010000 00000011 10001011
00011111 10
```

where S bits above are the zero bits "stuffed" into the user data. Of course, the octet boundaries are now meaningless, and this is just a stream of bits.

The receiver can easily decode this stream by counting consecutive ones. If this counter reaches five and the next bit is a zero, then that zero is an S bit and should be deleted. If this bit is one, the frame is complete.

An additional complication for the user who is decoding synchronous traffic is that many interfaces use only a subset of the bits on the wire. For instance, in an ISDN data-over-speech-bearer-service (DOSBS) application in the United States, the bits are presented from the hardware as 8 bits per sample at 8000 samples per second, but with the last bit in each octet possibly destroyed due to bit-robbed signaling. For voice applications, this limitation destroys only the least significant bit in some samples and adds some noise to the audio, since pulse-code-modulated (PCM) audio data are sent MSB first.

For PPP, though, this means that the data must be sent in 7-bit chunks with a dummy bit inserted after each chunk, which restricts the usable data rate from $8*8000 = 64000$ down to $7*8000 = 56000$ bits per second. Continuing with the above example, this same frame might, depending on the sender's initial bit alignment, be sent as:

```
0111111X 011111SX 11111S0X 0000000X 0000111X 0000100X
1000000X 0100000X 0000000X 0000111X 0000010X 0000001X
1000000X 0000000X 0000000X 0000000X 0000000X 0001110X
0000010X 0000000X 0100000X 1000000X 0000111X 0001011X
0001111X 110...
```

Or, reversing the bits and converting back to hex:

```
7E 3E 1F 00 70 10 01 02 00 70 20 40 01 00 00 00 00 38 20 00
02 01 70 68 78 03
```

Operating over fractional T1 is still more complex, since each T1 frame of 193 bits will contain some number of possibly noncontiguous 7 or 8-bit samples that must be extracted and concatenated to reconstruct the transmitted HDLC bit stream.

Octet-Synchronous HDLC

The third encapsulation technique, octet synchronous, is relatively rare. RFC 1662 simply describes this technique as an option, and RFC 1618 goes so far as to describe this as the "recommended" way of communicating over ISDN links, though not the default. In fact, all ISDN equipment in existence that uses PPP does bit-synchronous, not octet-synchronous framing since the former is far more efficient when implemented in hardware and reduces the system overhead to simply per-packet handling rather than per-octet processing for escape characters.

Octet-synchronous framing is essentially identical to AHDLC, with the same escape and framing codes. The only significant difference is that the ASCII control characters need not be escaped.

This technique is used on special media that present a buffer-oriented, rather than bit-oriented or octet-oriented, default hardware interface. RFC 1619 describes the only current such interface, which is the Synchronous Optical Network (SONET) and Synchronous Digital Hierarchy (SDH) family of media. One example member of this family is the SONET STS-3c interface, which provides a block of 9 by 260 octets at a rate of 8000 blocks per second, or 149.76 million bits per second usable out of a 155.52Mbps stream. The actual frames are located by row within the block but may span blocks. Some special values may be escaped to avoid undesirable data patterns, and 32-bit CRCs should be negotiated for use on high-volume links like this.

Despite the name, SONET and SDH can run over a variety of physical media, including various types of optical fiber, as well as cable television–grade coaxial cable. All of these interfaces run at very high speeds, generally a multiple of 51.840 million bits per second.

On these media, ATM (Asynchronous Transfer Mode) is a competitor to PPP. A great deal of effort has been spent developing specialized implementations of some of the ATM layers in hardware, while PPP implementations usually depend on general-purpose processor (CPU) speed.

Currently, three configurations are possible for these media with ATM and PPP:

1. PPP may be run directly over SONET/SDH.
2. Networking protocols may be run over ATM Adaptation Layer-5 (AAL-5) on SONET/SDH using Multi-Protocol Over ATM (MPOA) or Local Area Network Emulation (LANE).
3. PPP may be run over ATM virtual circuits using AAL-5 or Frame User Network Interface (FUNI).

Each solution may make sense in some particular set of circumstances. Usually the primary consideration is either compatibility with some set of existing equipment or network policy decisions. For instance, some carriers may offer ATM access priced above or below point-to-point optical links, and this kind of recurring charge, rather than the relative technical merits, can have a dramatic effect on the technology chosen.

Other Encapsulations

PPP runs over many other media types, such as Frame Relay (RFC 1973) and X.25 (RFC 1598). These encapsulations are mostly enhancements to the transmission methods already described. For instance, Frame Relay uses the HDLC Address field to direct traffic in a packet-switched environment, but it uses the same bit-synchronous HDLC format already described. These encapsulations impose additional restrictions on the options which may be negotiated. In particular, the Address and Control fields must not be negotiated away.

Translation

It is possible to translate between any two of the three forms of HDLC framing. Of course, translating between octet-synchronous and AHDLC, which are nearly identical, is rather trivial. The only serious concern would be the need for the octet-synchronous system to respect the additional transparency rules for AHDLC.

Translating between bit-synchronous and AHDLC is more interesting. Such a device will need to eavesdrop on the negotiation to discover which characters the remote system wishes to remove from the transparency rules (see ACCM in Chapter 3) and will need to perform the necessary octet escaping. In order to make this work, any system that supports bit-synchronous HDLC must accept the asynchronous ACCM option and acknowledge any value, but it must not escape any characters.

This kind of translation is popular for ISDN interfaces to personal computers. PCs usually are not equipped with the necessary synchronous hardware, and the software implementations of PPP found on PCs generally do not support such hardware, but these machines usually do have high-speed asynchronous ports. An ISDN Terminal Adapter (TA) can attach to the asynchronous port on a PC and place an ISDN call to a system running bit-synchronous PPP without user intervention. Examples of such TAs are the Motorola BitSurfr and the USR Courier I-Modem. These devices often go far beyond simple translation and offer additional PPP protocols like Multilink PPP (MP) and Compression Control Protocol (CCP). Doing this requires extensive processing of the PPP data during negotiation, such as adding a Maximum Reconstructed Receive Unit (MRRU) option to the LCP Configure-Request message as it passes by and to make things like security on multiple links for MP work transparently.

Statistics and Management

In addition to the standard SNMP MIB-2 objects for serial lines, a PPP implementation may include RFCs 1471 (LCP and LQM), 1472 (PAP and CHAP security), 1473 (IPCP), and 1474 (bridging). These Management Information Bases (MIBs) provide both statistics on the operation of PPP and, in some implementations, can control configuration.

Because PPP is often connected to external databases for authentication and user profile management, the configuration control options of these MIBs are not always able to set PPP variables.

Auto-Detecting

When a fixed set of protocols is expected to be used over a point-to-point link (for example, in a dial-up access device), it is sometimes convenient to discriminate the protocol in use by the peer automatically. This process is variously known as *auto-detecting* and *sniffing*.

Of course, the expected protocols depend on both the link level medium and the population of devices at the other end of the link. In this section, we will consider two scenarios, one in an asynchronous environment and one in a synchronous environment, which will illustrate the important ideas. None of these techniques is perfectly reliable in all situations since they rely on finding patterns in expected data and on timing. Systems that implement these detection algorithms should also have a means to disable their use.

Asynchronous Auto-Detect

In an asynchronous implementation, two forms of information are available: data patterns and timing. We will first consider the data patterns. Let us assume that we are implementing a device that can handle PPP, AppleTalk Remote Access Protocol (ARAP) versions 1 and 2, and SLIP, and that it is possible to read raw input data without alteration.

The initial packet from PPP is always a Link Control Protocol (LCP) frame (see the next chapter for details). This frame has one of these forms, depending on escaping configuration:

```
7E FF 03 C0 21 ...
7E FF 7D 23 C0 21 ...
7E 7D DF 7D 23 C0 21 ...
7E 7D DF 03 C0 21 ...
```

It is possible that an auto-detect routine could use the next two octets as well, which must be 01 01 for Configure-Request, although practice suggests that this is unnecessary.

SLIP and ARAP do not negotiate like PPP, but they do have known formats that allow their detection. These formats are:

```
SLIP:            C0 45 ...
ARAPv1:          16 10 02 ...
ARAPv2:          01 1B 02 ...
```

One possible way to build a detection routine would be to build a table containing each of these sequences and to run a state machine to recognize any of the given forms. At this point, though, it is a good idea to take a step back and consider the timing information available.

Reasonable implementations of either SLIP or PPP may have a delay between the initial 7E or C0 and the rest of the data, since this may actually be the trailing framing character from a previous (unrecognized) frame. However, no reasonable implementation should have a significant delay between characters midpacket. ARAP is even simpler, since the frame start and frame end characters are distinct.

Given this information, the following procedure suggests itself:

```
array of forms = list
  { FF 03 C0 21 }
  { FF 7D 23 C0 21 }
  { 7D DF 7D 23 C0 21 }
  { 7D DF 03 C0 21 }
  { 45 }
  { 16 10 02 }
  { 01 1B 02 }
listend
while (still in detect mode) do
```

```
set inter-character time-out
read until time-out keeping only first seven octets
if fewer than seven octets received then
  discard data read
  begin reading again
endif
set flag[0] through flag[6] to TRUE
if first octet read is 7E then
  set flag[4] through flag[6] to FALSE
  discard first octet
else if first octet is C0 then
  set flag[0] through flag[3] to FALSE
  set flag[5] through flag[6] to FALSE
  discard first octet
endif
compare remaining received data against list of forms
if matched one and flag[index of match] is TRUE then
  exit ; detected protocol
endif
enddo
```

This process can be altered to detect terminal-mode users by watching the received buffers for isolated characters or pairs of characters, since humans cannot type as fast as a computer. It is also worthwhile to emit a text message first saying, "Please start your network software now or press any key to bring up a menu." Peers that are already in PPP, ARAP, or SLIP mode will simply discard this text as a badly formed packet.

Synchronous Auto-Detect

Auto-detecting on a bit-synchronous link, such as an ISDN dial-up, is more complicated than on an asynchronous link but also more reliable. For this example, let us assume that we will be accepting both PPP and V.120 (a terminal adapter protocol) at either 56K or 64K data rates on a single bearer channel of an ISDN interface. Unlike AHDLC, there is only one PPP frame to consider, since no escape codes are used. This frame is:

```
FF 03 C0 21 ...
```

For V.120, either of two possible frames might be received first—a SABME (Set Asynchronous Balance Mode Extended) or a control frame. These two frames are:

```
08 01 7F
08 01 03
```

(Unlike normal HDLC, V.120 uses one bit, called "command versus response," or C/R, from the first octet of the address field to signal the direction of the data. The address field, termed Logical Link Identifier, or LLI, in V.120, has a default value of 256 decimal, which would be 04 01 in normal HDLC encoding but is instead 08 01 because the C/R bit has the value zero and is inserted as bit 1 of the octet, to the left of the Poll/Final bit. V.120's reply to these messages would then start with the C/R bit set, or 0A 01.)

Note that the first transmitted bit of the PPP frame (the LSB of FF) is one while the first bit of the V.120 frame (the LSB of 08) is zero. This means that only one bit of the message must be seen to identify which sequence to expect.

Now we will encode these values in bit-synchronous HDLC form without the initial flag sequence. The bit-encoded forms are:

```
PPP:                 11111011111000000000000001110000100
V.120 SABME:         0001000010000000111110110
V.120 control:       0001000010000000011000000
```

Since this is a bit-oriented protocol, the first task of the auto-detect routine will be to discover the bit offset of the initial flag sequence, or *sync marker*. Consider Table 2.1, which shows the data patterns to be expected for the sync marker with the first two octets of a valid frame, assuming either 64K "clear channel" or 56K restricted data path. The "v" bits in the table are valid data bits from the frame itself, "x" is arbitrary data, and "." is the unusable bit in each sample when using 56K service. (The bits here are again given in reversed order, as they would appear on the wire. HDLC devices transmit and receive the LSB first, so these values must usually be reversed to construct properly the software tables needed for decoding.)

Table 2.1 SYNC MARKER PATTERNS

64K Clear Channel		56K Restricted	
First	*Second*	*First*	*Second*
01111110	vvvvvvvv	0111111.	0vvvvvv.
x0111111	0vvvvvvv	x011111.	10vvvvv.
xx011111	10vvvvvv	xx01111.	110vvvv.
xxx01111	110vvvvv	xxx0111.	1110vvv.
xxxx0111	1110vvvv	xxxx011.	11110vv.
xxxxx011	11110vvv	xxxxx01.	111110v.
xxxxxx01	111110vv	xxxxxx0.	1111110.
xxxxxxx0	1111110v		

Now it is a simple matter to build a pair of tables of bit masks with 256 entries each for the first and second octet values above (filling in the "v" bits with bits from each of the protocol sequences in turn) and then to use these bit masks to detect the start of the data. If a sync marker is found, then the auto-detect routine must test the next two to four octets, depending on the protocol assumed and the bit offset. In fact, using just these two protocols causes the table to be unambiguous in determining the protocol to test in all but one case: the last 56K restricted case has no "v" bits in it, and thus all possible protocols (with just one alignment and encoding, however) must be tested. This means that after testing the bit mask indexed by each octet, a single two- to four-octet string comparison will uniquely identify both the protocol and the type of connection.

For example, seeing the octets FC BE should make the auto-detect routine expect to see 64K PPP data of 0F 00 0E after that sequence, since this pattern matches only the second row of the 64K encoding table with PPP data filled in for the "v" positions, and the one "x" value set to zero (this choice is arbitrary, and could have been set to one, so FD BE also leads to the same state and the same string comparison). The pattern substitution is shown in Figure 2.6.

Note that FC could also be the start of a 56K sequence (second row of the 56K table), but that would be eliminated as a possibility by BE, which could not be the second octet of either a PPP or a V.120 sequence with 56K encoding.

The construction of a suitable auto-detect procedure and complete tables is left as an exercise for the reader. (My reference implementation required 93 lines of assembly code.)

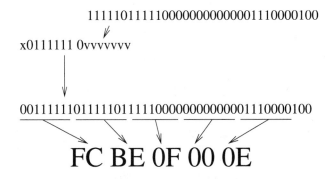

Figure 2.6: SYNCHRONOUS PPP DETECTION

AHDLC Start-Up Issues

The receiver of a PPP call over an asynchronous line generally has an easy task to perform, since the caller is usually expected to initiate the switch into PPP mode. At most, a simple auto-detect procedure may need to be run. Sometimes these devices are even configured to run PPP at all times.

The initiator has a more difficult task. Most consumer-grade modems use an in-band command channel (the familiar "AT" command set). Unfortunately, this same channel is also used for the user data, and no reliable synchronization mechanism is defined for switching from command to data mode and back. Worse, neither the commands the modem may accept nor the possible responses are well defined or even consistent between models of modems made by a single manufacturer.

This book is far too short to provide a comprehensive treatment of communications using modems, but here are a few suggestions:

- If you use hard reset on the modem, wait several seconds before attempting communication with it.

- Attempt to synchronize with the modem's autobaud mechanism first. This requires the sending of at least CR+"AT"+CR (0D 41 54 0D). Beware: some common brands of modems lock up if the first CR is too close in time to the "A." I recommend at least a 250 millisecond delay between these characters.

- Send an initialization string. "ATZ" or "AT&F" will usually do as a start. Some modems may glitch Data Carrier Detect (DCD) or Data Set Ready (DSR) when this is done, which may cause serial driver errors on some systems. Most modems then require a delay of 300 to 500 milliseconds after an "ATZ" is sent. This should then be followed by the parameter set-up string that includes settings to disable the in-band command mode break ("TIES"), to disable any software flow control, and any other special configuration necessary. Do not include "&w" as this unnecessarily stresses the modem's finite EEROM life span.

- Dial the line. A timer is very important here, since some modem firmware flaws can cause the modem to crash during negotiation.

- Wait for both DCD and a connect string. These may arrive in either order. Once both have been received, wait a short period (perhaps 250 milliseconds) before sending data. Sending data too early on some modems will cause connection drops.

- If a log-on script (sometimes known as a *chat script*) is required, run it.

- Start PPP. For several seconds after connecting (especially if a chat script was required), the remote system might not be running PPP. To detect this, one possible trick is to look for reception of frames where the CRC matches the last CRC sent. A more complex technique is to use the magic number negotiation procedure from RFC 1661. You may have to extend the counter limit for Configure-Request failures if you use this technique for detecting temporary loop-backs, since several requests may be sent before the peer even starts to run PPP.

It is also possible that either the serial ports or the modems themselves are misconfigured such that each character has fewer than 8 valid bits. PPP cannot run under these conditions at all. To detect this misconfiguration, use two variables, one set to 00 and the other set to FF. Logically OR all received data into the former and AND into the latter. If LCP fails, check these variables. If the OR variable is not set to FF or if the AND variable does have bits 6 or 7 set (hex C0), then it is likely that either the serial port or the modem is configured for 7-bit operation. An operator should be notified that the line is not 8-bit clean.

PPP Outline

PPP has three basic phases of negotiation: Link Control Protocol (LCP) negotiation, Authentication and Link Quality Management, and Network Control Protocol (NCP) negotiation. These three phases can be considered layers in the protocol design sense in that each layer sends Up and Down events to the adjacent layers (with a hypothetical additional "physical" layer below LCP and the network interfaces above the individual NCPs). These layers, though, have more in common than protocol layers normally do, so we will discuss them together.

Bringing a layer "up" is the result of three things; an "Open" request from a higher layer, an Up event from the next lower layer, and the successful negotiation of parameters at that particular layer.

Typically, either a user requests that the link be established through some sort of interface, or a network interface requests the establishment through a demand-dialing mechanism. This will cause an Open event to be sent to the authentication and LCP layers of the PPP stack.

When LCP starts, depending on the implementation, the physical link will be established. This may involve dialing a modem and waiting for the carrier, creating a Switched Virtual Circuit (SVC) over an ATM interface or, for hard-wired links, no action at all. Once this procedure is complete, it will send an Up event into LCP.

LCP then begins negotiation by sending out Configure-Request messages to the peer. Once the peers settle on a set of configuration values, LCP then sends an Up event into the authentication layer. If authentication is desired, then this layer runs until the link is authenticated. Otherwise, it just sends an "Up" event to the NCP layer.

Once authentication is complete, the link is generally considered to be "up." No user data yet flow across the link though. In order to bring up network interfaces that will pass user data on the link, the NCP for each network interface must be negotiated. The NCPs are independent and may join or leave the link as needed while the link is up. Often the link is torn down by sending a Close event to LCP when the last NCP closes, but this is not strictly necessary. If system resources permit, the link could be left up but idle until needed again by another network interface.

On tear-down, each NCP should separately terminate itself from the link, then LCP should terminate, and finally the physical layer should terminate in an implementation-dependent manner (hanging up the telephone call, for example). It is necessary for PPP implementations to handle termination of LCP without the termination of the NCPs and to handle termination of the physical link with no notification at all. These are very common error cases and generally require implementation-dependent handling.

State Machine

Each layer can be in any of ten different states. This leads to a rather difficult-to-interpret state table in RFC 1661. To simplify this, I will describe the establishment and tear-down sequences separately.

As a layer is brought up, there are two stages of the process. First, the state machine must make certain that the lower layer is already up and that the current layer should be started. This is done with states 0, 1, and 2, with 1 representing open requested and 2 representing lower-layer up. Then it is necessary to negotiate with the peer and converge on a set of parameters to use for the layer. This is done with Request, Acknowledge, Negative-Acknowledge, and Reject messages in states 6, 7, and 8, which synchronize the bidirectional negotiation so that both sides can finish. Finally, the layer is up when in state 9, and the next higher layer is then signaled. Refer to Figure 2.7.

Bringing a layer down (see Figure 2.8) is simpler and requires only sending a Terminate-Request, and listening for a Terminate-Acknowledge. The only complication in this process is that the peer may initiate the termination sequence rather than the local system-thus, the need for states 3 and 5, where the peer has brought the layer down, but locally both the next higher and the next lower layer are still up.

In the combined state machine, we are including notations from RFC 1661, which indicate the events that cause the transition as well as the resulting actions.

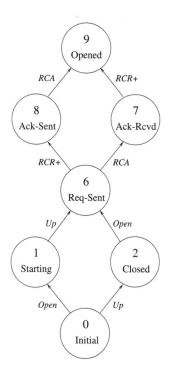

Figure 2.7: LAYER ESTABLISHMENT

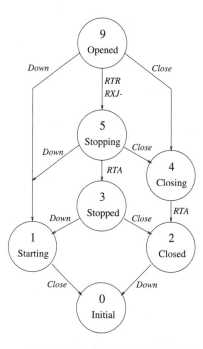

Figure 2.8: LAYER TEAR-DOWN

Do not be intimidated by Figure 2.9, a rather complex diagram. It is rarely necessary to debug a PPP implementation through this state machine. Instead, most of the work involved in an implementation, and most of problems that occur, are related to the negotiation exchange itself, which is covered in detail in the next chapter.

Note that a Terminate-Request received (RTR) during negotiation puts the state machine back into Req-Sent state. For this reason, the Close event should not be delivered to an NCP that is failing to negotiate. It is better simply to disable that NCP entirely so that Protocol-Reject will be sent.

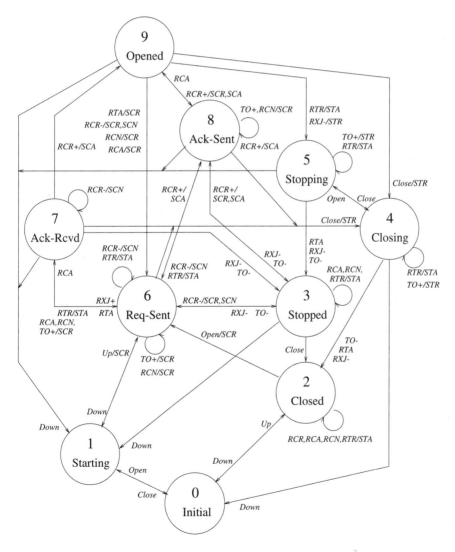

Figure 2.9: COMPLETE STATE MACHINE

Switched Circuit Integration

When used on a switched circuit, such as a modem on a telephone line, the up/down messages from the switching system may be translated into Up/Down events into LCP, though they need not be. A system that automatically maintains the link, such as a dial-on-demand system, might opt to wait for a short period before sending the Down event to LCP while a redial is attempted. The implementor of such a system should be cautioned that the price for faster reconnection is lowered security. Any such technique used must, of course, be configurable, since it is not the default.

Such a scheme greatly weakens security. Before considering any such "short hold" option, a cautious implementor would first exhaust all possible ways to speed up normal PPP authentication. On most media, this can be made to be much faster than any circuit-switched set-up time. In particular, ISDN call set-up time is in the hundreds of milliseconds, while PPP negotiation can be an order of magnitude faster when well implemented.

It is highly recommended that the system that initiated the link should also be the system that tears down the link to save toll charges when the link is idle. This rule avoids thrashing when demand dialing is used. Of course, in some unusual circumstances, such as "toll-reversing" lines, a separate negotiation of either callback or Bandwidth Allocation Control Protocol (BACP) might be needed.

Note that the distinction between caller and callee should be made available to the PPP authentication layer. See "Authentication Protocols" and "About Security" at the end of Chapter 3.

General Implementation Issues

Specific PPP implementation techniques vary widely, but good PPP implementations have a number of common attributes:

- **The Protocol Rule.** "Be liberal in what you expect and conservative in what you send." This is the golden rule of network software design, and good implementations follow it. In particular, it is worthwhile to study the various obsolete versions of a particular protocol before implementing it, including the Internet Drafts and obsoleted RFCs. Often products will be released that conform to these obsolete versions, and interoperability occasionally depends on behavior that is not documented in later versions. Even more important, following the protocol rule will allow your implementation to interoperate with flawed peers. There are, sadly, many PPP implementations in the world today that have glaring bugs. It is better for your reputation if your implementation logs the error but continues operation in a reasonable manner, if possible, rather than giving up.

- **Resilience.** PPP negotiation protocols have a number of different field length values and restrictions on the values of certain other fields. Good implementations will carefully check that these values are consistent with the type of data received and the overall packet length before acting on the data. It is quite common for errant PPP packages to send incorrect field lengths, and unfortunately it is more common for bad implementations to crash when presented with such data.

- **Renegotiation.** Any layer of the PPP protocol may be separately renegotiated at any time. Good implementations handle this gracefully and do not treat it as an error. In particular, options that require storage, such as data compression, will need to free the storage and reallocate it on successful renegotiation.

- **Loop Avoidance.** The standard PPP negotiation model can easily fall into nonconverging patterns, also called *loops*. Good implementations detect these by means of timers and counters.

- **Configurability.** Good implementations permit each supported protocol to be separately disabled and any variables be modified. A good implementation should not rest simply on the PPP negotiation mechanism, since it is occasionally true that another implementation will properly negotiate an option but will not properly implement that option itself. Being able to modify or eliminate an offending protocol or configuration option from negotiation is an effective work-around.

- **Event Logging.** Good implementations can log events at varying levels of detail to aid in debugging failed connections. It is especially helpful to log the state of each layer that is not in "Initial" state and to have the ability at least to log the raw data sent over the wire.

- **Legibility.** Good implementations provide error messages that are meaningful to both experienced and inexperienced users and may also suggest fixes. For instance, "could not negotiate a compatible set of protocols" is a particularly useless message. A better message might be, "IPCP failure—local address is not set and peer refuses to provide one."

- **Peer-to-Peer Design.** PPP is inherently a peer-to-peer protocol, and most emphatically not a client/server protocol. Good implementations will not make arbitrary distinctions based on the system on which it is executing. In particular, all implementations should offer authentication to their peers and demand authentication when so configured, and all should be able to configure desired values for all negotiable parameters rather than always conforming to the peer's demands.

As you read the following chapters, keep these issues in mind and compare them with the information presented. Where possible, I will provide hints and details from actual implementations to illuminate these concepts.

Chapter

3

Negotiation, LCP, and Authentication

IN THIS CHAPTER

This chapter covers the first protocol always negotiated, the Link Control Protocol (LCP), the basic methods of parameter negotiation for all of the PPP protocols, and the special negotiation required for authentication. Variations on the techniques described in this chapter are used for the rest of the protocols in this book.

The Negotiation Messages

PPP is a symmetric peer-to-peer protocol. There is no such thing as a "client" version or, for that matter, a "server." All of the protocol negotiation that follows reflects this fact.

PPP uses four messages to negotiate parameters for almost all protocols. These messages, documented with the LCP in RFC 1661, are called Configure-Request, Configure-Acknowledge, Configure-Negative-Acknowledge or Configure-Nak, and Configure-Reject, which are often abbreviated as Conf-Req, Conf-Ack, Conf-Nak, and Conf-Rej, respectively. This text, however, uses the standard terms. Each message contains within it a list of options and parameters, and all options in a given layer are thus negotiated simultaneously.

The system sending Configure-Request is telling the peer system that it is willing to receive data sent with the enclosed options enabled. The peer may then respond with Configure-Ack to indicate that all of the enclosed options were acceptable and all are now enabled. If some of the options were unacceptable with the supplied parameters, the peer would then respond with a Configure-Nak containing only the offending options and a suggested value for the parameters (called a *hint*). The receiver of the Configure-Nak then should decide if the hinted value is acceptable and, if so, send a new Configure-Request reflecting the requested changes plus the original values for the unchanged options. The sender of the Configure-Request may not send back any message other than Configure-Request in response to Configure-Nak, so the only recourse available if the hint is unreasonable is to drop the option from subsequent Configure-Request messages. Finally, if the peer does not recognize one or more of the options in the Configure-Request message, then it must return just these options in a Configure-Reject message, instead of a Configure-Nak, and the original sender must then remove the options from subsequent Configure-Request messages.

Note that both systems will issue Configure-Request messages. The negotiation procedure outlined is repeated in the opposite direction in order to negotiate the options in use in each direction on the link. Normally there is no need for the options negotiated in each direction to match, though some options do have usage restrictions.

In some situations, one peer will absolutely require the use of a particular option. If that option is not presented in the Configure-Request message from the peer, and no Configure-Reject is needed, then that peer may reply with a Configure-Nak hinting that this additional option (or options) is needed. This is often referred to as an *unsolicited Configure-Nak*. Of course, this rarely works to prod the Configure-Request sender to include the option. Instead it usually causes the link to fail to come up since it will get stuck in a Configure-Request/Configure-Nak loop. However, it is useful in that a well-written peer will log that the other system was sending Configure-Nak for an unknown option, which can allow an administrator at least to diagnose the problem. (Good implementations should not make undue restrictions on which options must be used, since such restrictions usually make an implementation prone to interoperability problems. In particular, some peers refuse to negotiate IPCP addresses for no good reason. If the necessary addresses are known from some other information—perhaps a database look-up on the authenticated peer name—then it is safe and reasonable to proceed with negotiation without this option.)

Note that if the unsolicited Configure-Nak does not cause the peer to change its Configure-Request, it is impossible to tell if the peer failed to receive the Configure-Nak or simply cannot honor it, since behavior when retransmitting Configure-Request due to a time-out after the loss of the response is identical to having the peer simply ignore the Configure-Nak. For this reason, most systems that send an unsolicited Configure-Nak in order to request an option will do so during the initial negotiation of a given protocol and not during any subsequent renegotiation. Some implementations even send the Configure-Nak message exactly once and then give up.

Some options do not have associated data values, but instead are "boolean" (on-off) switches. These options are generally not modified with Configure-Nak, except with possible unsolicited Configure-Naks as in the paragraph above, but are instead negotiated "on" with Configure-Ack and "off" with Configure-Reject.

Example Negotiations

This example uses a hypothetical situation with two peers, A and B, attempting to negotiate the use of several options in each direction. Following are the logs of the negotiation (the sender's name is given on each line):

1. A: Configure-Request   ID:1 [1 4:01010101 5:80 9]
2. B: Configure-Reject   ID:1 [1 5:80]
3. A: Configure-Request   ID:2 [4:01010101 9]
4. B: Configure-Nak   ID:2 [4:01010102]
5. A: Configure-Request   ID:3 [4:01010102 9]
6. B: Configure-Ack   ID:3 [4:01010102 9]
7. B: Configure-Request   ID:1 [2 9]
8. A: Configure-Ack   ID:1 [2 9]

Here they are rendered as English dialog:

1. A: "Please send me data with options 1 and 9 enabled, and with option 4 set to 01010101 and option 5 set to 80."
2. B: "I don't understand options 1 and 5 at all."
3. A: "OK, then, please send me data with option 4 set to 01010101 and option 9 enabled."
4. B: "I'd rather have option 4 set to 01010102."
5. A: "OK, how about sending me data with option 4 set to 01010102 and option 9 enabled?"
6. B: "I agree. I will now send you data with option 4 set to 01010102 and option 9 enabled."
7. B: "I want you to send me data with options 2 and 9 enabled."
8. A: "I will now send you data with options 2 and 9 enabled."

There are actually two independent conversations here, with one represented by the sequence 1 through 6 and the other by messages 7 and 8. These two could also be intermixed, with messages 7 and 8 appearing between any of the other messages, depending on timing. In messages 1 through 6, the options for data flowing from B to A are negotiated, while messages 7 and 8 negotiate the options for data flowing from A to B.

Assuming that the peers have received both the Up indication from the next lower layer and the Open indication from the next higher layer at the start of this conversation, and that peer B has sent a Configure-Request that was dropped by peer A before the first message shown, the corresponding state transitions are:

```
    Peer A                   Peer B
                             (->Req-Sent) (6)
1.  ->Req-Sent (6)
2.
3.
4.
5.
6.  Req-Sent->Ack-Rcvd (7)   Req-Sent->Ack-Sent (8)
7.
8.  Ack-Rcvd->Opened (9)     Ack-Sent->Opened (9)
```

Note that the state transitions are triggered by the Configure-Ack messages.

Packet Loss Scenarios in Negotiation

When packets are lost during negotiation, user data can be lost. Here are four scenarios, shown in Figures 3.1 through 3.4, showing how negotiation proceeds. Each line shows what is sent by that peer, and the numbers in parentheses show the state transitions.

In the simple case in Figure 3.1, one of the initial Configure-Request messages was lost. The sender times out (TO) first, and the negotiation then completes. In the example in Figure 3.2, one of the initial Configure-Request messages was again lost. However, in this case, peer A has a shorter time-out configured than peer B. The negotiation completes only after peer B has timed out. In the example in Figure 3.3, one of the Configure-Ack messages is getting lost. Note that peer A goes to Open state (9) until peer B's timer expires. If this is a Network Control Protocol (NCP), then any user data that might be sent by peer A will be lost. If it is LCP, then negotiation messages from the next higher layer will probably be sent by A but discarded by B.

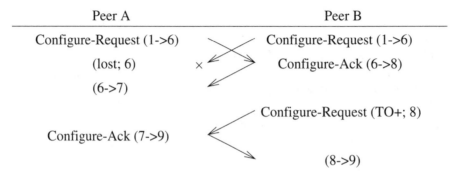

Figure 3.1: LOST CONFIGURE-REQUEST

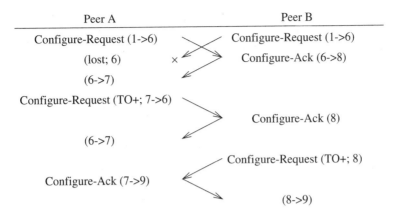

Figure 3.2: LOST CONFIGURE-REQUEST WITH PEER TIMEOUT

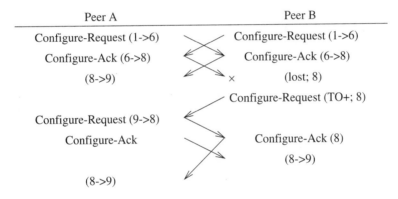

Figure 3.3: LOST CONFIGURE-ACK

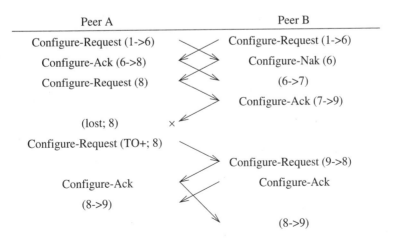

Figure 3.4: ANOTHER LOST CONFIGURE-ACK

This last example in Figure 3.4, shows another Configure-Ack message being lost in a slightly different case. Again, though, one of the peers (B) briefly proceeds to Open state before the other, and data may be lost.

Packet Formats

Each of these four messages follows the same basic packet format:

```
<Code> <Id> <Length> <Options...>
```

The Code field is a single octet with value 01 for *Configure-Request*, 02 for *Configure-Ack*, 03 for *Configure-Nak*, and 04 for *Configure-Reject*. The ID field is also a single octet and is a sequence number for the message. The Length field is two octets long and represents the length of the message, including all of the options that follow and the four-octet header (composed of Code, ID, and Length).

The ID field is changed for each new Configure-Request sent. Since timers are used by the PPP state machine, it is possible to receive a message in reply that refers to an "old" Configure-Request and must be discarded. Thus, it is necessary for the system generating the other three messages to insert the ID number from the Configure-Request message that is being interpreted, and the receiver of these messages must compare the ID number received against the ID of the last Configure-Request message sent. This will prevent accidentally delayed messages from confusing the system.

Some common PPP packages do not bother to check the received ID fields and happily accept and act on stale responses. This can cause trouble with authentication since a delayed response (common when external databases are used) can be misinterpreted as the reply to a later retransmitted request. When the retransmitted request is handled, the now-unexpected reply may cause the peer to disconnect.

Most PPP implementations start each layer's ID field at zero and increment when a new ID is needed. RFC 1661 does not specify this behavior, and incrementing should not be relied on. In fact, it is generally a good practice to choose the first ID number randomly if possible, since doing so tends to avoid problems when layer renegotiation is necessary. PPP analyzers (human and otherwise) should make no assumptions about the ID field, but rather treat it as a randomly generated number.

Also note that a system generating a Configure-Request message identical to the last sent Configure-Request message (when triggered by a time-out) may send the same ID number. Except for security protocols, doing this is legal and can help a link with long latency times establish itself correctly, although not quite in a foolproof manner. Consider the example in Figure 3.5, with the time-out configured to be less than the latency across the link. Either changing the ID on time-out or using an increasing time-out will prevent this behavior. Changing the ID value will cause this link to fail due to an excessive number of Configure-Request messages sent. Using an increasing time-out value is not required by RFC 1661 but will allow this link to settle and correctly establish itself.

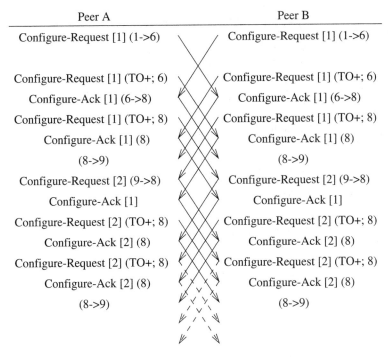

Figure 3.5: NEGOTIATION LOOP

If the peer ignores the ID field, as some nonstandard implementations do, then only an increasing or adjustable time-out can fix the above problem. No good implementation should ignore this field.

Option Encoding

The Options are a list of variable-length blocks in the following format:

```
<Type> <Len> <Data>
```

The Type field is a single octet and represents a single option for the protocol being negotiated. The Len field is also a single octet and is the length of the option block, including the two-octet header (composed of Type and Len). The Data field, if present, is information for the option being negotiated.

Returning to the example message used when describing HDLC encoding in the previous chapter, we can now begin to examine the components that make up this message:

```
FF  03  C0  21  01  01  00  0E  02  06  00  00  00  00  07  02  08  02  70  34
```

This frame consists of the following elements:

FF 03		–	Standard PPP HDLC address and control fields
C0 21		–	Protocol number C021 (LCP)
01		–	Code field; 01 is Configure-Request
01		–	ID field (number 1)
00 0E		–	Length field (14 octets)
02		–	Type field; option 02 for protocol C021
06		–	Len field (6 octets)
00 00 00 00		–	Data for this option
07		–	Type field; option 07 for protocol C021
02		–	Len field (2 octets)
08		–	Type field; option 08 for protocol C021
02		–	Len field (2 octets)
70 34		–	CRC

These structures are shown graphically in Figure 3.6. :

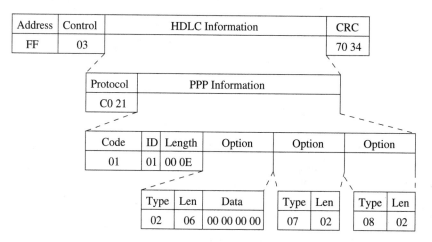

Figure 3.6: CONFIGURE REQUEST STRUCTURE

Notice that the length fields are redundant in many ways. The HDLC frame itself gives an indication of length by the framing marks. The Length field must be equal to the total length of the frame minus the HDLC overhead (four octets; Address, Control, and CRC) and the PPP Protocol number overhead (two octets), so for this 20-octet message, the Configure-Request message length must be 14. Each of the Option fields has a Len field, and the sum of all Len fields plus four (for the Code, ID, and Length fields) must be equal to the Length field. And, of course, most options have fixed lengths due to their definitions.

This redundancy helps an implementation do a number of sanity checks on the data before attempting to act on them. The PPP standard says that any malformed packets must be silently dropped. Thus, if any but the last test in the previous paragraph fails, the frame is ignored. If, however, an option has an improper Len field for that type of option but all of the lengths otherwise add up correctly, then the option should, according to RFC 1661, be included in a Configure-Nak message with the Len field changed to the proper length. (Dealing with a Len field set to 00 or 01 is a gray area in the standard. I recommend treating this as though it had been 02 for the sake of verifying the packet integrity when doing the length checks; if these checks succeed, a Configure-Nak should be returned with the correct Len field for those options. Other implementors reasonably argue that Configure-Reject is appropriate since the peer could not possibly implement an option correctly if it cannot even get the length right. Still others argue that such errors should result in Protocol-Reject, since the peer is obviously confused, and attempting to continue negotiation of a broken protocol may be unwise.)

Other Code Numbers

Besides the four main negotiation messages, several other codes can appear on the link. These additional messages all have the same basic format, which is very similar to the negotiation messages:

```
<Code> <Id> <Length> <Data ...>
```

Terminate-Request (Term-Req; code 05) and *Terminate-Ack* (Term-Ack; code 06) are used to tear down a link in a graceful manner. For LCP, these codes are most often useful on links that have no external control signals, like the DCD signal on a modem, to shut down operation. They are also useful in multilink PPP (MP) systems when tearing down an unneeded link since they can prevent packet loss. For the other protocols, they allow individual network protocols to be shut down to conserve resources or for security reasons. The length of these messages is usually 4, but some implementations put termination reason text into the data field that follows the length field. Any such message is implementation dependent but should be a printable text string.

RFC 1661 specifically indicates that a system sending Terminate-Request must begin discarding network layer data received since it must leave state Open. However, as long as the link is not being torn down due to authentication failure, I recommend instead that network layer data should still be properly handled in Closing state after having sent Terminate-Request until Closing state is exited. Although this is a violation of the RFC, it is well supported by many members of the IETF working group.

An exchange of messages for termination of the IPX protocol could look like this:

```
FF 03 80 2B 05 14 00 0D 49 27 6D 20 64 6F 6E 65 2E 0C 4F
FF 03 80 2B 06 14 00 04 A1 10
```

where the first message decodes as:

FF 03	–		Standard PPP HDLC address and control fields
80 2B	–		Protocol number 802B (IPXCP)
05	–		Code field; 05 is Term-Req
14	–		ID field (number 20)
00 0D	–		Length field (13 octets)
49 27 6D 20 64 6F 6E 65 2E			
		–	Text string saying "I'm done."
0C 4F	–		CRC

and the second as:

FF 03	–	Standard PPP HDLC address and control fields
80 2B	–	Protocol number 802B (IPXCP)
06	–	Code field; 06 is Term-Ack
14	–	ID field (number 20)
00 04	–	Length field (4 octets)
0C 4F	–	CRC

Code-Reject (Code-Rej; code 07) and *Protocol-Reject* (Proto-Rej; code 08) are used to indicate that the sender's code number or PPP protocol number is unknown. In these cases, the entire offending message is sent back to the sender (starting with the beginning of the PPP information field for Code-Reject and with the uncompressed PPP protocol field for Protocol-Reject). Generally Code-Reject should not occur in normal usage, and it means that the sender is running a much newer version of the protocol or that it is confused and sending corrupted packets. The Protocol-Reject message, relatively common while protocols are being negotiated, means that the sender does not know the given protocol at all. For example, a system may offer to handle AppleTalk (ATCP), IPX (IPXCP), and IP (IPCP) by sending Configure-Request for each of these NCP protocols. The receiver may elect to run just IP by sending Protocol-Reject for the other two Configure-Request messages.

Note that sending Protocol-Reject is quite different from simply sending a Configure-Reject for all requested options. Configure-Reject leaves the protocol enabled, while Protocol-Reject disables it.

Note also that section 5.7 of RFC 1661, which describes the usage of Protocol-Reject, is sometimes confused by developers. An implementation must reject a protocol that it does not understand. It must not, though, reject a protocol that it does implement but has not yet negotiated or initialized, unless it intends never to negotiate that protocol during the life of the link. In other words, you should send Protocol-Reject for any protocol not in your table of known protocols and for any protocol explicitly disabled by an operator, but send nothing at all for protocols you are not yet ready to receive. Code-Reject is sent from any protocol level. Protocol-Reject, though, is sent only from LCP, never from any other protocol level.

There is at least one very common implementation in use in central sites that occasionally gets confused and sends a Protocol-Reject for LCP itself. These messages should be ignored from a state machine standpoint but probably should also be logged where an administrator can see them. This same implementation occasionally generates erroneous configuration messages with the PPP Protocol field set to 0000, which usually leads to interesting exchanges with properly implemented peers.

Echo-Request (Echo-Req; code 09), *Echo-Reply* (Echo-Rep; code 0A), and *Discard-Request* (Disc-Req; code 0B) are generally used for monitoring link integrity and while debugging an implementation. Each of these messages has the same data format: four octets of the locally assigned magic number (see LCP negotiation option 05 below) followed by arbitrary text. Usually these messages are sent and received only from LCP.

Many implementations send periodic Echo-Request messages on idle links in order to check the viability and integrity of the link. This is done by setting one timer at, say, a 1-second interval to generate Echo-Request messages when the receive side is idle. A second, longer timer at, say, a 5-second interval, is also set on the receive side and restarted when any traffic is received. If this second timer expires, the link is probably not operational and should be dropped. On some media, like analog modems, the timers may need to be set much longer due to such phenomena as V.42 error correction and data pump retraining. On other media, such as wireless links, LCP echoes on an idle link may be expensive. Timing of Echo-Request messages tends to be application dependent.

One important implementation note is that it is necessary to place Echo-Requests at the front of the transmit queue, if possible, when they are used for dead link detection. If the queue is full, it is preferable to drop user data rather than to lose the link due to a lack of echo replies. This detail may vary depending on the system architecture.

On MP links, LCP Echo-Requests should be sent without MP encapsulation as normal LCP messages, and the reply should be sent on the same link over which the request was received. An implementation must not attempt to pass these replies through the normal MP output routine, which load-balances across the available links.

Identification (Ident; code 0C) is described in RFC 1570, "PPP LCP Extensions." There is no negotiation for this message, and no response is defined. This message has the same format as the above messages: four octets for the magic number followed by an arbitrary text string. The identification option allows an implementation to identify itself to the peer using a simple unauthenticated string. This string may include version numbers, manufacturer information, or any other data. It can be used for debug logs, enabling proprietary options, or licensing restrictions. This message can be sent before LCP is open and generally should be sent as early as possible in order to be most useful. (RFC 1570 recommends sending it when a Configure-Reject is sent, before disconnecting due to negotiation failure, and when LCP goes to Open state. I recommend sending it earlier as well—either before or after the first Configure-Request during LCP negotiation.)

Time-Remaining (Time; code 0D) is also described in RFC 1570. There is no negotiation for this message, and no response is defined. The message has a format similar to the messages above: four octets for the magic number plus four octets for an integer representing the number of seconds remaining for the link, followed by a variable-length text string. The Time-Remaining message allows a PPP system to notify its peer that the connection is subject to some kind of administrative control that will terminate the connection in a known amount of time. This message is handled by the peer in an implementation-dependent manner. If the peer has a user interface, then it should present this message to the user. If not, then it might generate a Simple Network Management Protocol (SNMP) trap or log a message for use by an operator. Unlike Identification messages, Time-Remaining may be sent only after LCP has reached Open state.

The *Reset-Request* (Reset-Req; code 0E) and *Reset-Reply* (Reset-Ack; code 0F) messages are used with data compression. See "Architecture" and "Error Recovery" for the CCP protocol in Chapter 5 for details.

The *Vendor-Extension* (code 00) message can be used for any proprietary purpose that requires sending a packet from one peer to the other. These messages may be sent at any time. The message format includes a four-octet magic number, three octets of vendor identification (which should contain the first three octets of an Ethernet address assigned to the vendor or, alternatively, a number assigned by the Internet Assigned Numbers Authority [IANA] which always begins with the value CF), and a variable-length data field for the proprietary message. This extension is described in RFC 2153.

The Identification and Vendor-Extension messages can cause negotiation problems if they are unsupported by the peer. If either is sent immediately after Configure-Request, the peer may respond with Code-Reject after sending its Configure-Ack. Receiving the Configure-Ack will put LCP in Ack-Rcvd state, but the Code-Reject will push it back to Req-Sent state. I recommend disabling these extensions if Code-Reject is received.

Peers based on the current RFC 1661 will not change state on receiving an unknown code number. Unfortunately, this is not true of peers based on older RFCs. Implementations based on RFC 1331 will tolerate unknown codes during negotiation but will restart negotiation if an unknown code is received while the layer is Open. Older implementations based on RFC 1171 or the original RFC 1134 will shut down completely on an unknown code in any state.

Since interoperability is an important goal, it should be possible on a good implementation to bar the transmission of potentially troublesome code numbers, such as Identification and Vendor-Extension.

Codes 00 (vendor-extension), 0B (discard-request), 0C (identification), and 0D (time-remaining) are rarely used. The others described are fairly common.

LCP Negotiation Options

There are quite a few LCP options—more so than any other protocol within PPP. This is true for a number of reasons. First, several of these options change framing-level details and are thus convenient to settle as soon as possible. Second, some imply changes in authentication methods or parameters and thus must take place before the authentication phase of the PPP session. And some are here for no good reason at all, except that LCP tends to be a catch-all for other options.

Conspicuously absent from the LCP negotiation is any type of peer identification and authentication. This means that LCP option settings must either be selected on a global basis or, where available, be based on external peer identification, such as call parameters or external prompting. Future LCP options may include authentication.

Options 01, 02, 03, 05, 07, and 08 are nearly universal. Options 11, 12, and 13 are common in MP implementations. The others are rarely used.

00 Vendor Extensions

This option is described in RFC 2153. It allows vendors to exchange proprietary options between devices of like kind. This option has the following information in its data field:

```
<OUI> <Kind> <Values>
```

where OUI is a three-octet Ethernet address prefix for the vendor or an identifier assigned by the Internet Assigned Numbers Authority (IANA), Kind is a single octet with implementation-specific meaning, and Values are vendor defined.

See also option 14, which does not require the use of an OUI.

01 Maximum Receive Unit (MRU)

This option, described in RFC 1661, has a two-octet data value associated with it. This value in a Configure-Request message is the maximum size of a PPP information field that the implementation can receive. (This value does not include the HDLC address, control, or check fields or the PPP protocol field, so typical implementations need room for at least another six octets.)

The negotiated MRU is used for both subsequent NCP negotiation messages and the actual user data. This means that the actual MRU negotiated must be at least as large as the largest negotiation message or user datagram sent. In particular, if the configured MRU is small, it may need to be altered to allow authentication to proceed.

It may seem at first glance rather illogical ever to send a Configure-Nak for this option unless the message itself is corrupted. If the peer sends a Configure-Request with a small MRU, then any reasonable implementation should be able to limit its messages to the requested size. If the peer indicates a larger-than-expected MRU, there is no harm in sending Configure-Ack for this value but then sending only the largest messages possible, even though these messages may be less than the requested MRU. In other words, reasonable implementations should reply with Configure-Ack if the offered value is any value greater than some small lower bound (say, 64 octets).

There is, though, at least one case where Configure-Nak is useful for MRU. Since the MRU requested by the peer often maps locally into the interface MTU as long as MP is not in use, this means that systems with preconfigured and unchangeable interfaces, such as most systems doing dial on demand, may need to use Configure-Nak to inform the peer that a particular MRU is required if the offered MRU is too small. In practice, if this value is over 1500, this tactic often fails, but it does prevent unusable links from being established.

Note also that all implementations are required to accept a PPP information field of at least 1500 octets at all times, regardless of the negotiated value. If the peer requests an MRU that is too small for any reason and the MRU you want to have is 1500 octets or fewer, then it is reasonable to send Configure-Reject to the peer's MRU option, which will force the peer to use the default of 1500.

Some implementations calculate an MRU to offer based on connection speed. This is generally not worthwhile at or above 14.4Kbps for TCP/IP connections.

Choosing a good MRU turns out to be quite complicated due to compression protocols, which may inflate rather than compress some types of data, because of link layers that have intrinsic MTUs, and because of optional network layers that cannot handle fragmentation. Regardless of any automatic MRU selection implemented, user controls that allow tuning of both the advertised (via Configure-Request) and required (via Configure-Nak) MRUs should be provided in any good implementation. Choosing good defaults based on possible protocol overhead, such as with MP, CCP, and Encryption Control Protocol (ECP), is a good practice. These headers can add as many as 20 octets to the messages. Other protocols, such as bridging, can add more.

In order to be as compatible as possible with existing implementations, it is reasonable to allow for a maximum MRU of 1600 (unless Fiber Distributed Data Interface (FDDI) bridging is in use; see Chapter 4). Do not trim the input data to the negotiated MRU since some broken peers may go slightly over this amount in some cases. Trimming output data is also not necessary, but detecting cases where the output message is too large for the peer's MRU should be done and should be logged since it is indicative of internal errors.

Some implementations, such as SGI's IRIX, will change the MRU requested when other options are changed. For example, if it is configured to run RFC 1990 MP, it will send an MRU of 1505. If the MRRU is rejected (disabling MP), it will drop back to a default MRU of 1500. This means that implementations must be prepared to receive an MRU in one Configure-Request but then to have it absent in a subsequent Configure-Request. When this happens, the implementation must drop back to the default. Some systems fail to implement this correctly. Good implementations set all option values to the default on reception of a Configure-Request before processing the request itself.

02 Asynchronous Control Character Map (ACCM)

This option is described in RFC 1662. Its value is a four-octet bit map that enables (bit set) or disables (bit clear) character escapes (the AHDLC 7D code) for the 32 ASCII control characters in the range 00 to 1F. The first octet of the value has the bits for control characters 18 through 1F, with the most significant bit representing 1F and the least 18, the second octet has bits for characters 10 through 17, and so on. The default is FFFFFFFF, or all control characters escaped. Values typically negotiated are 00000000 for links that can handle arbitrary data and 000A0000 for links with standard XON/XOFF software flow control. Unlike the pseudo-code in the previous chapter, the implementation in Appendix A properly handles ACCM.

The ACCM negotiation handler should combine the value received in a Configure-Nak via a logical bitwise OR operation with the last Configure-Request value. This result should then be sent in the next Configure-Request message. If a Configure-Request is received whose bit mask includes cleared bits for characters that the local implementation knows to be problematic (perhaps by way of an administrative option or some kind of hardware information), then it should send a Configure-Nak with the prior value modified to have these bits set.

When negotiating LCP, be careful to set the ACCM at the proper point in time. The RFC indicates that this is to be done as LCP transitions to Open state. In order to be as compatible as possible with poorly written implementations, I recommend that the receive ACCM be set immediately on reception of Configure-Ack or Configure-Nak from the peer. The transmit ACCM should be set only after LCP has transitioned to Open state and all pending output has been sent. (Waiting to set the transmit ACCM until the peer begins negotiation of the next layer is even better, as it eliminates the possibility of confusion due to a lost Configure-Ack message but is often impractical in most implementations.)

When renegotiating LCP, the transmit ACCM should first be set to the default. The receive ACCM, however, should be left at its previous value since the peer may miss the first LCP Configure-Request or simply fail to reset its transmit ACCM.

Instead, the receive ACCM should be set based on the received Configure-Ack or Configure-Nak from the peer.

An implementation may instead choose to detect the use of LCP (perhaps by testing the PPP Protocol field) and temporarily force the transmit ACCM to FFFFFFFF. This may be simpler than dealing with the timing issues but does mean that the AHDLC driver must "know" a little bit about the protocol running above it. It would be a slight layering violation.

Synchronous implementations should not negotiate this parameter by default but must accept any parameter sent by the peer without actually acting on the value. This requirement allows interoperability between synchronous devices and asynchronous devices through translators, as mentioned in Chapter 2. The tests for escape characters are implemented by the translating device, not by the synchronous device.

Developers and testers should be aware that some modern synchronous systems still violate this requirement. These systems are not compliant with the current RFC 1662, the prior RFC 1331, or even the original RFC 1172 for PPP.

03 Authentication Protocol

This option is described in RFC 1661. Its value is a two-or-more octet field. The first two octets are the PPP protocol ID of the desired authentication protocol, and any additional octets are described by the particular RFC for that authentication protocol.

Receiving a Configure-Request for this option means that the peer wants the receiving system to identify itself using the indicated protocol. The receiver of Configure-Request may reply with Configure-Nak to request use of a different protocol, but the sender of Configure-Request may simply reply by terminating the link. Once a system sends Configure-Ack, it must then identify itself using the chosen protocol. The receiver of Configure-Ack should verify that the peer does indeed do this and should not allow network protocols to be negotiated until this identification is complete.

Current common values are C0 23 for PAP (RFC 1334), C2 23 05 for standard MD5 CHAP (RFC 1994), C2 23 80 for Microsoft CHAP, C2 27 for EAP, C0 27 for SPAP, and C1 23 for the old version of SPAP. See the authentication discussion after the LCP option list for more information on these protocols.

04 Quality Protocol

This option is described in RFC 1661. It is negotiated in exactly the same manner as the authentication protocol above, where the first two octets are the desired link quality monitoring protocol to use. Currently, only protocol C025 (Link-Quality-Report), specified in RFC 1989, is defined. The negotiation for this particular protocol includes an additional four octets after the protocol number specifying the maximum time between quality reports in hundredths of a second.

RFC 1989 describes the reports given, which are packets with PPP protocol C025 and an information field with 12 4-byte integers (48 octets). These integers give information on the number of octets and packets lost in both directions. The RFC specifies the meanings of these numbers and directions on handling them, but analysis and policy decisions (such as what constitutes a "bad" link and what action to take) are left to the implementor.

Some implementations send LQM messages without negotiating LQM in LCP. These implementations depend on Protocol-Reject to disable LQM if necessary.

05 Magic Number

This option is described in RFC 1661. It contains a four-octet data field, called the *magic number*. This is a random number chosen to distinguish the two peers and detect error conditions, such as looped-back lines and echoes. The negotiation of this option is a little different from other options. In particular, each peer must compare the magic number received in a Configure-Request with the last magic number sent in a Configure-Request, and likewise for the corresponding Configure-Nak messages. If either pair is equal, then a new magic number must be chosen and sent by Configure-Request. Also, Configure-Reject is taken to mean the same thing as Configure-Ack for this option, since the sender of Configure-Request for this option must never reject it.

If the line is looped back, this will result in an endless loop of Configure-Request and Configure-Nak messages. Implementations should detect this with counters and log this specific error. (Generally, looped-back lines occur most often on asynchronous dial-up when one side of the connection is in PPP mode, but the other side is still in some kind of command-line mode, since command lines usually echo user input.)

An implementation that does not include this option should send 0 in all cases where a magic number is required (such as with the Echo-Request message). This is a generally useful and easy-to-implement option, however, so all implementations should support it.

06 Reserved; Not Used

This was originally the link-quality-monitoring proposal. It has since been renumbered.

07 Protocol Field Compression (PFC)

This boolean option is described in RFC 1661. When this option is negotiated, the sender of the Configure-Request indicates that it can receive "compressed" PPP protocol fields. To compress a PPP protocol field, the protocol number must have a most-significant octet of zero; that is, it must be in the range 0000 to 00FF (remember, of course, that neither 0000 nor 00FF is a legal PPP protocol number). The compressed protocol is sent as a single octet containing just the least-significant portion of the protocol number.

After sending Configure-Ack, the sender is not obligated to compress the PPP protocol field, although it is expected to do so. Uncompressed PPP protocol fields must always be accepted.

The receiver of compressed PPP protocol field messages can detect the compressed protocol since the least-significant octet of a protocol is always odd (has its least-significant bit set) and the most-significant octet is always even (has its LSB clear).

A robust implementation may decide to handle arbitrary-length PPP protocol fields by using the standard HDLC integer-reading procedure (read an octet, append to prior octets read, stop when LSB is nonzero). If so, beware that all protocol numbers specified in the RFCs are in encoded form. Doing this is plainly not required by RFC 1661 and may result in an unnecessarily complex implementation but does allow for some elegant solutions to alignment restrictions. In particular, encryption would have benefited from such an implementation to meet the 8-byte alignment restriction, had the protocol designers made use of it.

A suggested procedure to handle compression is:

```
if protocol <= 00FF and PFC negotiated then
   write protocol as one octet
else
   write protocol as two octets
         (most-significant first)
endif
```

A suggested decompression procedure is:

```
if LSB of octet is set then
   if PFC negotiated then
         protocol = value of first octet
   else
         discard frame
         record receive error
   endif
else
   protocol = value of first two octets
endif
```

Appendix A has C language examples.

These procedures may need to be modified if CCP-STAC compression using extended mode is negotiated. See Chapter 5 for details.

08 Address and Control Field Compression (ACFC)

This boolean option is described in RFC 1661. Negotiating this option indicates that the sender of the Configure-Request wishes to receive messages without the leading HDLC address and control fields (normally set to FF 03). The system sending Configure-Ack for this option may send subsequent frames without these octets (beginning each frame with the PPP protocol field) but is not required to do so.

This option cannot be used with RFC 1663 numbered mode or with any of the encapsulations that use the PPP NLPID (hex CF), such as RFC 1973 PPP in Frame Relay and RFC 1598 PPP in X.25.

The Address and Control fields must always be included on LCP messages, regardless of the negotiation of this option. Receivers must always be prepared to receive and handle these octets, again regardless of the negotiation. A suggested procedure to handle compression is:

```
if ACFC negotiated and not (protocol = C021) then
   do nothing
else
   write FF 03 as first two octets of frame
endif
```

A suggested decompression procedure is:

```
if first two octets of frame are not FF 03 then
   if ACFC negotiated then
        continue with PPP protocol field
   else
        drop frame
        record receive error
   endif
else
   remove first two octets
   continue with PPP protocol field
endif
```

09 FCS Alternatives

This option is described in the "extensions" RFC 1570. It allows the default 16-bit CRC to be negotiated into either a 32-bit CRC or disabled entirely. At one point, a 48-bit CRC was also considered, but it was dropped from consideration due to a patent held by Digital Equipment Corporation.

0A Self-Describing Pad (SDP)

This option, described in the "extensions" RFC 1570, describes a simple method for placing unambiguous padding octets at the end of the PPP information field in order to cause messages to fall on "natural" boundaries (typically, a power of two). When this option is enabled, packets are padded by adding the octet sequence 01 02 03, and so on, until the boundary is reached. If the packet falls on the boundary and the final octet is not in the range 01 through the boundary number, nothing is done. If it ends in such an octet, it is padded out to the next possible boundary.

The option negotiation contains a single octet of data that specifies the boundary, called the Maximum Pad Value.

The receiver checks the final octet of the frame (before the CRC) on reception. If this octet is in the range 01 through the boundary number, then octets are stripped and checked until 01 is removed or until an out-of-order octet is found, which is an error that results in dropping the frame.

There are currently two uses for this procedure. One is with the rarely used Compound-Frames option. The other is with encryption via ECP. Many encryption algorithms require the source data to fall on some kind of natural boundaries, like the US Data Encryption Standard (DES), which requires 8-byte boundaries.

Note that this boundary requirement is placed on the network layer data presented to the DES algorithm but that SDP pads only the link-level data. Negotiating the SDP option is therefore not useful for ECP. (Indeed, since the output of DES is always aligned, SDP is counterproductive in this case.)

0B Numbered Mode

This option is described in RFC 1663. It uses the ISO 7776 (LAP-B) standard for reliable data transport. This means that the implementation must maintain a queue of messages for retransmission and must implement a number of special timers.

Using this option means that the upper-level protocols will not see frame loss if errors occur, unless, of course, the link itself goes down. It also means that the upper-level protocols will experience relatively large variances in latency times over the link, which can have a severe impact on the performance of reliable transport protocols, like TCP.

I recommend limiting implementation of this option to rare circumstances, such as, perhaps, PPP over spread-spectrum radio. In particular, it is not worthwhile over typical modem connections (which usually already have error-correcting features, like V.42) or over common synchronous connections, which are usually highly reliable.

0C Multi-link Procedure

This option, briefly mentioned in RFC 1663, was intended to be used along with Numbered-Mode in order to enable the ISO 7776 Multi-link Procedure, which increases bandwidth by aggregating multiple serial links. With the advent of standard PPP Multi-link in RFC 1990, it is no longer necessary to support this feature.

0D Call-back

This option is described in RFC 1570. It allows a way for a peer to indicate that it wishes to have the link terminated after authentication and to have the other system call it back in an implementation-dependent manner, for either security reasons or as a toll-saving feature.

Unfortunately, this option is somewhat flawed. It is negotiated at LCP time when the peer has not yet been authenticated. In most cases, this means that it is not possible to determine whether the callback will be authorized at the time this option is acknowledged. The only realistic option in the cases where callback is available but the peer is not authorized to use the service is to terminate the link after going through authentication, possibly with a meaningful error message in the LCP terminate request, or renegotiate LCP and send Configure-Reject for the option when next requested. LCP renegotiation, though a mandatory part of the PPP standard, is not well tolerated by many implementations. In particular, according to engineers from Shiva, both ShivaRemote and Windows 95 will hang up the telephone if LCP renegotiation is attempted.

A proposed solution to this problem, which involves the use of an NCP-like protocol called Call-back Control Protocol (CBCP), is documented in the draft draft-ietf-pppext-callback-cp-02.txt. This proposal, discussed in more detail in Chapter 6, is strongly tied to machines with a CP/M lineage and to analog modems with Hayes-compatible command sets. This draft has expired, and no replacement has been proposed as of late 1997. It should not be implemented in new systems because no general consensus exists on how its features should be supported.

0E Connect Time

This was originally part of the PPP AppleTalk Control Protocol and was briefly changed into a configuration option and then into a separate code number to become the Time-Remaining message. This option is now obsolete.

0F Compound Frames

This boolean option is described in RFC 1570. It specifies a standard way to encapsulate multiple PPP frames within a single link-layer frame. This could be used, for instance, to save on per packet charges incurred on some kinds of packet-switched networks by sending fewer, larger packets. Its use was shaped by the IP over Large Public Data Networks (IPLPDN) working group.

10 Nominal-Data-Encapsulation

This option is described in the expired Internet Draft named draft-ietf-pppext-dataencap-03.txt. It specifies a way for data frames that would normally travel within PPP to use instead some other encapsulation technique (called *nominal encapsulation* by this draft). The goal of the draft was to introduce the use of PPP parameter negotiation to existing systems that exchange network data. The exchange of the data would not be altered and would stay in its possibly proprietary format, but PPP would also be negotiated over the link in order to establish security and other parameters.

This option has been officially dropped by the IETF pppext working group.

11 Multilink-MRRU

12 Multilink-Short-Sequence-Number-Header-Format

13 Multilink-Endpoint-Discriminator

These three options together are described in RFC 1990. These options form the basis of MP. In particular, negotiation of an MRRU means that this link is one of possibly several links to be aggregated together into a single bundle.

Frames are sent in MP by breaking them into small fragments, which are sent in parallel over all participating links and then reassembled at the remote end. Like IP fragmentation, there is no retransmission if a fragment is dropped. Instead, the entire frame is lost.

See Chapter 6 for a detailed description of this protocol.

14 Proprietary

This option is proprietary to Funk Software. Its format was discussed by Funk on the IETF PPP mailing list in June 1996. The option contains the following fields:

```
<ID Type> <ID Length> <Vendor ID> <Data>
```

The ID Type is a single octet with the value 00 if the Vendor ID is an Organizationally Unique Identifier (OUI; the first three octets of an Ethernet address) or 01 if the Vendor ID is a unique string, generally containing a company name or trademark. The ID Length is a single octet with the length of the Vendor ID string in octets. Its value should be 03 if ID Type is 00.

All information in the Data field is in a proprietary format defined by the indicated vendor and need not be interoperable with any other system or publicly documented.

Funk uses this format for its Data field:

```
<Sub-option Type> <Length> <Sub-option Data>
```

The Sub-option Type field is a single octet with the values 65 (Node Type), 66 (Authentication), 67 (NodeID™), 68 (Name), 69 (Container Control), 6A (Proprietary Flags). The Length is also a single octet representing the length of the entire option.

For the Node Type suboption, data field is a single octet set to 01 for WanderLink Server, 02 for WanderLink Free Client, and 04 for WanderLink Paid Client. The Name suboption allows the name to be used for authentication to be queried before starting authentication. The other suboptions are not documented.

15 DCE-Identifier

This option is described in the Informational (non-standards-track) RFC 1976. It specifies a way to distinguish communications devices, like CSU/DSUs from regular PPP bridges and routers. The intent of this option proposed by engineers at Adtran, a manufacturer of telecommunications equipment, is to have devices like CSU/DSUs communicate using a stripped-down version of PPP. This would provide a standard means of negotiating desirable features, like data compression and encryption. It is intended to be used with RFC 1963, which specifies a way to transport ordinary serial data over PPP using a form of V.120.

16 Multi-Link-Plus Procedure

This option negotiates the use of Ascend's proprietary MP+ protocol, which is documented in RFC 1934. The option currently has two octets of data, which are unused. See Chapter 6 for more details.

17 Link Discriminator

This option negotiates a two-octet integer used by the Bandwidth Allocation Protocol (BACP) to distinguish links in a multilink bundle. See Chapter 6 for more details.

18 LCP Authentication Option

This option was proposed in September 1996 by Funk Software as Internet Draft draft-ietf-pppext-link-negot-00.txt. This is an elegant scheme to incorporate security within LCP negotiation itself using a challenge-response model based on Configure-Nak. Implementation of this option would make the separate authentication stage unnecessary and simplify the implementation of callback and Multilink. It is currently being debated within the IETF.

Authentication Protocols

The authentication protocols generally do not follow the negotiation model laid out in the previous section. They are in a sense special protocols because portions are nonnegotiable by design and because they do not have many optional parameters but, rather, consist of an exchange that leads to either confirmation of identity or failure.

The base RFC for PPP authentication is 1334. This RFC covers Password Authentication Protocol (PAP) and the original version of Challenge-Handshake Authentication Protocol (CHAP). The current RFC for CHAP, though, is number 1994 and does not include PAP. The Extensible Authentication Protocol (EAP) is still in I-D stage (draft-ietf-pppext-eap-auth-02.txt and draft-ietf-pppext-eaptsa-

04.txt) with the IETF as of this writing. The two other protocols in use, the nonstandard Shiva-PAP and Microsoft-CHAP, are described last.

The protocol to use for authentication is negotiated during LCP option negotiation. A PPP implementation should be prepared to offer its strongest option first and to be able to accept only options that have been configured as acceptably secure by a system administrator. Authentication is often computationally expensive, requiring database look-ups and long calculations. For this reason, good implementations should relax retransmit timers and counters for these protocols.

Password Authentication Protocol (PAP)

PAP is protocol number C023, and its packets have the format:

```
<Code> <Id> <Length> <Data ...>
```

where Code is 01 for *Authenticate-Request* (Auth-Req), 02 for *Authenticate-Ack* (Auth-Ack), and 03 for *Authenticate-Nak* (Auth-Nak).

In the Authenticate-Request message, the Data has two counted strings, which are regular ASCII strings with a single octet prepended indicating the length of the string. The first string is the "Peer-ID," which is commonly, though incorrectly, referred to as a user name, and the second is the password. An example PAP Authenticate-Request looks like this before HDLC framing:

```
FF 03 C0 23 01 01 00 0F 03 7A 6F 65 06 53 65 63 52 65 74 D7 B9
```

which decodes as:

FF 03	–	Standard address and control field
C0 23	–	PPP Protocol field for PAP
01	–	Authenticate-Request
01	–	ID number
00 0F	–	Length
03	–	Peer-ID length — three octets
7A 6F 65	–	The letters "joe"; the peer's name
06	–	Password length — six octets
53 65 63 52 65 74		
	–	The letters "SecRet"; Joe's password (He's apparently not too concerned about security!)
D7 B9	–	CRC

The possible replies to this message are the Authenticate-Ack or Authenticate-Nak messages, where the data field contains an optional message for the human user (if any exists). If authentication fails, the system sending Authenticate-Nak should also attempt to terminate the link to frustrate a would-be system cracker, though a small number of attempts are often permitted, since some peers will have an interface to a human user and will permit retries. Systems that do not expect to have users actively typing in passwords during the establishment of the link need not support any retries.

Note that the authentication session is controlled by the authenticatee's sending requests, rather than by the authenticator, and that PAP authentication, if used, can usually be used only once during the lifetime of a link. To reauthenticate using PAP on a live link, it is necessary to renegotiate LCP in order to trigger PAP authentication again. Figure 3.7 shows the standard state machine marked up for use with PAP authentication.

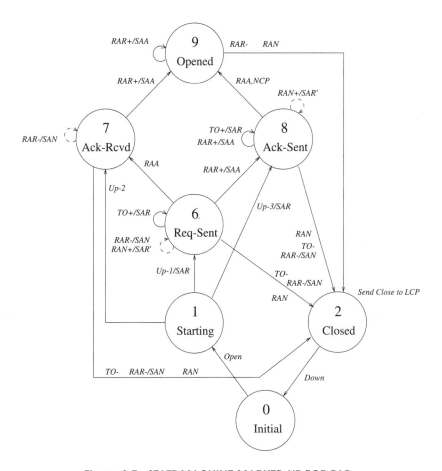

Figure 3.7: STATE MACHINE MARKED UP FOR PAP

The notations are the events and actions to be performed:

- Up-1: LCP Open on a system doing bidirectional PAP.
- Up-2: LCP Open on a system demanding PAP from its peer (sent LCP Configure-Request with PAP) but not providing its identity to its peer; sometimes referred to as a server.
- Up-3: LCP Open on a system supplying its identity to its peer (sent LCP Configure-Ack with PAP) but not demanding identification from the peer; sometimes referred to as a client.
- RAR+:Receive a good Authenticate-Request (validation succeeds).
- RAR-: Receive a bad Authenticate-Request (validation fails).
- RAA: Receive Authenticate-Ack.
- RAN: Receive Authenticate-Nak.
- TO+: Nonfatal time-out (retransmit).
- TO-: Fatal time-out (limit reached).
- NCP: Receive any NCP negotiation message (optional; allows negotiation to proceed quickly when Authenticate-Ack is lost).
- SAR: Send Authenticate-Request.
- SAA: Send Authenticate-Ack.
- SAN: Send Authenticate-Nak.

The transitions shown with dotted lines are optional. They represent the actions necessary for support of retries. RAN+ is a received Authenticate-Nak within the retry limit. SAR′ is a new Authenticate-Request generated after requerying the user for a new peer name–password combination.

In all cases, on failure PAP sends a Close message to LCP to tear down the link.

With PAP, you are necessarily giving away a peer name and password to any peer that requests it. It should be immediately obvious that the peer name and password sent out by an implementation should not be a valid peer name and password accepted by that implementation. This implies that for each connection, a separate peer name and password must be configured at each peer or that PAP should be used in only one direction. A separate pair of passwords, one for each call direction, should be used for each pair of peers if the link may be initiated by either peer, as in symmetric demand dialing. This means that the hardware must keep track of which peer dialed in order to select the password to use. If this is not done, then a third party may trivially break security by calling both parties and relaying the messages between them. This problem does not occur if only one peer will answer the call and the other ignores incoming calls.

Challenge-Handshake Authentication Protocol (CHAP)

CHAP is protocol number C223 and uses two basic packet formats. For the *Challenge* (code 01) and *Response* (code 02) messages, that format is:

```
<Code> <Id> <Length> <Value-Size> <Value> <Name>
```

where Value-Size is a single octet representing the length of the Value field in octets, and the Value field is the randomly generated challenge or the encoded response.

The Name field identifies the system performing the authentication for the Challenge message, and in the Response message it supplies the name of the system proving its identity. Unlike PAP, this allows a system automatically to use different CHAP secrets for different peers without relying on external information since the peers identify themselves by name. An example CHAP Challenge looks like this:

```
FF 03 C2 23 01 00 22 10 F7 11 7A E8 5A EE A7 05 83 33 F0 34
60 CB 49 44 44 69 61 6C 2D 75 70 20 53 65 72 76 65 72 39 E2
```

which decodes as:

```
FF 03          –    Standard address and control field
C2 23          –    PPP Protocol field for CHAP
01             –    Challenge
01             –    ID number
00 22          –    Length (34 octets)
10             –    Value-Size (16 octets)
F7 11 7A E8 5A EE A7 05 83 33 F0 34 60 CB 49 44
               –    Randomly generated value
44 69 61 6C 2D 75 70 20 53 65 72 76 65 72
               –    Name "Dial-up Server"
39 E2          –    CRC
```

For the *Success* (code 03) and *Failure* (code 04) messages, that format is similar to the PAP response codes:

```
<Code> <Id> <Length> <Message>
```

As in PAP, the message supplied, if any, should be a human-readable string. Usually systems supporting CHAP do not permit retries, so a failure message should be followed immediately by link termination.

Unlike PAP, the conversation is controlled by the authenticator sending a Challenge message, and CHAP may also be renegotiated at random during the life of a link without renegotiating LCP to lessen the chance that a hacker could successfully "hijack" a connection.

The operation of CHAP is quite a bit more complex than PAP. First, the system that wants to identify its peer using CHAP must generate a random sequence of octets (called the *challenge*) and send this along with an identifying name (which may not necessarily be the same as a user or peer name at that site). Only then may the recipient of this message respond; thus, the authentication session is controlled by the authenticator, not the authenticatee. The recipient uses the given name to look up a plain-text secret to use with this peer (perhaps in a local database or by asking a human user) and then uses the hash algorithm negotiated at LCP time to generate a response from the secret and the challenge value and then transmits this value back as the Value field in a Response message, along with the real peer's name.

The system that sent the challenge then performs the same hash algorithm (currently, MD5 is required for any implementation that supports CHAP). If the result matches the Response value, it sends a Success message. Otherwise, it sends a Failure message.

It is essential that this validation of the peer's Response be done using a database of secrets separate from that used to generate CHAP Response messages on a system. If a CHAP implementation both generates and validates Responses using a single secret, it has effectively no security at all. As with PAP, symmetric demand-dialing systems must use separate secrets depending on which system originates the call.

Figure 3.8 shows the standard state machine, which I marked up for use with CHAP authentication.

The notations are the events and actions to be performed:

- Up-1: LCP Open on a system doing bidirectional CHAP.
- Up-2: LCP Open on a system demanding CHAP from its peer (sent LCP Configure-Request with CHAP) but not providing its identity to its peer, sometimes referred to as a "server."
- Up-3: LCP Open on a system supplying its identity to its peer (sent LCP Configure-Ack with CHAP) but not demanding identification from the peer, sometimes referred to as a "client."
- RC: Receive a Challenge message.
- RR+:   Receive a good Response message (validation succeeds).
- RR-:   Receive a bad Response message (validation fails).
- RS: Receive a Success message.
- RF: Receive a Failure message.
- NCP: Receive any NCP negotiation message (optional).
- TO+:   Nonfatal time-out (retransmit).
- TO-:   Fatal time-out (limit reached).

- SC: Send a Challenge message.
- SR: Send a Response message.
- SS: Send a Success message.
- SF: Send a Failure message.
- SLR: Send last-generated Response message (if any).
- TMR: Rechallenge timer event. Unlike most state machines, CHAP should not signal a Down event to the NCPs when leaving the Opened state on a TMR event.

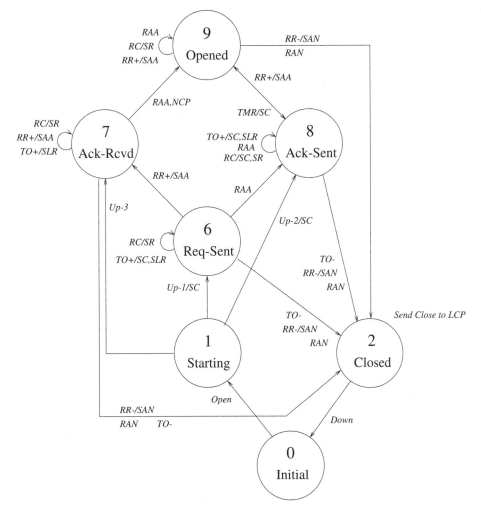

Figure 3.8: STATE MACHINE MARKED UP FOR CHAP

This state machine is not marked up for retries on authentication failure, since systems using CHAP often do not permit retries. Such a modification, though, is rather simple and analogous to the PAP changes.

PAP versus CHAP

Good implementations should support both CHAP and PAP authentication methods, even though the PAP protocol has been officially deprecated by RFC 1994. Many users believe that CHAP is always "better" than PAP. This is not the case. Each of these two protocols has its own advantages and failings. In CHAP, the secret never appears on the wire in any form, but the failing is that both sides must keep a clear-text version of the password in order to calculate the response value, and this password could be compromised. In PAP, this particular problem can be avoided by the use of one-way hashing, which cannot be used with CHAP, but using PAP means that the clear-text password must be sent over the wire and that a rogue peer could be used to extract a user's password.

The RFC does not state that the PAP password must be a fixed value or even that it must come from a user. One way to use the password, which makes PAP more secure than CHAP, is to use it with a token card, such as Enigma's SafeWord or Security Dynamics' SecurID. These hardware devices (which resemble credit cards with LCD numeric displays) give one-time passwords, which are useless to an attacker if intercepted. Since the validation routines for these cards can check a given value but will not reveal the current password for use with other calculations, these cards cannot be used with CHAP at all, but they do work perfectly well with PAP using the password field for the one-time key value. Such a system usually needs prior arrangement to signal the use of this validation scheme, often based on the peer name.

Of course, such a scheme is impractical if periodic reverification is desired. For these applications, specialized hardware with interfaces to smart cards might be employed to generate secure responses.

MS-CHAP

MS-CHAP is just regular CHAP with algorithm 80 negotiated at LCP time instead of 05 for MD5. When this option is accepted, the MS-CHAP documentation, which is publicly available on Microsoft's FTP site but not in any standard RFC, gives a complex set of possible ways to form a response from an eight-octet challenge value. The two main options are LAN Manager– and Windows NT–type responses. When using the LAN Manager form, the user's password is hashed by using it as a key to encrypt a well-known string with DES. For the Windows NT form, the user's password is hashed by running it through the public MD4 algorithm.

In either case, the response value to the challenge is generated by using DES to encrypt the random challenge value from the peer using the hashed password as a key. For this step of the operation, standard CHAP does the same but uses MD5 instead.

When using MS-CHAP with non-Microsoft software, be aware that the user name and Windows network domain strings must be concatenated to form the peer name passed to an NT host. For example, if the domain is "office" and the user name is "mary," then the peer name passed to NT should be "office\mary." In a pppd configuration file on Unix, the backslash in this string will need to be escaped, so the peer name for this case appears in the file as "office\\mary." Also note that NT systems do not identify themselves. The peer name from the NT system will be zero length.

Standard versus MS-CHAP

Of course, there is no way for a system implementing this protocol to "know" whether the peer system actually started with the user's password and did the initial DES or MD4 hash starting with the user's typed password, or just used a stored copy of the hash value. Indeed, the Windows NT dial-in system stores the hashed password value as the key for the user, in exactly the same way a CHAP system must store the shared secret. In truth, this system does not differ much from regular CHAP in that both use a shared secret, which is a string for regular CHAP and the output of a hash routine for the MS-CHAP system. If one were to break into a Windows NT password registry using the readily available PWDUMP utility and steal the hashed user passwords, one could then successfully authenticate PPP connections into that system using a modified PPP client that does not implement the hash function, and thus have complete access to the target network.

The claimed advantage for this variant of CHAP, other than the incorrect claim of stronger C2-compliant security, is one of simplicity. Users can reuse their dial-in password as the simple password for other applications (such as logging into the NT system itself for file access), since the system is not storing this password in the clear and any compromise of that hash value does not reveal this "upper-level" password. However, since using the same password for PPP link authentication as is used for access to other systems is generally a bad idea, this is a dubious advantage at best.

Worst of all, MS-CHAP provides a way to change the stored password from within PPP. After having broken into the system using the technique given above, a trespasser can use this flaw to set the user's real password to any convenient value in order to gain complete access.

MS-CHAP also declares that the peer name is in an international character set known as "UNICODE." Standard CHAP makes no such restriction.

Extensible Authentication Protocol (EAP)

EAP (protocol C227) is a new authentication scheme for PPP and is not yet in wide-spread use. The packets have the same basic code numbers and a format similar to CHAP. The packet format is:

```
<Code> <Id> <Length> <Message>
```

with valid codes defined as 01 (*Request*), 02 (*Response*), 03 (*Success*), and 04 (*Failure*). The message format depends on the code number. No message is present for codes 03 or 04. The message format for codes 01 and 02 is:

```
<Type> <Type-Data>
```

where Type is one octet indicating the contents of the Type-Data field that follow, and is one of 01 (*Identity*), 02 (*Notification*), 03 (*Nak*), 04 (*MD5-Challenge*), 05 (*S/Key RFC 1760*), or 06 (*Generic Token Card*).

The operation of this protocol is quite different from PAP or CHAP. The peers hold a conversation consisting of several Request and Response messages (Requests come from the system performing the authentication, and Responses come from the system being authenticated) until the authenticator is satisfied that the peer has been identified or has failed identification, at which point it sends either the Success or Failure message instead of the Request message.

Since this protocol is still in Internet Draft stage, it will not be further described here. Interested readers are encouraged to retrieve the latest draft from any of the standard FTP sites listed in Chapter 8.

Shiva Password Authentication Protocol (SPAP)

SPAP is protocol number C027, or the illegal protocol number C1 23 for the older version. On the IETF PPP mailing list, Shiva engineers discussed a few of the features of this protocol, such as support for token cards. However, no documentation for this protocol exists in any of the standard public sources, and it appears that Shiva intends to license this protocol to selected companies rather than placing it in the public domain, as is usually done.

As documented by the Klos sniffer (see Chapter 7), the LCP option to request SPAP is C027 plus four octets of unknown data set to 01000002. The LCP option for the old SPAP is C123 plus two octets of unknown data set to 0000.

Old SPAP appears to use a message format identical to regular PAP, except for the protocol number. The password field contains an obscured (though not quite encrypted) version of the text password.

Regular SPAP uses a message format modeled after the option format used for the NCPs. Codes 02 (*Ack*), 03 (*Nak*), and 06 (*Request*) are used. The option numbers are 01 (*Peer-ID*), 02 (*Password*), and several unknown options. The Peer-ID contains just the name of the peer as text. The Password contains two octets that form a "secret" value, perhaps similar in function to the Unix password "salt," plus the obscured password.

Other Security Protocols

A number of security protocols are defined for PPP, including these:

- C225: draft-ietf-pppext-public-key-00.txt, a protocol developed by Novell but apparently now abandoned.
- C229: Mitsubishi's Security Information Exchange Protocol.
- C26F: Stampede's Bridging Authorization Protocol.

There are as well several proprietary protocols, such as C281, C481, and C283, which are generally not seen in the field.

About Security

There are two facets of security, authentication and privacy, that are intimately related. Measures that provide for one facet usually depend on the other, and both must be considered together during system design. Successfully decrypting valid data, for instance, often implies something about the peer's identity, and, conversely, verifying the identity of the peer prevents the accidental release of private information.

Security is hard. Replacing the front door with a solid steel version with electronic locks will encourage burglars to try the windows. Barring the windows might encourage the more enterprising ones to take a chainsaw to the exterior walls. Similarly, employing complex security measures in a telecommunications system may cause a hacker intent on gaining access to employ what is sometimes known as *social engineering*—a simple telephone call to an administrator or other legitimate system user can reveal the secrets necessary for access.

Security is therefore a system issue. Employing the most cryptographically secure authentication and encryption methods is a wasted effort if the building doors are not locked or an administrator is willing to change a password based on a telephone conversation. Worse yet, some seemingly good methods are actually counterproductive. In order to use more secure methods, longer keys and frequent changes are usually necessary. Users, however, have limited memories, and forcing the use of these supposedly more secure methods often causes them either to write down their passwords in a convenient location or to choose easy-to-remember, and therefore easy-to-break, ones.

It is far too easy for implementors to expend great effort on minutiae. Worrying, for instance, about the predictability of the plaintext padding used might not be worthwhile if a VLSI device that can crack DES becomes available. The effort should be commensurate with the value of the data and the likelihood of attack.

PPP Security Pitfalls

A comprehensive list of the ways security in PPP can fail is probably impossible to produce. The following cautions relate to common implementation and usage errors for switched access systems, such as dial-up servers and PCs with modems:

- **Do not use a PAP peer name and password combination on more than one system.**
  Doing so means that a caller requesting authentication will receive information that is also valid on that system.

- **Do not use the same PAP password or CHAP secret for both dial-in and dial-out when offering credentials to the peer.**
  Doing this means that an attacker can call one peer to get the other's PAP password or can relay the challenge from one called system to another to get authenticated.

- **Pay close attention to switched-access features and interactions among them.**
  For instance, glare, which occurs when a line being used for dial-out receives a call at the same time it attempts to dial, can be exploited in a number of ways. Consider a PC-based system that uses a modem to call a central system. Many PCs automatically redial the central system if the connection is lost. Unfortunately, many telephone lines in use with modems also have a "call-waiting" feature, which can cause a modem to disconnect in a predictable way. A viable, and difficult-to-detect, attack would be to call the PC's modem once briefly to cause the connection to drop, then to redial as the PC starts its automatic redial attempt and thus force an intentional glare. At this point, the PC modem will "think" it is reconnected to the host system, when, in fact, it is attached to the attacker's system. Using authentication in both directions generally alleviates this problem but is unfortunately not common in dial-up PPP implementations. Special telephone lines, such as ground-start, can also help by eliminating glare, as can use of features to disable call-waiting (usually "*70") and randomly delaying automatic redial or requiring user intervention instead.

Following is a similar caution for unswitched (leased-line) systems:

- **Bidirectional authentication and random challenges are still important.** Good authentication prevents simple problems, such as wiring errors, as well as more complex problems, such as attackers who have access to the telephone company routing tables, which establish leased-line connections.

And the following are for any kind of system:

- **Do not use the same CHAP secret to validate both ends of a link.** Doing this enables a particularly simple break-in technique. The attacker echoes back the Challenge it receives from its peer. When the system issues its response, this is then replayed back as the attacker's response. If the CHAP secrets for each direction are the same, then these responses, given the same challenges, will be the same. This implies, for the general case, that a system that has relationships with many peers must use separate lists of secrets for generating CHAP Response messages and validating received Response messages and that users must be carefully warned against having the same secret in both lists. Violating this rule effectively disables all CHAP security.

- **If you support both PAP and CHAP, do not use the same secret for both.**

- **Limit the number of CHAP Challenges per second that are accepted.** Challenges can be used for password guessing.

- **Do not respond correctly to Challenges with a different peer name from the first Challenge seen.** This tactic is used by peers using your system as an *oracle*. The attack is made by authenticating with some unprivileged account, then using periodic but altered rechallenges on the connection to yield valid responses for a more privileged account being attacked on a separate simultaneous connection. Failing to respond will give useful clues to the attacker. Generating a meaningless random number or even a simple fixed string for the Response will frustrate the effort. In any event, such Challenges should be logged for review by an administrator.

- **Be very careful with pseudo-random-number generators.** Protocols, like CHAP, that rely on the apparent unpredictability of these numbers as viewed from outside the system are compromised if these numbers are predictable, by either time of day (or time since boot) or prior challenge values. One good source of random numbers is to use a cryptographic hash of some secret along with the last number generated and the time of day.

- **Consider the system security and the PPP line security together.**
  If the system to which you are authenticating yourself is accessible to a
  large number of possibly untrusted people, then consider using PAP instead
  of CHAP. With PAP, your password need not be stored in a reversible format
  on that possibly insecure system, while with either standard CHAP or MS-
  CHAP a copy of your password must be kept. For a system that only dials
  out, PAP is exactly equivalent to the traditional "user name" and "password" prompts from a text-mode system. It is neither more nor less secure.

- **If using CHAP, invest as much effort as possible making the inevitable
  list of secrets inaccessible in any form.**
  Reversible encryption helps only a little. Hiding the secrets on a dedicated challenge-response generating machine (perhaps running RADIUS) is much better.
  (Of course, this solution would require extensions to RADIUS, which does not
  support symmetric CHAP.)

Security References

Security is a broad and complex topic. Interested readers may wish to explore this
topic through some of the many books written on the subject. Following is a list of
suggested starting points:

- Denning, D. E. *Cryptography and Data Security*. Addison-Wesley, Reading, MA,
  1982.
- Garfinkel, Simson, and Gene Spafford. *Practical Unix and Internet Security*.
  O'Reilly & Associates, Sebastapol, CA, 1991.
- Hsiao, D. K., D. S. Kerr, and S. E. Madnick. *Computer Security*. Academic Press,
  New York, 1979.
- Rivest, R. L., A. Shamir, and L. Adleman. On Digital Signatures and Public Key
  Cryptosystems. *Communications of the ACM* 21, no.2 (February 1978): 120–126.
- The IPSEC draft documents (draft-ietf-ipsec-isakmp-07.txt, et al).

Fast Reconnect

An example in Chapter 7 shows that PPP can fully negotiate even in complex cases
within a few round-trip times and that this negotiation is easily faster than
switched-circuit set-up times, even on ISDN. Some users, however, view PPP negotiation as too slow for some applications, perhaps based on their experience with
bad PPP implementations. These designers have many times proposed complex
mechanisms to maintain state across sessions in order to bypass normal PPP negotiation. These proposals are usually termed *fast reconnect* or *short hold*. These pro-

posed protocols, such as draft-ietf-pppext-scm-00.txt, greatly weaken security and are completely unnecessary.

As the example in Chapter 7 shows, PPP is already faster than the inherent delays in circuit set-up, but PPP can be made faster still, if necessary. A technique proposed by Vernon Schryver reduces this delay to a single-round trip time, at the expense of a minor but generally compatible violation of RFC 1661 and a possible time-out delay with some peers. It does not require any new PPP options or protocols. The technique is to send without delay all of the Configure-Request and Configure-Ack messages that should bring up the link rather than waiting after each message for the peer to respond. As long as both sides are in the right state (LCP transitioning to Req-Sent) at the start, the link will be up as soon as this burst is over. To the peer, it will seem as though the necessary negotiation messages are always immediately available when it goes to read the next one. In the worst case, if the receiving peer requires a delay while switching state, this technique will cause LCP to reach Open state, and the extra messages will get silently discarded. Negotiation will then proceed in the usual fashion after a time-out.

Implementing this technique requires prior knowledge of the messages that will be sent by the peer and the options it will attempt. This can be done by saving the negotiation options in stable storage during a "regular" call. For CHAP, it also requires prior knowledge of the CHAP challenge value, which can be achieved by prior agreement between the peers to use a secure pseudo-random-number generator for the hash values. A possible algorithm would be an MD5 hash of the last challenge, the peer's secret, and the time of day to the nearest ten minutes. Another good algorithm would be to encrypt the last challenge using DES and a key known only to the peers.

Chapter

4

The Network Layer Protocols

IN THIS CHAPTER

This chapter covers the network layer protocols, which form the links between PPP and the software outside PPP that handles the networking protocols, like IP and AppleTalk. The network layers are where the real work of PPP is done. These are the connections to the client protocols run over PPP. All common networking protocols, and many uncommon protocols, are represented, and new protocols are added as existing proprietary systems are converted over to standards-based protocols.

This chapter covers many of the more common network layer protocols for PPP, but new protocols continue to be introduced at a steady pace. Check with any of the standard document repositories listed in Chapter 8 for more information on particular protocols.

For each network protocol, there are usually two PPP protocol numbers. The first is the network control protocol (NCP), which is distinguished by being chosen from the range 8000 through BFFF. The NCP is used by PPP to negotiate the use of any parameters necessary for that network protocol. The second protocol number assigned is in the range 0000 through 3FFF and is the same as the NCP number minus 8000. This protocol is the network protocol itself and carries the user's data. For instance, the IP network protocol is assigned 8021 for IPCP, which negotiates IP addresses and other parameters, and is assigned network protocol 0021 for the IP data.

An implementation could use the range of the protocol numbers received to direct the data intelligently through either a high-priority path for user data or a low-priority path for negotiation data. Such a split is common in embedded systems, such as routers. (Such an implementation would, of course, need to be extremely careful with the timing considerations between the data and the negotiation. In general, one must be ready to receive data when one sends the Configure-Ack message and must stop sending data when a Terminate-Request or Configure-Request is received.)

Of these protocols, IPCP is most common. IPV6CP has been proposed to supplant it but is rare as of this writing. IPXCP is next most common. The others are less common although not quite rare.

Internet Protocol (IPCP)

IPCP, described in RFC 1332, is protocol 8021, and the corresponding network protocol is 0021. This network layer transports IP version 4 datagrams across a PPP link. See also RFC 791, which describes IPv4 itself, and the primary transport-level protocols ICMP (RFC 792), TCP (RFC 793), and UDP (RFC 768). Options 02 and 03 are common. Options 81, 82, 83, and 84 are specific to PCs. The others are rare. The negotiable IPCP options follow.

01 IP-Addresses

This option is described in the obsolete RFC 1172. The option contains eight octets of information: four for an IP source address and four for an IP destination address. This option should not be implemented by any new PPP system. Rather, the IP-Address option should be negotiated instead. It has been deprecated due to convergence problems in some cases.

02 IP-Compression-Protocol

This option is described in RFC 1332. The data field of this option contains two octets for the compression protocol number and any additional octets defined by that protocol.

The only current value for this option is 00 2D MM PP, where 002D is the protocol number for Van Jacobson (VJ) Compressed TCP/IP, MM is a single octet representing the maximum slot ID (number of slots minus 1), and PP is a flag set to 00 if the slot identifier must not be compressed and 01 if it may be. When this option is in use, three network protocols are used:

0021	Regular IP data (could not be compressed)
002D	Compressed TCP
002F	Uncompressed TCP

VJ compression can reduce the standard TCP and IP headers from 40 octets to 1 octet under favorable conditions. It does not affect UDP or other IP protocols, and it does not compress the actual user data. The net effect is to improve latency greatly for interactive applications, such as TELNET, and to improve slightly throughput for bulk data applications, such as FTP.

This compression technique is intricate, and a discussion of it is outside the scope of this book. RFC 1144 contains both a detailed description of the protocol and C language source code.

03 IP-Address

This configuration option is documented in RFC 1332. It contains a single four-octet IP address representing the address of the local system. The address may be sent as 00 00 00 00, in which case the peer is requested to send a Configure-Nak specifying the address of the local system, perhaps by looking up the authenticated peer name from PAP or CHAP in a database. If such a look-up fails, the IPCP protocol should be shut down with a simple Protocol-Reject or by sending a Configure-Ack to go to Open state and then sending a Terminate-Request message. (Although more complex, many common implementations, including the freely available pppd [see Chapter 8], will do the latter. Thus, the usual interpretation of IPCP going to Open state and then immediately terminating is that the addresses negotiated were not acceptable.)

This option may be omitted from the Configure-Request and rejected with Configure-Reject if received. In this case, no IP addresses are negotiated on the link. This is occasionally done by intelligent half-bridge devices that do not have IP addresses assigned. However, I strongly recommend against this practice for three reasons. First, negotiation of addresses does not imply that the addresses are not in use for other purposes. In fact, it is quite reasonable to borrow the local IP address of another interface for IPCP negotiation purposes. It is explicitly not necessary to create a separate "subnet" for the link. Second, even if the addresses are not needed for any purpose, such as with half-bridges, it is still a good idea to negotiate for the addresses to avoid configuration and wiring errors. Finally, virtually all devices that speak IPCP have at least one IP address assigned that could be used for negotiation. For instance, any device manageable via SNMP must have a configured IP address. Sending this IP address to your peer via this option is a good practice.

An IP address of all zeros is often the source of trouble. Implementors should be aware that some systems send an unsolicited Configure-Nak with 0 if the peer attempts to negotiate without revealing its address in a Configure-Request message. Such a Configure-Nak does not imply, as the RFC would seem to indicate, that offering an IP address of all zeros to this peer is an acceptable response. Instead, a proper nonzero address should be returned if possible. Also, some implementations (such as Windows 95) erroneously send Configure-Ack with a zero IP address in response to a zero Configure-Request. IPCP should be shut down if this is detected, since it indicates a configuration error.

Good implementations allow both the local IP address (sent in Configure-Request) and the remote IP address (sent in Configure-Nak, if necessary) to be configured by an administrator. Depending on network topology and address assignment practices, it may be wise to allow a range or list of addresses to be specified in each case to allow for some latitude in the addresses requested by the peer.

The Unnumbered Mode Controversy

Many implementations and implementors wrongly confuse the IP routing notions of "numbered" and "unnumbered" with the presence or absence of the IPCP IP-Address option. This issue probably causes more IPCP interoperability problems than any other.

To understand the confusion, it is necessary to understand some IP routing basics. There are two fundamental types of links[1], called *broadcast* and *point-to-point*. On a broadcast interface, such as Ethernet, a given node will have at least one local address and a subnet mask. The local address on the interface must exist in order for the node to transmit on the link and receive data. The subnet mask segregates the world into those several nodes that are also on the same link and those many that must be on different links. When the node wants to send data to a particular IP address, it can use the subnet mask to determine if the message can be sent directly to the recipient on the same link or, if it is not on the subnet, if it must go through an intermediate router first. This test is done by comparing the destination address with the source address after logically AND-ing both with the subnet mask value.

An interesting corollary to the same link–other link distinction made by the subnet mask on broadcast interfaces is that no separate link (unconnected by bridges) may exist anywhere in the Internet that overlaps any portion of a given subnet. In other words, all IP addresses within that subnet must be reachable by a broadcast on that interface. If splitting of the subnet were permitted, then IP addresses would be ambiguous, at least for hosts not running a routing protocol. How would a router determine where to send a packet whose destination address lies in the overlapped region? It could not reasonably resolve the next hop because the address would belong to two separate links (A or B in Figure 4.1) according to the subnet mask comparison. Worse, consider what happens when a host unaware of this misconfiguration attempts to contact an address in the disputed region. It will use local address resolution (such as ARP) instead of forwarding to a router, as would be required.[2]

---

1. There are, of course, variants, such as the nonbroadcast LAN emulation used on ATM networks. These variants function in ways similar enough to the two fundamental types that they can be ignored for simplicity.

2. For a few restricted cases, it is possible to do this by having the router respond to all ARP requests on the larger network on behalf of the smaller network. This solution does not scale as well as traditional routing and generally has little to recommend it.

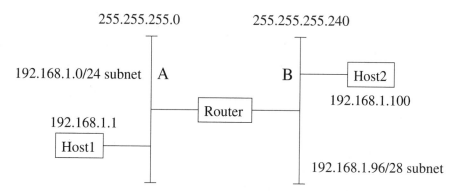

Figure 4.1: ILLEGAL CONFIGURATION

Host1 here will attempt to ARP for Host2 rather than sending packets for Host2 to the router. Host2 will never see the ARP request and never be able to reply to it. Broadcasts and protocols that rely on them are even more adversely affected.

From this restriction, it follows that no broadcast interface can be configured whose local address lies within another interface's subnet, since this would clearly mean that any subnet mask given to the former would surely overlap some or all of the latter's subnet. Some IP implementations, though, have taken this idea to an extreme by prohibiting any interface—not just broadcast interfaces—from having a local address within another interface's subnet.

This extreme is clearly wrong for point-to-point links. Consider the configuration of routers connected only by point-to-point links in Figure 4.2. Node A could quite reasonably use the same local address for its links to both C and G, since that local address would define A's identity and would not be part of a subnet definition.

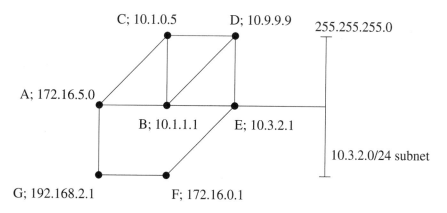

Figure 4.2: BOTH POINT-TO-POINT AND BROADCAST

Each node in this network may have a single unique and arbitrary IP address, and the entire configuration would still function as part of an internet. The fact that node B has four links, each with the same local address, causes no harm. Even node E, which uses the same local address on a broadcast interface, is in no trouble, since the addresses are still distinct and the subnet does not overlap any address not physically connected to the broadcast link.

IP implementations that require the local addresses to differ will force the administrator to assign separate local addresses for each link. Node B in Figure 4.2 would consume at least four IP addresses. Usually this software flaw is the result of the lack of a broadcast point-to-point flag in the link interface. Thus, since all links look like broadcast interfaces, a separate subnet must be created for each link even though there are only two peers, and the notion of "broadcasting" inherent in a subnet definition is irrelevant.

Note that for three nodes, as in Figure 4.3, a minimum of 12 IP addresses (4 per link) is used if this problem exists. This mode of operation is known as numbered mode to most router manufacturers, because each link is identified with a subnet number and a unique local address. The prior example, where each node had only a single local address, is known as unnumbered mode, since the point-to-point links do not use unique local addresses. Clearly, for point-to-point links such as PPP, numbered mode need not exist.

The confusion in IPCP is that some vendors have integrated the IP-Address option into this routing software design flaw. Normally the IP-Address option serves only to ease configuration errors and to simplify administration. When this option is not negotiated, IPCP falls back to a mode of operation similar to SLIP; addresses must be carefully configured at both ends of the link or dynamically discovered through some other means (BOOTP and monitoring the source address on RIP updates are two popular techniques). Either way, the IPCP option is not intended to affect routing issues. However, on the implementations with this flaw, enabling IP-Address negotiation will also configure the unit for numbered mode, and disabling it reverts to unnumbered mode. Either way, the administrator must give up important functionality.

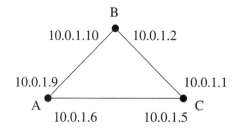

Figure 4.3: NUMBERED MODE LINKS

All subnet masks set to 255.255.255.252

Good PPP implementations with IPCP should separate these two options. If numbered mode is necessary for interoperating with broken peers, then it should be configured separately from the option that controls whether IP-Address is included in the Configure-Request message. If the peer sends a Configure-Reject for IP-Address, then the obsolete IP-Addresses option may be tried. If both are Configure-Rejected, then, just like SLIP, any local address may be used without notifying the peer. If the peer refuses to send a Configure-Request with the IP-Address option, then after trying an unsolicited Configure-Nak, a guess at the peer's address may be taken (perhaps based on a database look-up of the authenticated peer name), or any reasonable address may be chosen.

Note that the Terminate-Request message will not terminate IPCP if it has not yet reached Open state. If IPCP must be terminated due to addressing problems, then either use Protocol-Reject or allow it to reach Open state with any options (send Configure-Ack for any received Configure-Request) and only then issue Terminate-Request.

Since this routing flaw is unfortunately common and shows no signs of repair in the near future, I recommend going to great lengths to attempt to interoperate with peers that unwisely choose to reject the IP-Address option.

81 Primary-DNS-Address

82 Primary-NBNS-Address

83 Secondary-DNS-Address

84 Secondary-NBNS-Address

These four options are described in Informational (non-standards-track) RFC 1877. Each carries a single four-octet IP address for the indicated type of name server, where DNS is the standard Domain Name Service, and NBNS is the NetBIOS name server.

Unfortunately, these options have two rather severe flaws. First, they are nego-tiated at the wrong level, since DNS and NBNS are application-level services and IPCP is a network-level negotiation. Second, they duplicate, at least for IP users, a service that already has a long history, which is BOOTP (RFC 951) over PPP. Instead, the author of this RFC probably should have described options to transfer NBNS addresses via BOOTP in order to implement these features.

To understand the layering flaw, consider a network in which a remote office has a small router attached to a wide-area link via PPP and a local network with a few devices attached via Ethernet. When IPCP is negotiated by the router, what name server address should be sent? If addresses are received, what should be done with them? In fact, this small router would neither know nor care about the location of any name servers, since this is, for many routers, an irrelevant application-level detail.

The local systems on the Ethernet will need to resort to using a BOOTP proxy across the PPP link to find this information, if necessary.

Consider also what happens when a PC implementing these options is disconnected from its PPP link and is plugged into an Ethernet or Token Ring network. If neither Token Ring nor Ethernet interfaces (which do not implement a similar negotiation) will be able to supply these addresses, where will the PC find them? It will then be necessary to statically define the addresses through a user interface or use a standard protocol like BOOTP (or its cousin DHCP) to get them. But if BOOTP is available for the Ethernet connection, then why not also use it for the PPP configuration?

The advantage these options allow is a slight simplification of those few systems that have monolithic software architectures, where the applications and network layers are mixed together into a single program. This is often the case on personal computers. The disadvantages, which generally include the lack of usefulness on many common architectures, argue that these options should not be implemented.

89 Mobile-IPv4

This option is described in draft-ietf-pppext-ipcp-mip-02.txt. The value contained in the option is a four-octet IP address of the home agent for a mobile host. This option is sent in a Configure-Request message only by a mobile node requesting a tunneled connection back to its home network. It is not modified by Configure-Nak. If the peer is willing to establish the tunnel, a Configure-Ack should be sent. Otherwise, Configure-Reject is used to signal that tunneling is unavailable.

Internet Protocol Version 6 (IPV6CP)

IPv6, also known as IPng, has gone by several names during its development as the next-generation replacement for IP. It provides significant enhancements over the venerable IPv4 protocol, including expanded addresses, automatic configuration, and better security. This network protocol is 0057, the control protocol is 8057, and the negotiation options are covered in RFC 2023. See also RFC 1883 for a description of IPv6 itself. The current IPV6CP options follow.

01 Interface-Token

This option negotiates a four-octet randomly chosen nonzero number at each end of the link. This number is then used to create the interface addresses by prepending FE0000000000000000000000 to it, making it into an RFC 1884 "local use" address. (IPv6 addresses are 16 octets long, giving roughly $4 \cdot 10^{20}$ available IPv6 addresses per square inch on Earth.)

02   IPv6 Compression Protocol

The data field of this option contains two octets for the compression protocol number, plus any additional octets defined by that protocol. The only current value for this option is 00 4F MM PP, which is the IPV6 header compression protocol. MM is the maximum slot number, and PP are option flags.

As of this writing, header compression is the subject of at least two Internet Drafts (draft-degermark-ipv6-hc-03.txt and draft-simpson-ipv6-hc-00.txt).

Internetwork Packet Exchange (IPXCP)

Despite its name, IPX is generally not used on the global Internet. It is instead a protocol used chiefly by personal computers running software from Novell on corporate networks (although there are at least partial implementations available for other types of computers). IPX is virtually an exact subset of Xerox's original XNS protocol, which has a separate PPP protocol number. IPXCP, which is described in RFC 1552, has been assigned PPP protocol number 802B, and the corresponding network layer for user data is 002B.

In addition to the following options, an implementation may need to include Novell's IPX WAN protocol, documented in informational RFC 1634. This RFC describes an application-level protocol used to maintain routing information on Novell wide-area links and restricts some of the information given in the following options. It is not possible to connect to a Novell MPR (Multi-Protocol Router) using IPX without IPXWAN support, though most other routers accept connections with or without IPXWAN. If your target market does not include connecting directly to Novell dial-up routers over PPP links, the IPXWAN extension is not necessary for IPX support.

All options except 04 are common to IPXCP implementations.

01 IPX-Network-Number

This option negotiates a single four-octet number representing the network number assigned to the link itself. If both peers send Configure-Request messages for this parameter, then the numerically larger network number is chosen. The network number may also be configured as zero, which means that the link is not used for IPX routing but is instead a link to a single node that is logically located on the peer's configured network. The receiver of a Configure-Request specifying zero may also reply with a Configure-Nak specifying a different number if routing is desired by one peer.

This option is not symmetrically negotiated in each direction like other PPP options. There is only one network number for a given physical link, and the Configure-Request generating code in an implementation should take information from both received Configure-Naks and received Configure-Requests from the peer.

02 IPX-Node-Number

This option negotiates a unique six-octet number, which generally has a format similar to an Ethernet address, for the local system. This number must be unique for the given network negotiated. Often a system that implements IPXCP will use an installed Ethernet adapter as the source for this number. Unlike the network number, this number is unique for each end of the link and is negotiated in each direction.

03 IPX-Compression-Protocol

This option negotiates a header compression protocol. The negotiated value is two octets specifying the compression protocol, plus additional octets determined by the desired protocol. There are two currently valid compression protocol values:

0002: Telebit RFC 1553 compression. Two additional octets of information are given: one specifying the maximum slot ID number, and the second specifying a number of boolean option flags.

0235: Shiva Compressed NCP/IPX (Proprietary).

Like IP compression, this option compresses only header overhead and not the user data. Unlike IP compression, though, IPX compression is mandatory once negotiated. The same protocol number (002B) is then used for the compressed data.

04 IPX-Routing-Protocol

This option negotiates the routing protocol to be used over the link. The value contained in this option is a two-octet integer representing a single routing protocol to be used, plus a variable-length data field for information specific to that protocol. By default, a combination of Novell Routing Information Protocol (RIP) and Server Advertising Protocol (SAP) messages are expected. Unlike many other options, this one may appear more than once in a Configure-Request message in order to request the use of multiple protocols on a link.

The routing protocol numbers are as follows:

0000   None

0002   Novell RIP/SAP

0004   Novell Netware Link State Protocol (NLSP).

0005   Novell Demand RIP required

0006   Novell Demand SAP required

0007   Novell Triggered RIP required

0008   Novell Triggered SAP required

Numbers 5 and 6 are allocated in order to implement the RFC 1582 extensions to RIP for demand circuits. Numbers 7 and 8 are allocated for implementation of the RFC 2091 extensions to RIP for triggered updates. It is likely that the triggered version will supplant the demand version.

05 IPX-Router-Name

This option provides a means for sending the name of the local IPX system (the file server name) to the peer via Configure-Request. Since this option is simply advisory and is meant for logging functions, it is not actively negotiated. In particular, Configure-Nak must never be sent for this option.

06 IPX-Configuration-Complete

This is a boolean "option" meant to speed negotiations when convergence is not possible. If an option necessary for operation has been rejected by the peer or if the last message from the peer was a Configure-Nak that changed the value of an option to an unacceptable value, then this option is not included. Otherwise it is included with any Configure-Request message that could be acknowledged with Configure-Ack and would result in a viable link.

Relying on this option is not recommended. A good implementation should offer this option in a Configure-Request sent but should not expect the peer to include it in any Configure-Request received. Some implementations do not include it at all.

NetBIOS Frames Control Protocol (NBFCP)

NetBIOS (formerly known as NetBEUI) is an older, nonroutable protocol used mostly with PCs. NBFCP is described in RFC 2097. The control protocol is 803F, and the network protocol is 003F. NetBIOS itself is documented in IBM's *Local Area Network Technical Reference*, SC30-3383-2.

Two special modifications to an otherwise straightforward implementation are necessary to support NBFCP. First, instead of requiring an implementation to negotiate a large enough MRU before using this protocol, the RFC requires that implementations disregard the negotiated MRU to send the required data. 1512 bytes of space for the PPP information field are required regardless of negotiation. Second, some of the actions required during negotiation can take a long time to complete. Implementations will need an adjustable Configure-Request time-out to support this. The negotiated options follow.

01 Name-Projection

This option is implemented strangely in that the value returned in the Configure-Ack message is not the same as the data in the corresponding Configure-Request due to the use of a result-code field. The negotiated value is a sequence of 17 octet blocks. The first 16 octets of each block are a network name string padded with null characters and not prepended with a length field as are other PPP strings. The 17th octet is a "type" field (01 for Unique, 02 for Group) in Configure-Request and Configure-Reject but is changed to a result-code in Configure-Ack and Configure-Nak.

02 Peer-Information

This is used as a means for one peer to inform the other of its software version and type numbers plus an identifying name. It should not be included in Configure-Nak, since it informational only and is not subject to negotiation.

03 Multicast-Filtering

This option allows the sender of Configure-Request to ask its peer to limit the rate of NetBIOS multicasts forwarded over the link. To ask a peer to indicate how often it wants to receive multicasts, an unsolicited Configure-Nak for this option with the rate control set to the reserved value FFFF is used. By default, all multicasts are forwarded.

04 IEEE-MAC-Address-Required

This boolean option enables the sending of MAC addresses as the first 12 octets in each frame. If the source of the forwarded data is on Ethernet, this will expand the forwarded frame size to as large as 1512 bytes, regardless of the negotiated MRU. The RFC indicates that the bits within each byte of address are to be swapped. This is not true. The addresses are sent as they would be over a standard Ethernet interface.

AppleTalk (ATCP)

AppleTalk is the native protocol for Apple MacIntosh computers. The AppleTalk Control Protocol for PPP is described in RFC 1378. The control protocol is 8029, and the network protocol is 0029.

The data packets transferred via protocol 0029 begin with the extended Datagram Delivery Protocol (DDP) header. Fragmentation is not supported in AppleTalk, so implementations must support reception of AppleTalk frames with up to 599 octets in the PPP information field. Implementors and testers of this protocol should refer to *Inside AppleTalk* 2d ed., by G. Sidhu, R. Andrews, and A. Oppenheimer (Addison-Wesley, May 1990), for information on AppleTalk protocols and routing.

Options 01, 06, 07, and 08 are common to ATCP implementations. Devices that implement ATCP often also implement the older proprietary ARAP protocol.

01 AppleTalk Address

This option indicates the AppleTalk network and local node number when sent as part of a Configure-Request message. The data in this option consist of an ignored octet, two octets for the network number, and one octet for the node number. The network and node numbers must be in "nonextended" mode.

The network and local node numbers may be requested from the peer by sending a Configure-Request message with either network, node, or both set to zero. The peer should reply with a Configure-Nak message containing the correct network and node numbers, perhaps derived from a database look-up. A system that does not use AppleTalk addresses, such as a "half-router," will Configure-Reject this option. As with IP addresses, this is a useful option to detect configuration errors and should be implemented.

Note that only a single network number is negotiated for the link, but that a separate node number is negotiated for each end of the link. As with IPXCP, this means that the network number used in generating Configure-Requests should reflect the latest Configure-Nak or Configure-Request received from the peer. The node number, however, is symmetrically negotiated, so Configure-Requests must take only Configure-Nak values into consideration.

02 Routing Protocol

This option negotiates the routing protocol to be used on the link. By default, AppleTalk Routing Table Maintenance Protocol (RTMP) is expected. This option has a two-octet routing protocol number plus a variable-length data field that depends on the particular routing protocol. The defined routing protocol numbers are 0000 for no routing information, 0001 for RTMP, 0002 for AURP, and 0003 for ABGP. None of these routing protocols uses the variable-length data field.

03 Suppress Broadcast

This option specifies a variable-length list of octets. Each octet is a DDP type code. The sender of Configure-Request for this option is requesting that the peer suppress transmission of any DDP packet that was sent to the broadcast address and has any of these type codes. This suppression may interfere with the selected routing protocol if it is not carefully chosen.

If the list is empty, the peer is requesting that all DDP broadcasts be suppressed. An implementation that cannot filter based on DDP type code but can filter out broadcasts might return an empty Configure-Nak in response to a Configure-Request list.

Reasonable implementations should not implement this option at all, should implement it as a simple on-off flag to drop all broadcasts, or should permit an arbitrary list of protocol numbers to be specified. Otherwise, modifying the list and sending a Configure-Nak can lead to nonconvergence.

04 AT Compression Protocol

This option would negotiate the desired header compression protocol to be used, if any existed for AppleTalk. It defines a two-octet protocol number field followed by a variable-length data field for the particular protocol chosen.

This option is not yet used.

05 Reserved

This option was originally derived from the old AppleTalk Remote Access Protocol (ARAP) connect-time feature. It was removed from ATCP by the IETF and placed into LCP as the Time-Remaining message, since it is generally useful for many kinds of systems, not just Apples.

06 Server Information

This option provides information about the local implementation of AppleTalk to the peer. It should not be returned in a Configure-Nak. The data in this option include a two-octet "server class" number, a four-octet implementation ID, and a variable-length field for the name of the implementation in AppleTalk ASCII.

The server class number can be 0001 for an AppleTalk PPP Dial-In Server, 0002 for a generic AppleTalk PPP, or 0003 for a Dial-In Server and Router. The implementation ID is a software version number and, if the server class is 0001, is specified as a single octet for the major version number and a single octet for the minor version number followed by two zero octets. Otherwise, the implementation ID is vendor specific for other server classes.

07 Zone Information

This option provides information about the local AppleTalk zone name to the peer. It should not be returned in a Configure-Nak message unless its format is corrupt. The data field of the option contains the name of the zone in AppleTalk ASCII.

08 Default Router Address

This option is in the same format as the AppleTalk Address option. It specifies the network and node number of the local default router.

Systems Network Architecture (SNACP)

SNA is a protocol primarily used by IBM mainframe computers. The SNA encapsulation for PPP is defined in RFC 2043.

There are two protocols in use for SNA: raw SNA (used by IBM's Advanced Peer-to-Peer Networking High Performance Routing [APPN-HPR]) and SNA over LLC 802.2. These are assigned independent PPP protocol numbers 004D and 004B, respectively. 804D and 804B are the control protocols for these, although neither protocol has any negotiable parameters. Instead, only an empty Configure-Request is sent, and the reply is either an empty Configure-Ack or a Protocol-Reject.

Open Systems Interconnection (OSI; OSINLCP)

The OSI Network Layer Control Protocol is described in RFC 1377. The control protocol is 8023, and the network protocol is 0023. The first octet of the network layer data is the Network Layer Protocol Identifier (NLPID), which indicates which OSI protocol is contained in the rest of the packet. See ISO 9577 for these protocol numbers.

There is only one option negotiated for OSINLCP.

01 Align NPDU

This option requests alignment of network protocol data units (NPDUs) within the PPP information field by insertion of zero octets. The data field of this option is a single octet whose value indicates the desired alignment. When this value is 01, 02, 03, or 04, then that offset (modulo 4) from the beginning of the HDLC frame is requested. For instance, a value of 01 would result in the following alignment for the four ACFC and PFC combinations:

```
FF 03 00 23 00 <NPDU>        (neither ACFC nor PFC)
FF 03 23 00 00 <NPDU>        (PFC only)
00 23 00 00 00 <NPDU>        (ACFC only)
23 <NPDU>                    (both ACFC and PFC)
```

The 00 octets past the protocol number (23) are the added padding octets. Note that the example alignment of the NPDU is either 5 or 1 with a negotiated value of 01. The special value FF indicates that odd alignment (modulo 2) is necessary, and FE indicates even alignment.

If this option is negotiated, the sender must transmit data with the indicated alignment. However, all receivers must be able to receive packets with any alignment. If the Configure-Request option is rejected by the peer, data will be received without alignment changes, and the RFC requires that the link must operate in spite of the failure of this option.

Xerox Network Systems Internet Datagram Protocol (XNS IDP; XNSCP)

The XNS network protocol is 0025, and the control protocol is 8025. The protocol is described in RFC 1764. Like SNA, XNS has no configuration options. To transport XNS data, each peer simply sends an empty Configure-Request and Configure-Ack, like this:

```
A: FF 03 80 25 01 01 00 04 10 9A
B: FF 03 80 25 02 01 00 04 DD BF
B: FF 03 80 25 01 01 00 04 10 9A
A: FF 03 80 25 02 01 00 04 DD BF
```

Like AppleTalk, there is no way to fragment XNS IDP datagrams, so all implementations must support a minimum MRU of 576.

Documentation on XNS IDP itself is available from Xerox as XNSS 029101, *Internet Transport Protocols.*

DECnet Phase IV Routing Protocol (DNCP)

DECnet over PPP is described in RFC 1762. It is assigned network protocol number 0027 and network control protocol 8027. PPP supports only the routing messages, and not the other Phase IV messages, such as MOP, LAT, and the maintenance protocols.

DECnet has no configuration options. Like SNA and XNS, negotiation of DECnet consists simply of an empty Configure-Request and Configure-Ack message. The network protocol messages consist of a two-octet length field, which is in reverse byte order (LSB first), followed by the DECnet data field.

Documentation on the DECnet protocol itself can be ordered from Digital Equipment Corporation, as AA-X436A-TK, *DNA Routing Layer Functional Specification.*

Banyan Vines (BVCP)

RFC 1763 describes the standard method for carrying Banyan Vines data over a PPP link. The network protocol number is 0035, and the control protocol is 8035.

Because of its history as a PC-based protocol, Vines is somewhat Ethernet-centric. Its MRU is fixed at 1500 octets, unless FRP is negotiated (see the options below). The negotiable BVCP options follow.

01 NS RTP Link Type

This boolean option configures the behavior of the nonsequenced routing update protocol (NS-RTP). If it is present, then LAN-type updates are sent (a full table update every 90 seconds). If it is not present, then by default wide area network–type updates are sent (a full table for the first three updates, then only changes for the next five updates, in a repeating pattern). This option has no effect if the newer (version 5.5) sequenced routing update protocol (S-RTP) is used.

02 FRP

This boolean option configures the use of Vines fragmentation protocol (FRP). By default, no FRP header is sent with the Vines packets, and fragmentation is not possible.

The FRP header is a two-octet field prepended to the data packets and includes fragment begin and end flags and a sequence number, making it similar to standard PPP MP (RFC 1990; see Chapter 6). FRP is described in the Banyan documentation.

03 RTP

This boolean option suppresses the use of routing updates. By default, routing updates are sent on links. The sender of Configure-Request for this option is requesting that RTP messages not be sent to it. This is useful for dial lines with static routes, where RTP would use up a significant portion of the bandwidth with no visible benefit.

04 Suppress Broadcast

This boolean option suppresses Vines broadcast messages, except for ARP and RTP. Most such messages are not useful to simple dial-in systems, and suppression saves bandwidth. By default, all broadcasts are forwarded. The sender of Configure-Request for this option is requesting that broadcasts not be sent to it.

Bridging (BCP)

Bridging is a technique for forwarding messages from one physical network to another without reference to their network layer information. In particular, bridging is useful in PPP for handling protocols that are otherwise unimplemented in a given machine.

The PPP bridging control protocol is described in RFC 1638. It is assigned "network" (data) PPP protocol number 0031 and control protocol number 8031. It also makes use of several special spanning tree protocol numbers, documented with that option below.

Two models of operation are supported by the standard. One is the half-bridge model, where the two sides agree to behave as though they were a single larger bridge and the PPP link is invisible for spanning tree calculations. The other model is the full, independent bridge, where the PPP link is visible as a separate segment in the spanning tree.

Usually the default MRU of 1500 octets is not sufficient for BCP support. No standard exists for fragmentation at the MAC level, so the MRU must be large enough to handle a message forwarded from any interface that might be actively in use for bridging. For reference, a bridged Ethernet packet (including PPP bridging headers) is 1524 octets, and a bridged FDDI packet is 4377 octets with IP, or potentially as many as 4506 octets for arbitrary data (including 4500 octets of data plus PADS/MAC-type and LAN ID fields).

Alternatively, if the MRU cannot be negotiated large enough due to hardware or driver-imposed restrictions, MP with a large MRRU may be negotiated. MP can be used as a simple link-level fragmentation mechanism on a single link. See Chapter 6.

The negotiable BCP options follow.

01 Bridge Identification

Negotiation of this option implies that the half-bridge model is in use. This option is mutually incompatible with the Line Identification option. The data in this option consist of a two-octet field containing a 12-bit local area network (LAN) segment number and a 4-bit bridge ID (both from IEEE 802.1D).

There is only one value for the bridge ID number for a given PPP link. This option is not negotiated symmetrically like most other PPP options. Instead, systems must either agree to disconnect if the configured number does not match or select the higher ID number of the two proposed in each Configure-Request.

02 Line Identification

Negotiation of this option implies that the full-bridge model is in use. This option is mutually incompatible with the Bridge Identification option. The data in this option consist of a two-octet field containing a 12-bit LAN segment number and a 4-bit bridge ID (both from IEEE 802.1D).

There is only one value for the LAN segment number for a given PPP link. This option is not negotiated symmetrically like most other PPP options. Instead, systems must either agree to disconnect if the configured number does not match or select the higher segment number of the two proposed in each Configure-Request.

If neither this nor the Bridge-Identification option is negotiated, then the full-bridge model is assumed, and it is also assumed that the LAN segment number is correctly configured on both ends by an administrator. I do not recommend this mode of operation due to the likelihood of undetected misconfiguration.

Misconfiguration may cause the creation of forwarding loops, which will make the attached networks unusable.

03 MAC Support

This option in a Configure-Request message announces support for a single MAC type to its peer. Since this is only an announcement, it must never be included in a Configure-Nak message. The data field of the option is a single octet representing the MAC type, which is currently one of the following:

01   IEEE 802.3/Ethernet (with canonical addresses)

02   IEEE 802.4 (with canonical addresses)

03   IEEE 802.5 (with noncanonical addresses)

04   FDDI (with noncanonical addresses)

0B   IEEE 802.5 (with canonical addresses)

0C   FDDI (with canonical addresses)

Zero, 05-0A, and all numbers above 0C are reserved.

Multiple copies of this option will be sent in a Configure-Request message, with one for each supported MAC type.

04 Tinygram Compression

This option is a nonstandard boolean flag. Unlike standard PPP boolean flags, this option contains a single octet of data set to 01 to enable compression and 02 to disable it. The sender of Configure-Request for this option is declaring its support for decompression on input.

Tinygrams are padded messages that appear on certain types of media, such as Ethernet. On Ethernet, the minimum PDU is 64 octets, but common frames in interactive applications are about two-thirds of that size, so many frames are padded out to meet the minimum PDU requirement. Compression of these frames means detecting and stripping out this padding and reconstructing it on the other side of the link.

05 LAN Identification

This option is also a nonstandard boolean flag. The data field, as with the Tinygram-Compression option, is 01 to enable and 02 to disable. This option is an announcement only and must never be included in a Configure-Nak message.

When LAN identification is enabled, the LAN ID field must be checked to separate traffic destined for separate interfaces. When identification is disabled (the default), any traffic carrying a LAN ID field must be dropped.

This option permits the implementation of multiple virtual LAN groups over a single bridging link.

06 MAC Address

This option announces the local Ethernet MAC address or is used to request that the peer assign the address. It is useful only with small bridges that have only a single Ethernet interface and is not defined for other media types. The data in the option consist of six octets, which are the Ethernet address in canonical format. If all six octets are zero, the sender of Configure-Request is asking the peer to send a Configure-Nak with the correct Ethernet address, perhaps derived from a look-up based on the system name provided during authentication. Otherwise, if it is nonzero, then the peer should not send a Configure-Nak.

07 Spanning Tree Protocol

This option negotiates the spanning tree protocol in use. A spanning tree protocol detects and eliminates forwarding loops when multiple bridges are in use on a network.

There is only one protocol negotiated for a given link, and in case of a conflict, the lower-numbered option of the two is chosen. This may result in no spanning tree protocol being selected. The RFC is somewhat unclear on the intention in this case, but a reasonable implementation should not bring up the link if it knows any spanning tree protocol at all. The link should be established with no spanning tree protocol only in the case where both peers have no protocol at all available.

All systems must support either no protocol or IEEE 802.1D, which are options 00 and 01.

The option data consist of a list of one or more protocol numbers represented as single octets chosen from the following list:

00   Null—no spanning tree protocol supported (required)

01   IEEE 802.1D spanning tree protocol (required)

02   IEEE 802.1G extended spanning tree protocol

03   IBM source route spanning tree protocol

04   DEC LANbridge 100 spanning tree protocol

The actual spanning tree protocol messages are sent using the following PPP protocol numbers:

0201   IEEE 802.1 (either 802.1D or 802.1G)

0203   IBM Source Route Bridge

0205   DEC LANbridge 100

Documentation for the IEEE protocols is in the following sources:

Media Access Control (MAC) Bridges, ISO/IEC 15802-3:1993, ANSI/IEEE Std 802.1D, July 1993.

Draft Standard 802.1G: Remote MAC Bridging, IEEE P802.1G/D7, December 30, 1992.

Documentation for the IBM protocol is in:

Token-Ring Network Architecture Reference, 3d ed., September 1989.

Documentation for the DEC LANbridge protocol is not available.

Chapter

5

The Transforming Layers

IN THIS CHAPTER

The two transforming layers defined are data compression (Compression Control Protocol, or CCP) and encryption (Encryption Control Protocol, or ECP). Technically, these layers are considered to be NCPs, but they are discussed in this separate chapter because they share some unusual properties:

- *No associated network interface.* These protocols, unlike the NCPs documented in the previous chapter, do not have an interface to a networking system outside of PPP, as do IP and IPX.

- *Reprocessing of data from other NCPs.* Data transmitted from other running NCPs are routed through these layers when they are active. The other NCPs process only user data.

- *Special definitions for use with multilink PPP (MP).* These protocols define special protocol numbers to indicate their position in the flow of PPP data processing. They may be implemented logically above (at the aggregate link level) or below MP (in the multiple individual links).

- *Patented error-recovery techniques used (Reset-Request / Reset-Ack).* Both protocols can make use of techniques for which Motorola claims patent rights. However, unpatented work-arounds do exist, and not all algorithms use this mechanism.

- *Patented algorithms used for all compression schemes.* Normally these kinds of restrictions are not permitted for IETF protocols (see RFC 1602), but a special variance for CCP and ECP was issued as RFC 1915. The existence of these patents means that implementors of these protocols may need to consult with a patent lawyer before developing products. (See also the pointers to the LPF in Chapter 8.)

- *Parallel negotiation of multiple protocols* (shown later).

The two relevant RFCs are 1962 for CCP and 1968 for ECP. I recommend reading both together, even if only one is to be used, since they are very similar and each can be used to clarify points made in the other.

Architecture

Architecturally, there is only one possible legal implementation when these protocols are not used with MP, according to RFC 1968. (See Chapter 6 for architectural details for CCP and ECP when used with MP.) The non-MP implementation corresponds to the diagram in Figure 5.1.

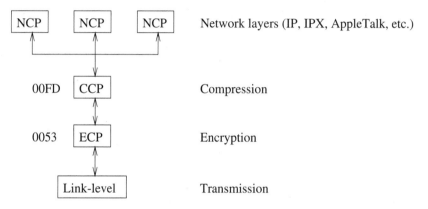

Figure 5.1: NON-MP COMPRESSION AND ENCRYPTION

The encapsulation performed on transmit is shown in Figure 5.2.

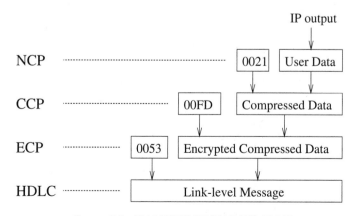

Figure 5.2: ENCAPSULATION DATA FLOW

Of course, it is not necessary to use both protocols in all implementations. If both are used, though, data must first be compressed and then encrypted.

One major router vendor uses 00FB instead of 00FD on a single synchronous link even when MP is not in use. Designers considering CCP on a synchronous interface may need to support this.

Negotiation Features

In both protocols, the goal of negotiation is to determine a preferred common algorithm for compressing or encrypting and to determine parameters for that algorithm. In both CCP and ECP, the algorithms listed in the configuration messages take the familiar variable-length Type-Len-Data option format, with a single octet each for Type and Len and a variable number of octets for the Data field, depending on the parameters defined for the algorithm indicated by the Type field.

To negotiate the common algorithm, the decryptor or decompressor (let us call this peer the *decoder* for simplicity) sends a Configure-Request listing the algorithms it wishes to decode, in descending order of preference. The receiver replies with Configure-Reject if any of these algorithms is unknown or, if all are known, then Configure-Nak if any is specified with unusable parameters. Finally, the encryptor or compressor (the *encoder*) replies with Configure-Ack to agree to begin encoding.

These algorithms can be negotiated serially, with a separate Configure-Request sent for each single algorithm known by the decoder, or in parallel, with all algorithms listed at once. Although serial negotiation is simpler to implement, parallel negotiation usually converges faster, especially if a large number of algorithms are implemented.

An example negotiation for either CCP or ECP protocol might go as follows (watching only one side of the symmetric negotiation, with peer A as decoder and peer B as encoder):

```
A: Configure-Request ID:1 [ 1 2 15:0C 12:05 ]
B: Configure-Reject  ID:1 [ 1 2 12:05 ]
A: Configure-Request ID:2 [ 15:0C ]
B: Configure-Nak     ID:2 [ 15:09 ]
A: Configure-Request ID:3 [ 15:09 ]
B: Configure-Ack     ID:3 [ 15:09 ]
```

In this example, peer A offered to decode four algorithms, numbered 1, 2, 15, and 12. B does not implement 1, 2, or 12, so it Configure-Rejects these first. A offers the remaining algorithm 15 with parameter 0C. B does implement this algorithm but does not agree to the parameter 0C, so it sends Configure-Nak with a hint of 09 instead. Finally, A offers 15 with 09, and B accepts.

It is also possible for peer A to offer several algorithms that are all known to B and that all have acceptable parameters. In this case, B has two choices: send

Configure-Ack for all of these acceptable algorithms offered, in which case the actual algorithm used for decoding on A and encoding on B will be the first one in the list, or use Configure-Reject to disable the algorithms no longer wanted. B cannot send a Configure-Ack containing only the single desired algorithm from the list, because it is not legal to send a Configure-Ack with data that differs from the corresponding Configure-Request. The first possibility appears as:

```
A: Configure-Request ID:1 [ 1 2 15:09 12:05 ]
B: Configure-Reject  ID:1 [ 2 12:05 ]
A: Configure-Request ID:2 [ 1 15:09 ]
B: Configure-Ack     ID:2 [ 1 15:09 ]
```

The second appears as:

```
A: Configure-Request ID:1 [ 1 2 15:09 12:05 ]
B: Configure-Reject  ID:1 [ 2 12:05 ]
A: Configure-Request ID:2 [ 1 15:09 ]
B: Configure-Reject  ID:2 [ 15:09 ]
A: Configure-Request ID:3 [ 1 ]
B: Configure-Ack     ID:3 [ 1 ]
```

The first option is fully supported by both of the RFCs, but the second is safer with peers that may not necessarily implement this feature correctly and also allows the encoder to choose a preferred algorithm that may not be the same as the decoder's preferred algorithm. In both cases, algorithm option 1 has been negotiated. (It is even possible to send a Configure-Ack if only the first option is acceptable even though the others are not. Doing so is faster but is risky and is not recommended.)

It is possible for there to be no common algorithm. For ECP, which is generally concerned with security, this means that the encryptor should tear down the link. For CCP, which generally has little security implication, either end may choose to terminate the CCP protocol using Protocol-Reject in response to Configure-Request or simply to complete negotiation with no algorithms supplied in the Configure-Request and Configure-Ack messages. If the latter is done, CCP proceeds to Open state but does not compress any data.

Although somewhat controversial, proceeding to Open state in CCP with no chosen algorithm is often wise because the peer that is sending Configure-Request and finds no algorithms left to negotiate has no other option but to send an empty request. The implementor may want to send Protocol-Reject for the preceding Configure-Reject that caused the problem, but doing so will prohibit compression in the opposite direction as well, which may be an undesirable side effect.

Once a single algorithm is decided on, that algorithm is used to send data from the encoder (sender of Configure-Ack) to the decoder (sender of Configure-Request).

Each direction must be separately negotiated and may well use different algorithms due to differing configurations or system capacity. Compression may even be run in only one direction if desired.

Error Recovery

Both protocols make use of a pair of special code numbers, called Reset-Request (0E) and Reset-Ack (0F), to recover from lost or corrupted messages. When the decoder detects a lost or corrupted packet, it sends a Reset-Request to the encoder. When the encoder receives a Reset-Request, it clears any stored history and sends Reset-Ack to the receiver, then resumes encoding.

This mechanism implies that in a typical implementation, several resets will occur when there is an error, depending on the queuing and transmission delays in the system (see Figure 5.3).

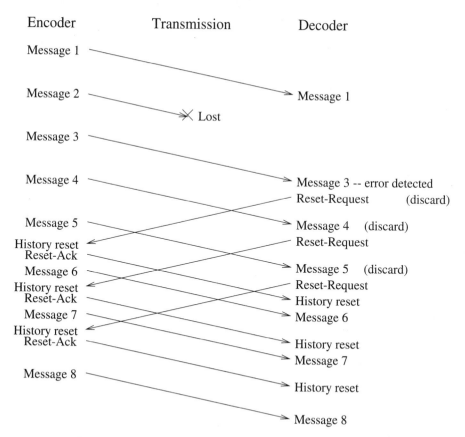

Figure 5.3: ERROR RECOVERY WITH TRANSMISSION DELAYS

The decoder may elect not to send a Reset-Request for each failing message if it has an estimate of the round-trip time for the link. In this case, the decoder should silently discard the bad messages received until the round-trip time expires. If the Reset-Ack is not received within the estimated round-trip time, then another Reset-Request must be generated, since the prior request may have been lost.

US patent 5,130,993, assigned to Codex Corporation (a subsidiary of Motorola), and entitled, "Transmitting encoded data on unreliable networks," claims to cover this Reset-Request and Reset-Ack technique of synchronization. I have reservations about this claim due to the apparent prior art available. Implementors nevertheless must investigate this claim and license or fight it as they deem reasonable. I can provide no guidance on this.

Other available techniques can be used as alternatives to the Reset-Request and Reset-Ack mechanisms. For instance, the decoder can reset the encoder by sending a new Configure-Request message, which will take the encoder out of Open state and cause encoding to be renegotiated. Several of the algorithms also define embedded flags for the internal request and ack states, which also make Reset-Request and Reset-Ack unnecessary.

Compression Negotiation

The CCP negotiations, described in RFC 1962, are done with protocols 80FD, both for non-MP implementations and for compression above MP, and with 80FB, for MP implementations that compress at the link level. The data are passed with protocols 00FD and 00FB, respectively.

The single-octet Type field indicates the algorithm, as selected from this list:

```
00  Organization Unique Identifier (OUI)
01  Predictor type 1 (RFC 1978)
02  Predictor type 2 (RFC 1978)
03  Puddle Jumper
10  Hewlett-Packard PPC (draft-ietf-pppext-hpppc-00.txt)
11  STAC Electronics LZS (RFC 1974)
12  Microsoft PPC (RFC 2118)
13  Gandalf FZA (RFC 1993)
14  V.42bis compression
15  BSD LZW Compress (RFC 1977)
17  LZS-DCP (RFC 1967)
18  Magnalink MVRCA (RFC 1975)
19  Not used (assigned as DCE for RFC 1976)
1A  Deflate (RFC 1979)
```

Codes 04–0F were originally reserved by RFC 1962 for freely available compression algorithms without license fees, although this scheme appears to have been abandoned. Codes 16 and 1B–FE are unassigned, and FF is reserved. Code 00 allows a vendor to use any proprietary algorithm desired without needing a number assigned by the IANA.

When a message is sent through CCP for transmission from an upper-level NCP, the protocol number is usually first checked. I recommend that if the protocol number is in the range 0001 through 3EFF, it should be compressed. Otherwise, it should be passed through to ECP or the link level without modification. I also suggested that NCPs be able to specify when network layer data should not be compressed; this is a design and administrator interface issue for implementors. Unfortunately, each compression algorithm defines a slightly different method for determining which data to compress.

Generally, in order to compress the data, the original PPP protocol number, often referred to as the *inner protocol number*, is prepended to the user data, often using standard protocol field compression (PFC) even if PFC was not negotiated in LCP, and this entire message is then compressed using the chosen algorithm. The modified packet is then passed down to ECP or the link level for transmission with the CCP protocol number (00FD or 00FB), which is often referred to as the *outer protocol number* (see Figure 5.4). At the receiver's side, the packet is demultiplexed using the PPP protocol number, as usual. If that number is the CCP protocol number, then the data are decompressed. The real NCP protocol number is then removed from the beginning of the resulting decompressed data, and the data are then passed back through the normal demultiplexing procedure. Note, though, that this is only a general outline. Each compression algorithm defines its own means of encapsulating the data for transmission.

Compression Algorithms

Choosing compression algorithms to implement and use depends strongly on the environment. There is no one best algorithm, even for a specific purpose. The factors an implementor must weigh include availability and cost, since some algorithms are available only under license from the inventor and all are subject to patent concerns, memory consumption, CPU loading, compression ratio for various types of data, and asymmetry of compression and decompression.

As of this writing, STAC compression is the most popular algorithm, in part because of its sparing memory requirements (20KB for both transmit and receive) and because a C code implementation is available from STAC for use in PPP without a license fee. Other algorithms do have strong adherents, and some market research may be required before choosing which algorithms to support. In particular, note that Windows NT, unlike Windows 95, supports only MS-PPC and does not support STAC.

Many of the algorithms are mathematically similar and are based on original work by Lempel-Ziv (LZ) and later extensions by Welch (LZW). These techniques make use of dynamically constructed tables of substrings of the compressed message, and compress the message by producing pointers into these tables as output. In general, this class of algorithm uses more CPU time to compress than to decompress.

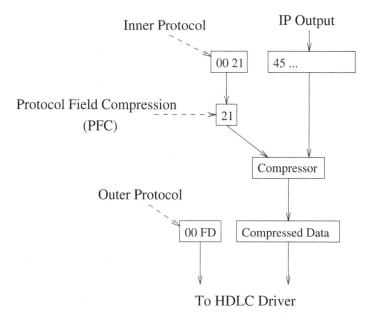

Figure 5.4: CCP DATA HANDLING EXAMPLE

Many of these algorithms also have hardware implementations available. These hardware devices can greatly increase the speed of a system using the compression algorithms, which are often highly computationally intensive. Devices are also available that implement several algorithms simultaneously.

Motorola claims patent rights to much of the idea of compressing data and allocating memory for it through US patent 5,245,614. Implementors of any data compression algorithms should investigate this claim first.

00 Organization Unique Identifier (OUI)

The data for this option consist of three octets of identifier information, defined to be the first three octets of the manufacturer's assigned Ethernet physical address. Presumably a future draft of this RFC will permit the use of IANA-assigned identifiers as well. The next octet is a subtype field for discriminating different algorithms supported by that manufacturer, and any additional octets are parameters for that algorithm.

01 Predictor type 1

02 Predictor type 2

These two algorithms are described in RFC 1978, which includes C source code. (Implementors should refer to the example source code distributed on SGI's ftp site [ftp://ftp.sgi.com/other/ppp-comp/predictor1.c], as it correctly implements the handling of incompressible data and is representative of a real implementation. The code in the RFC is based on a demonstration program that compresses and decompresses files, not packets.)

Predictor types 1 and 2 are basically the same, except that type 2 is a stream-oriented protocol that can pack multiple compressed frames into a single PPP frame or segment a single compressed frame into many PPP frames. For simplicity, most implementations use type 1. Since there are no options for this protocol, the negotiation consists of just the type and length fields.

This algorithm may infringe on US patent number 5,229,768. Novell, the author of the implementation in the RFC, has decided to allow copying of this source code without a license, but implementors wishing to use this algorithm may need to consult with a patent attorney because of this separate claim.

A standard CRC-16 is calculated with this algorithm. This is done by first adding an optionally compressed (PFC) PPP protocol field to the input data (as described in the general CCP section). Then the length of this combined data is expressed as two octets in network byte order, and the CRC is calculated over these two octets followed by the combined protocol field and original data. Next, the data starting with the protocol field (not including the length field) are compressed using the Predictor algorithm. Finally, if the data did not expand in compression, then the most significant bit of the two-octet length (the "compressed" flag) is set to indicate that the data are compressed, and the CRC is appended to the end of the message. If the message is larger after compression, then it is sent with the "compressed" flag clear and with the same CRC.

Normally, of course, a Predictor implementation will combine the CRC calculation with the compression encoding. The implementor must take care to start the CRC calculation with the length information, then continue with both the CRC and the compression on the rest of the data.

If the data must be sent uncompressed and the addition of the Predictor length and protocol number header and CRC trailer would put the message over the peer's MTU, I recommend sending the data without Predictor encapsulation and simply allowing the dictionary to become corrupt and reset itself. It is, of course, better to negotiate an MRU of 1506 when Predictor is in use and set an MTU of 1500 on the network interfaces (or, of course, negotiate 1500 and use 1494) to avoid the problem entirely.

The algorithm itself is based on a hashing scheme that uses a value calculated from adjacent bytes in the message to predict the next byte. If the prediction is successful, then a single bit is used to indicate the value. Otherwise, nine bits are used. Thus, in the best case, this could compress a message by a factor of eight to one or, in the worst case, expand it by 12.5 percent. Of course, if the data expand as a result of compression, the compressed flag should be cleared and the original uncompressed data sent.

03 Puddle Jumper

This algorithm was published in a now-obsolete Internet Draft. The algorithm was based on Huffman coding and allowed the table sizes to be negotiated. The author of the draft reports that it compressed about 10 to 15 percent better than Predictor 1.

No known implementations exist, and the author has abandoned work on it.

10 Hewlett-Packard PPC

This algorithm, which requires a license from Hewlett-Packard, is still in Internet Draft stage as of this writing. The draft is draft-ietf-pppext-hpppc-00.txt.

No parameters are negotiated, so the option appears in the list as just a type and length entry. As with other compression methods, the optionally compressed (PFC) PPP protocol field is prepended to the data, and this entire message is compressed. Then a two-octet header similar to that used with Predictor is added, consisting of two octets of original length (including the PPP protocol field), with the most significant bit set if the data are compressed.

The draft does not describe the compression algorithm itself, though it does note that it is based on a variant of LZ, called LZ2.

11 STAC Electronics LZS

STAC compression is documented in RFC 1974. Implementors of this algorithm must execute a license with STAC Electronics. Fortunately, the license is available free of charge when the "low-performance" version of the STAC code is used as part of a PPP implementation. See Chapter 8 for more information. As its name suggests, this is another variant of LZ compression. Implementations of this compression algorithm are available from STAC and several other vendors as hardware devices.

The negotiation information consists of a two-octet history count followed by a single-octet check mode value. The history count is used to allow multiple compression histories to be maintained by a compressor. This could be used, for instance, to separate data from certain network addresses or protocols to be compressed independent of other data on the link. Such use is up to the implementor to define. By default, and in most cases, the history count is one to signify a single compression history. It can also be negotiated as zero to compress each packet independently without maintaining a history. If this is done, then Reset-Request and Reset-Ack are not used.

The RFC erroneously describes this check mode octet as containing either left-aligned or right-aligned information (the text and diagram do not agree). The author of the RFC originally intended this to be a bit field. Instead, it is now by general agreement simply a single-octet value. The check mode is one of the following:

```
00  No checking
01  Longitudinal Check Byte
02  Cyclic Redundancy Check
03  Sequence Number
04  Extended
```

All implementations are required by the RFC to implement at least mode 3; however, several common implementations violate this requirement. In particular, Windows 95 implements only mode 4.

The check modes are used to verify the integrity of the data so that a Reset-Request can be generated when a packet is lost or damaged. The generated Reset-Request and Reset-Ack, despite the text of the RFC, must contain the affected history number, even if only one history is used, since some existing implementations were based on one of the earlier drafts, which required this number. The receiver of these messages should, though, allow the two-octet history number to be omitted.

The compressed packet format varies by the check mode and by the number of compression histories supported. The following list includes all legal formats:

Mode 0, 0 or 1 history:	`(Compressed data)`
Mode 0, 2 to 255 histories:	`HH (Compressed data)`
Mode 0, 256 or more histories:	`HH HH (Compressed data)`
Mode 1, 0 or 1 history:	`LL (Compressed data)`
Mode 1, 2 to 255 histories:	`HH LL (Compressed data)`
Mode 1, 256 or more histories:	`HH HH LL (Compressed)`
Mode 2, 0 or 1 history:	`CC CC (Compressed data)`
Mode 2, 2 to 255 histories:	`HH CC CC (Compressed)`
Mode 2, 256 or more histories:	`HH HH CC CC (Compressed)`
Mode 3, 0 or 1 history:	`SS (Compressed data)`
Mode 3, 2 to 255 histories:	`HH SS (Compressed data)`
Mode 3, 256 or more histories:	`HH HH SS (Compressed)`
Mode 4, 1 history:	`YY YY (Compressed data)`

HH is the history number, in network byte order when expressed as more than one octet; LL is the XOR of hex FF and all of the uncompressed data (including the PPP protocol number); CC CC is the standard HDLC CRC-16 of the uncompressed data (stored in LSB-first format, as with PPP HDLC framing); SS is a sequence number (starting with 01 and wrapping from FF to 00); and YY YY is special 16-bit flag word for extended mode which is in this format (bit-wise, most significant bit on left):

A B C D c c c c c c c c c c c c

The A bit is set to one if the compressor was reset before compressing this packet. C is set to one if the packet is compressed. Both B and D are zero. The c bits constitute a sequence number, starting at zero. For interoperability, packets that fail to compress are sent outside of compression through the normal data path. Thus, an observer will never see a packet with bit C set to zero when this mode is used.

Extended mode is unlike most of the other compression techniques. The inner PPP protocol number prepended to the data before compression may not be compressed, regardless of the negotiation of Protocol Field Compression (PFC) in LCP. More strangely, the RFC requires that the outer 00 FD protocol number itself not be compressed using PFC, regardless of the state of PFC. This means that if STAC mode 4 is implemented, then ECP, MP, and the HDLC driver must all check for STAC mode 4 packets and temporarily disable PFC. Alternatively, an implementation may elect to disable all use of PFC if STAC mode 4 is negotiated. The original proponents of this algorithm state that their systems that support STAC mode 4 do not support PFC, so no conflict exists. However, to comply with the RFC does pose interesting implementation problems for others with a higher level of functionality.

When in any of the other modes, the use of PFC on the inner protocol number is oddly conditional on the negotiation of PFC in LCP. If it is negotiated on, then it may be used in CCP-STAC. If not, then it must not be used.

When in extended mode, CCP Reset-Request is used to signal decompression failure or a missing sequence number, but CCP Reset-Ack is not issued by the compressor in response. Instead the A bit is set on the next compressed packet to indicate that the compressor has been reset.

STAC-compressed data may be sent without negotiation using PPP Protocol 4021. If the peer replies with an LCP Protocol-Reject then this mode must be disabled. The encapsulation for this mode is very simple. No header is used. The user data are prepended by the protocol number, STAC compressed, and sent. Use of this mode is rare.

12 Microsoft PPC (MS-PPC; LZM)

This algorithm, which also requires a license from STAC Electronics, is documented in RFC 2118. It is generally known as MPPC or MS-PPC, but within STAC and Microsoft it was known as LZM, since it is a variation on STAC's LZS technology.

There are a few hardware devices available as of this writing that support this compression algorithm.

The negotiated value for this protocol consists of a single integer encoded as four octets in network byte order. This integer is intended to be a bit-encoded mask of features supported. Currently, only the least significant bit is defined, and it must be set to negotiate MS-PPC.

The data encapsulation is similar to STAC mode 4, except that the B bit is set if the packet was moved to the front of the history buffer, and the strange restriction prohibiting compression of 00FD down to FD at the link level has been removed. As with STAC mode 4, the inner prepended PPP protocol field, which is passed through MS-PPC compression along with the user's data, may not be compressed.

If both STAC and MS-PPC are implemented, be very careful with the ordering of options presented in the Configure-Request message. Windows 95 will terminate CCP if it sees these options in some certain orders. Putting MS-PPC first seems to cure the problem.

13 Gandalf FZA

This algorithm, which must be licensed for a fee from Gandalf, is described in RFC 1993. This algorithm also is a variant on LZ compression. It requires the use of RFC 1663 reliable transmission and RFC 1570 self-describing padding.

The negotiated values consist of a single octet representing the size of the history table as a power of two and an optional octet representing a version number, which is omitted for FZA and set to 01 for FZA+ (two variants of the algorithm). The history size value must be in the range 0C (4096 bytes) to 0F (32768 bytes).

Unlike other compression algorithms, which either require or prohibit PFC-style compression of the PPP protocol field prepended to the data before compressing, the RFC for FZA indicates that the protocol field may be compressed using PFC only if PFC is negotiated by LCP. Also, data that expand beyond the peer's indicated MRU are sent in multiple consecutive frames. Since the algorithm may be run only on links with reliable transmission enabled, such frames can be unambiguously detected by the receiver during decompression based on features of the algorithm itself. Tracing and test equipment, though, generally cannot handle these data correctly.

14 V.42bis compression

This algorithm is available for a fee from several sources, including British Telecom. It is also a derivative of LZW. Unfortunately, no draft or RFC exists describing the encapsulation or negotiation options. Since this compression algorithm is substantially similar to other algorithms already implemented, it has been abandoned.

15 BSD LZW Compress

This algorithm is described in RFC 1977, which includes C source code for a vaguely BSD-like Unix implementation with STREAMS buffers. It is available to anyone without a license. However, the basic LZW algorithm itself is subject to US patent numbers 4,464,650 and 4,558,302 assigned to Unisys. Unisys has asserted its rights over other uses of LZW, such as the CompuServe GIF graphics file format. Implementors should be aware of this restriction. IBM's US patent 4,814,746 also covers the basic technology. (This list is incomplete. Designers must obtain competent legal counsel to avoid problems in this area.)

The negotiated value consists of a single octet. The most significant three bits are a version number and must be set to binary 001. The least significant five bits represent the size of the compression dictionary as a power of two. Valid values for this octet range from hex 29 (512 bytes) to hex 30 (65536 bytes).

The data packet format is a two-octet sequence number (starting with zero) followed by the compressed data, formed from the original data prepended with a PFC-compressed PPP protocol field. Unlike other compression schemes except Deflate, this one requires the use of PFC on the inner protocol field.

Also unlike other compression formats, this one requires the decompressor to monitor the reception of uncompressed data as well as compressed data. When uncompressed data are received that would normally (based on the PPP protocol number) be compressed, the decompressor's dictionary must be updated as though the compression took place. Alternatively, an implementation could renegotiate compression in these cases.

If compression fails due to a lack of buffers or expansion of the data, then the original message is sent without compression. Note that Reset-Ack, which normally will reset the decompressor's dictionary, cannot be sent unsolicited, since the ID number must be copied from the corresponding Reset-Request, so all input data from the NCPs must pass through the compressor even when no output space is available in order to keep the dictionaries in synchronization.

17 LZS-DCP

This algorithm, described in RFC 1967, is just a variant packet format for the same STAC compression algorithm used in RFC 1974.

The negotiated values are a two-octet history number, a single-octet check mode, and a single-octet process mode. The history number is defined as in RFC 1974. The check mode is one of the following:

    00 No checking
    01 Longitudinal Check Byte
    02 Sequence Number
    03 Sequence Number and Longitudinal Check Byte

The default is 03. The process mode is either 00, to indicate that uncompressed packets are not examined by the decompressor (the default), or 01, to indicate that the decompressor updates its state based on any uncompressed data received.

After prepending the PPP protocol field and compressing, the data are then prepended with a single-octet header whose bits are defined as:

```
E C/U R-A R-R 0 0 0 C/D
```

The E (extension) bit is always set to 1. The header can be extended to multiple octets by setting this bit to zero in the future. C/U indicates whether the enclosed data are compressed and is set to one for compressed data. R-A (Reset-Ack) is used to signal the decompressor that the compressor was reset before this packet was generated (as with RFC 1974 STAC mode 4 bit A). R-R (Reset-Request) is set to one in a message from the decompressor to the compressor to indicate that a reset is required. C/D is used for Frame Relay in other implementations and must be set to zero.

Unlike other compression algorithms, this one requires a connection between the compressor and decompressor in a given implementation. The compressed messages will be normally received by the decompressor, but the R-R bit received must be used to reset the compressor. This algorithm does not make use of the CCP Reset-Request and Reset-Ack messages.

18 Magnalink MVRCA

This algorithm, which must be licensed from Telco Systems, is described in RFC 1975. The negotiated values are two octets. The first octet contains two bits used for undocumented features, a single bit to indicate if packet-by-packet compression is supported, and five bits that specify the size of the history buffer in an undocumented manner. The second octet contains a value in the range 01 to 3F and indicates the number of contexts for which history is maintained. This number includes context zero, which by definition does not have a history, and is used for packet-by-packet compression.

IBM and other vendors have compression devices that support this algorithm in hardware.

19 DCE

This option number was apparently mistakenly allocated for RFC 1976, which defines an LCP (not CCP) option hex 19 (decimal 25). That RFC actually specifies a number of RFCs that should be supported by a class of equipment that includes CSU/DSUs.

1A Deflate

This algorithm is documented in RFC 1979. It is available without licensing restrictions, though source code distributions should include credit to the authors listed in the RFC. The algorithm is based on an LZ variant known as LZ77, which is used in

Gnu's "gzip" and PKWARE's PKZIP file compressors. The patent status of this algorithm is uncertain at this time, but it is believed to be free of such restrictions. Source code is freely available over the Internet.

The negotiated values are two octets long. The first octet contains two 4-bit integers. The upper half is the window value, which is expressed as a power of two, and ranges from binary 0000 for a 256-byte window to 1111 for an 8-megabyte window. The lower half is the method number, which must be 1000 for "zlib" compression, which supports a maximum window size of 32 KB.

The second octet contains six reserved bits. The least significant two bits are the check mode, which must be 00 to specify the sequence-number mode.

The values negotiated thus range from 08 00 to 78 00.

The data format is identical to the format used by BSD LZW Compress in RFC 1977. It consists of a two-octet sequence number field, which starts with zero. The compressed data contain the inner PPP protocol field, which must be compressed with PFC plus the original data. An implementation must also process uncompressed packets, which would normally have been compressed, by updating its dictionary.

Encryption Negotiation

The ECP negotiations, described in RFC 1968, are done with protocols 8053, for both non-MP implementations and encryption above MP, and with 8055, for MP implementations that encrypt at the link level. The data are passed with protocols 0053 and 0055, respectively. ECP is not very popular and has few interoperable implementations. There are also many proprietary link-level encryption schemes in use by major vendors.

The single-octet Type field indicates the algorithm, as selected from this list:

00 Organization Unique Identifier (OUI)
01 Data Encryption Standard Encryption (DESE)

Codes 02 through FE are unassigned, and FF is reserved. Code 00 allows a vendor to use any proprietary algorithm desired without needing a number assigned by the IANA.

As in CCP, the data received (either from the NCPs or from CCP) are generally prepended with the protocol number then encrypted, and the receiver employs the reverse process and sends the result back through the demultiplexing procedure. This may vary depending on the algorithm chosen.

Unlike CCP, encryption algorithms often have special requirements for the input data. DESE requires that the data prepended with the protocol number must be a multiple of eight octets. Unfortunately, the RFC does not specify exactly how this is to be done in a conforming implementation. The result is that this topic is currently under discussion within the IETF. One proposal with a number of adherents (including myself) is to use self-describing padding (SDP; RFC 1570) to pad the input data without explicitly negotiating for the use of SDP. If SDP is negotiated, then it is additionally used at the link level, as described in the original RFC.

ECP fits in as one part of the security puzzle. Unlike authentication, it does protect against a "man in the middle" attack and against most forms of wiretapping. But it does so only on the PPP link itself. Real security depends on additional encryption at the network layer, such as with IPSEC, and within applications themselves, such as with PGP.

There are other considerations for implementors. Quite unfortunately, many governments consider this type of technology to be of national security interest and classify systems containing encryption as "munitions" for export purposes. Protecting your customer's right to privacy may well cost you a stint in prison. I can recommend only caution. Don't dabble with this unless you are certain of what you are doing.

The encryption algorithms follow.

00 Organization Unique Identifier

This option is identical to the OUI option described for CCP.

01 Data Encryption Standard Encryption (DESE)

This algorithm is described in RFC 1969. It is based on the US National Bureau of Standards "DES" algorithm (FIPS PUB 46) in cipher block chaining (CBC) mode.

The negotiated value is an eight-octet nonce (one-time password; essentially just a random number) provided by the decryptor to the encryptor, which is used to seed the encryption algorithm in the same way that each packet seeds the encryption of following packets. This is used to prevent "replay" and chosen plaintext attacks, among others.

Since each decryption depends on only one prior packet, losing a single packet means that two packets will be lost by the receiver, but that the receiver will recover without other intervention. For this reason, Reset-Request and Reset-Ack are not used.

The data packet format contains a simple sequence number, starting at 0, prepended as two octets to the ciphertext. The RFC complicates matters by attempting to document the standard RFC 1661 headers and both ACFC and PFC options as well.

The RFC generally recommends padding the input data from the NCPs with random data where feasible based on the upper-level protocol, such as with IP, and using SDP where this is not possible, such as with bridging packets. (A better method would be to pad the PPP protocol number with leading 00 octets, as is legal with any HDLC integer. Unfortunately, this solution is not under consideration since it would require changes to RFC 1661, and the leading proposal is to use mandatory SDP-like encoding before running DES.)

A shared secret (a key) must be held by both ends of the communication. Distribution and storage of this key is not covered by the RFC and is left to the implementor. Distribution of keys is usually the most complex and vulnerable part of any encryption system. If it is not done often enough, then key material that "leaks" into the data stream can allow an eavesdropper to decode the data. If it is done too often, the key distribution system itself can be more easily attacked.

Chapter

6

Bandwidth Management

IN THIS CHAPTER

Bandwidth management is an active area of both research and marketing. This situation is a result of pricing policies of telephone companies and governments, which generally mandate per-time-unit or per-information-unit charges rather than flat connectivity fees. These variable charges drive users to search for means to limit measured usage to the minimum amount necessary.

Bandwidth management techniques in PPP are fairly new and somewhat unsettled. This area is likely to change dramatically in the face of newer technologies such as Cellular Digital Packet Data (CDPD) and higher-speed dedicated lines to residences. There are many bandwidth management techniques in use with PPP today—for example:

- **Demand dialing.** Many PPP implementations can automatically establish a link when network traffic is present and tear it down when idle. This is known as *dial-on-demand* or *dynamic dialing*. These techniques often require sophisticated traffic filtering and protocol spoofing.

- **Aggregation of multiple links.** Frequently, acquiring several low-speed links, such as modems, will cost less than the equivalent high-speed link, such as a dedicated line. Aggregation, which also goes by various other names (e.g., *multilink*, *load balancing*, *bonding*, and *inverse multiplexing*, depending on the underlying technology), allows an administrator to configure multiple low-speed links to behave as though they were a single higher-speed link. Aggregation is also used to maximize bandwidth over certain types of individual lines, such as Basic-Rate ISDN (BRI), which inherently carry multiple independent data channels.

- **Active bandwidth management.** A number of protocols have been invented to handle more gracefully the ebbs and flows of network traffic when used with

111

dial-on-demand links. By dropping individual links as soon as they become idle and avoiding dropping links that will soon be active, these techniques claim to reduce expenses.

- **Cost shifting.** In some economies, large companies have less expensive access to the public networks than do individuals. In others, reverse-toll lines (known in the U.S. as 800 numbers and the U.K. as 0800) are more expensive than directly placed calls. In either case, it can be advantageous to have a designated party to the call pay for it, regardless of who initiates the contact.

- **Multiplexed use of a single link.** Sometimes a higher-speed link, such as a Frame Relay connection, may be less expensive than a large number of individual slower links. Many variations of tunneling are used to support this technique, including ATM virtual circuits and L2TP.

These techniques are not mutually exclusive. In fact, they each complement the others in sometimes surprising ways, as we will see later.

Demand Dialing

Demand dialing is generally a proprietary technology, although the principle is simple. Filters that designate certain traffic as worthy of initiating a link and other traffic as important enough to keep the link up are normally required. For instance, with IP it is generally not desired that the link be brought up or kept up to send RIP updates. It may also be desired to keep the link up while SMTP (email) is transferred but not to bring the link up if only SMTP traffic is detected.

In some protocols, such as IPX and Windows Domain Naming, extensive work is required to make demand dialing function properly. This is because both of these systems are designed for LAN use and send frequent messages to detect what is available on the network and to detect failed connections (called *keep alive messages*). These messages must be spoofed and filtered from the demand-dial system.

Spoofing

As of this writing, only a single proposal has been made to negotiate use of spoofing with PPP links. This proposal, called the PPP Protocol Spoofing Control Protocol (PSCP), was presented as an Internet Draft in February 1996 (draft-ietf-pppext-spoof-00.txt).

Spoofing is the deliberate falsifying of protocol and application time-outs. It is done when these time-outs, which are often not under the user's control, would cause an unconnected dial-on-demand link to dial even though no data need to be transferred.

This proposal, which has since expired and has not been advanced, provided a means to negotiate which protocols should be spoofed when the link was down, a means to identify the "same" link being brought back up, and a means to set various timers. Unfortunately, the proposal contained extraneous matter, such as callback numbers, and was fairly ISDN specific.

As of this writing, spoofing and filtering for demand-dialed links is generally handled using proprietary configuration parameters rather than any standard protocol.

Aggregation of Multiple Links

This particular wheel has been invented many times, with varying results. Some of these inventions are:

- **Inverse multiplexing.** This is a rather generic term that is often applied to physical layer solutions. These solutions generally consist of some component, external to PPP, that uses proprietary means to spread traffic across multiple links. Since this is invisible to PPP, except perhaps for the latency variances that occur when an individual link is added or dropped, it will not be discussed further here. Two examples are a short-haul modem, which is able to use multiple channels or frequencies to transmit but has a single serial port, and ISO LAPB multilink.

- **Bonding.** This is a particular hardware-based inverse-multiplexing scheme invented, in general terms, for use with consumer-grade ISDN lines. Bonding is done at the bit level and requires tightly controlled timing relationships between the two B channels being bonded. These restrictions, which must also be supported by each of the telephone company switches in the path between caller and callee, using special call set-up commands, make this a niche solution. In general, it is far more expensive, less often available, and less capable than the other PPP-based solutions. It does have the benefit of the lowest possible latency.

- **Load balancing.** This technique is not specific to PPP and can be used by any point-to-point technology, such as SLIP or ATM. The general technique, as it concerns PPP, is to run separate copies of PPP on each of the individual links but to insert a layer between these PPP implementations and the network layers. This inserted layer then parcels out outgoing packets bound for a single "virtual" link (which represents the load-balancing group) among the individual links. This technique has the drawback of occasionally reordering messages, even with very cautious implementations, which can have dramatically bad interactions with a TCP implementation that includes standard fast retransmit. The load-balancing layer usually must run above (and outside of) PPP, since

PPP cannot tolerate reordering of its negotiation messages. Some network layers and routing technologies, such as OSPF, implement load balancing themselves through evaluation of multiple paths to the same destination along with cost, congestion, and other metrics.

- **Multilink.** This is the name given to the standard (RFC 1990) protocol used in PPP to spread traffic over multiple links. It does not suffer from packet reordering, as does load balancing, nor does it require special telephone company support, as does bonding, and it runs over existing equipment, unlike inverse multiplexing. It does have drawbacks, such as multiplying the error rates for interfaces that drop packets with a given probability rather than corrupt individual octets, and having indeterminate latency on some types of media, but these drawbacks are usually outweighed by the benefits. It does require specific support in both peers' implementations of PPP. It is not possible to run MP if one of the two peers does not support the protocol.

Multilink PPP (MP)

This protocol is described in RFC 1990. It specifies a means to negotiate MP mode, detect the establishment of new links (termed *bundling*), detect fragment loss, and fragment and reassemble messages. It does not specify when (or even if) additional links should be established, or when to drop links, or how to acquire necessary telephone numbers. These other tasks can be handled by configuration parameters, rules of thumb, or special protocols, as described later. The architecture is shown in Figure 6.1.

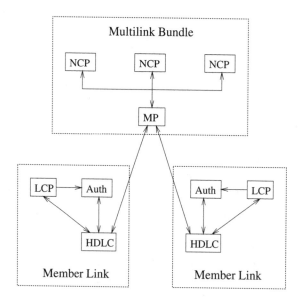

Figure 6.1: MP SYSTEM ARCHITECTURE

When used with CCP or ECP, there are three possible configurations. The most common is with both CCP and ECP at the bundle level (Figure 6.2).

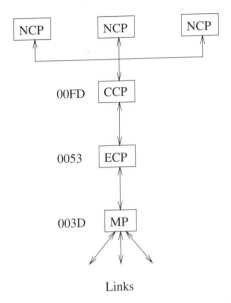

Figure 6.2: MP WITH CCP AND ECP ARCHITECTURE

For transmission, the data flow for this case is as shown in Figure 6.3.

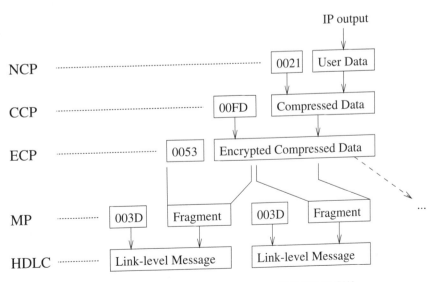

Figure 6.3: MP WITH CCP AND ECP DATA FLOW

Less commonly, ECP is moved to the member links, as in Figure 6.4.

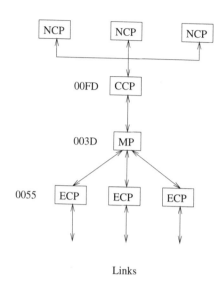

Figure 6.4: LINK-LEVEL ECP ARCHITECTURE

This is usually done because of the use of a link-level hardware encryption device, since encrypting at the bundle level requires that the hardware be separate from the link-level drivers. The data flow is shown in Figure 6.5.

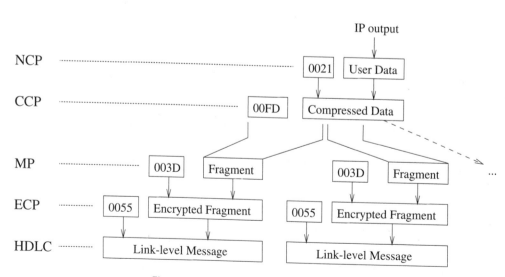

Figure 6.5: LINK-LEVEL ECP DATA FLOW

Least commonly, both CCP and ECP are done in the member links as in Figure 6.6.

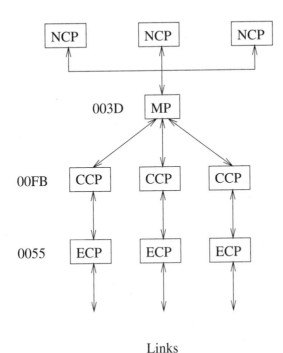

Links

Figure 6.6: LINK-LEVEL CCP AND ECP ARCHITECTURE

The corresponding data flow is shown in Figure 6.7.

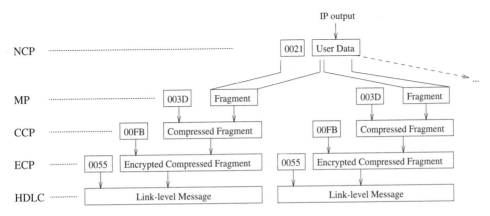

Figure 6.7: LINK-LEVEL CCP AND ECP DATA FLOW

When CCP and ECP are used with MP, the compress-then-encrypt semantics must be retained, but it is possible to negotiate separate compression and encryption at the aggregate level and at each link level. This can lead to explicitly illegal (by RFC 1968) states where, for instance, encryption is negotiated at the aggregate level and compression at the link level.

To minimize memory usage and the number of security relationships, preserve security in distributed MP systems, and maximize the compression ratio, I recommend implementing both CCP and ECP at the aggregate level with MP. Implementations at the individual link level might be desirable in systems with special link-level compression or encryption hardware, but this is the exception rather than the rule, and is often not interoperable.

As a PPP protocol, MP is an oddball. The parameters for it are negotiated using LCP options, not NCP options, and the data are passed using a network layer protocol (003D) without a corresponding NCP negotiation after authentication is complete. The reason is that when MP is negotiated, the link becomes part of the bundle where there is only one set of NCPs. If MP were an NCP by itself, then it would be negotiated alongside the other NCPs, and joining an existing bundle would be much more difficult since it would involve merging or terminating duplicate NCPs.

Normally, all data received by the member links except authentication (such as CHAP challenges) and LCP negotiation messages are forwarded to the bundle level. (Note that special code is required to segregate the LCP messages that a member link handles—usually codes 01–07 and 09–0B—and those that are forwarded to the bundle for processing. In particular, Protocol-Reject—code 08—must be forwarded.) If CCP or ECP is done at the member link level, then protocol numbers 0055, 00FB, 8055, and 80FB must be handled at the member link level, while others are forwarded.

MP may also be used on a single link to increase the effective MRU for the network layer protocols when the LCP MRU is too small for the intended application and when the LCP MRU cannot be changed due to hardware or serial driver restrictions. Usually the MRRU has no such restrictions and can be made as large as desired. In this case, MP functions as a link-layer fragmentation mechanism.

The parameters negotiated with LCP for MP follow.

11 Multilink Maximum Receive Reconstructed Unit (MRRU)

The MRRU is the number of octets an implementation can concatenate together for a given reconstructed frame. It is analogous to the MRU at the link level. In a non-MP system, the MRU is the maximum PPP information field size at the link level and is used as the MTU advertised to network layer interfaces, such as IP, on the peer's side. In an MP system, the MRRU sent by the peer's Configure-Request is used as the MTU for the network level interfaces, and the MRU is used as the maximum message size within MP fragmentation. If the MRRU given by the peer is less than or equal to its MRU+6, then it is not necessary to support fragmentation (though reassembly will still be required).

Unlike MRU, this parameter must be actively negotiated in order to enable MP, even if the desired value is the default (1500 octets). The presence of this option in a Configure-Request signals the desire of that peer to initiate MP mode. If the sender is joining an existing bundle, then the MRRU offered must be same as the MRRU initially negotiated for the bundle. It must be negotiated in both directions or not at all, since MP cannot be run unidirectionally on a link.

The developer implementing MP should refer to the obsolete RFC 1717 for MP, since this RFC recommended slightly different rules for initiating MP. (In particular, it specified that the presence of the following short-sequence-number option was enough to enable MP.) These differences may affect compatibility in some cases.

12 Short Sequence Number Header Format

This boolean option allows a 12-bit sequence number instead of the default 24-bit sequence number to be used for efficiency on low-speed links.

The default long-sequence-number MP header is four octets long. The first octet contains just two bit flags defined as follows:

40 End-of-fragment (E bit)
80 Beginning-of-fragment (B bit)

The remaining three octets are the sequence number of the fragment in network byte order. The MP header with short-sequence-number mode enabled is two octets long. The first octet reserves the most significant four bits for flags, of which two are defined as above. The remaining four bits plus the second octet form the sequence number in network byte order.

As long as the peak rate of transmitting fragments (in fragments-per-second) is less than 4096 divided by the maximum time delay skew between the links, short sequence numbers are viable. If the skew becomes too large for the transmit rate, then the sequence numbers will become ambiguous and reassembly will fail.

13 End-Point Discriminator (ED)

This option acts as a unique system identifier to disambiguate links from two separate peers with the same authenticated name. The negotiated value is intended to be simply accepted by the peer and is not intended to be included in a Configure-Nak. This value consists of a single octet encoding the discriminator class followed by a variable-length address field. The class options are:

00 Null class (equivalent to not specifying ED)
01 Locally assigned address (any value up to 20 octets)
02 IP address (four octets of address)

03 Ethernet MAC address (six octets of address)
04 Magic number block (four to 20 octets)
05 Public switched network directory number (up to 20 octets)

I recommend using these values only as suggested methods of displaying the negotiated parameters for diagnostic purposes. The class and address values have no defined usage in the protocol other than as a "magic cookie" used to identify links that should be bundled together. A reasonable implementation may therefore treat the value (both the class and the address) it receives from its peer for this option as an opaque object, which is simply compared for strict byte-for-byte equality with other ED objects.

Some implementations, however, do use the enclosed values for special purposes. For instance, the directory number (telephone number) class can be useful to supply a new telephone number for the peer to use for subsequent links. This is done when a general telephone number is configured on one side, and this number maps into a telephone company–controlled rotary spanning many separate units on the other side. Since the links cannot normally terminate on separate units, a direct telephone number that bypasses the rotary for the unit reached on the first call is supplied through the ED; then subsequent calls are placed through this number. Such usage, though, is generally obsolescent given the release of multichassis MP by many manufacturers (see the L2TP section below).

Another view of this option is that it forms an unauthenticated extension of the peer name, which is normally established during authentication. In fact, a reasonable implementation could concatenate the ED and the peer name together in some form when forwarding the data to an authentication server, and base its authentication decisions on the complete value.

Detecting New Links

Detecting that a newly negotiated link is actually a new link in an existing bundle is accomplished by scanning an internal list of established bundles. This scan terminates when the same combination of peer name and peer-supplied end-point discriminator is found or when no matching bundle can be found. When comparing peer name and discriminator, it is possible for some bundles to have either no peer name (security was not enabled) or no discriminator (none was supplied by the peer during LCP negotiation), or neither of these. These cases will still match an identical link being established if it lacks the same information. Thus, if neither a peer name nor an end-point discriminator is known, then all such links are simply bundled together. In this way, the peer name and end-point discriminator can be thought of as being logically concatenated for purposes of comparison.

Many implementations have timing problems with this algorithm. Note that it is necessary to do the scan and either establish a new bundle (if none matches) or join an existing bundle (if a match is found), all without permitting other processes to do the same scan concurrently. Otherwise, it is possible for two links from the same peer brought up at the same time to establish separate bundles mistakenly. This timing situation is very common with ISDN, since many TAs immediately dial both B channels when a link is requested. It is also necessary to be prepared to handle MP encapsulated data immediately, as soon as security is complete, whether or not the link is joining an existing bundle, since NCP negotiation is done over the bundle.

It is possible to defer the encapsulation of data transmitted in MP headers until more than one link is in use. If this is desired, MP headers must be enabled as soon as the second link is detected and joins the bundle. The first MP packet sent should also be sent over the newly established link.

Fragmentation and Reassembly

The RFC does not specify an exact method for fragmenting the message for transmission. It does specify the header formats and the correct way to handle these headers, but it does not specify exactly how large to make each message or how to distribute the message among the member links, though it does include some suggestions. This imprecision is intentional. The authors wish to allow implementors to decide what fragmentation policies are acceptable to them and to allow for possible future innovation.

As fragments are received over the member links, they are placed in a reassembly queue, sorted by sequence number. As the messages are reconstructed, they are removed from this queue in sequence number order. Thus, as long as the fragments are numbered correctly by the sender, the messages will be delivered in the same order as they were sent, even if some links experience delays. This property is very important, since out-of-order delivery will break CCP and ECP at the bundle level, as well as many network protocols.

For readers interested in IP, this description of MP should sound familiar. IP fragmentation performs a similar function in a similar manner: both adapt a large MTU to a smaller MTU, and neither relies on retransmission or acknowledgment. They are different in the following ways:

- IP fragmentation and reassembly may reorder packets by default.

- IP fragmentation uses timers to discard stale fragments in place of MP's increasing-sequence-number rule.

- IP fragments may be reordered during transit by an intermediate router or even refragmented. MP fragments are not routed and may not be reordered on any link.

- IP fragmentation is end to end, so a lost or delayed fragment does not affect delivery of other packets in the intermediate routers or in other applications on the same host. MP fragmentation is on a single virtual link only and can cause delays for all traffic over that link when a single fragment is lost or delayed.

Implementation Issues

A large number of issues must be addressed when implementing MP—for example:

- **Idle links.** Idle links hamper the effectiveness of the fragment loss detection logic and increase the buffer space required by the peer. This is because the algorithm specifies that sequence numbers newer than the oldest sequence number last seen on all links must be kept. If one link is not receiving new fragments, then its last sequence number will not change, and no more lost fragments will be detected and dropped. Any lost fragments at that point will cause all subsequent fragments to be buffered indefinitely and cause in-order reassembly to stop. Thus, a good implementation should attempt to avoid ever allowing a member link to go idle for an extended period. Fragments should be fairly distributed among the member links, and occasional null fragments, which have both the B and E bit set but contain zero data bytes, should also be sent.

- **Link loss.** In the event of catastrophic loss of a link, there may still be fragments enqueued for transmission on that link. These fragments cannot in general be requeued on another link because of the increasing-sequence-number rule. Thus, it is important to make use of the LCP Terminate-Request and Terminate-Ack messages to remove a link from a bundle gracefully. In this case, LCP Terminate-Request is sent on a link that is no longer needed. Received data from that link are still processed, but no new fragments are sent over it. When LCP Terminate-Ack is received, the link is finally dropped from the bundle. This procedure violates RFC 1661's rules on the use of LCP Terminate-Request since this is only to be sent when leaving Open state, but this modification is quite common to MP implementations, eliminates unnecessary data loss, and is generally regarded as safe by most members of the IETF PPP working group. If the link lost is the last link in the bundle, then it is safe to turn off MP encapsulation (if desired for efficiency reasons) when the LCP Terminate-Ack is received or when half of the current round-trip time elapses.

- **Out-of-order delivery.** MP is permitted to deliver some network layer data out of normal order, either by removing it from the reassembly queue early or transmitting it without the normal MP header. Implementations that do this for some defined purpose, such as meeting performance constraints, must also consider the effects on layers above MP. In particular, out-of-order delivery breaks most CCP and ECP implementations, breaks Van Jacobson compression in TCP/IP (although IP by itself tolerates reordering), and breaks several entire network protocols, such as SNA. The example MP code given in Appendix B avoids out-of-order delivery by doing fragment enqueuing, reassembly, and frame loss detection in a single pass.

Although reordering plain TCP itself is generally permissible, reordering can cause very poor performance by disabling common header-prediction-based optimizations and triggering TCP's fast-retransmit mechanism.

- **Synchronization.** Many systems support multiple concurrent tasks, and some support multiple processors. These systems pose special problems for MP implementations. For instance, when fragmenting a message for transmission, it is necessary to assign sequence numbers to the fragments and transmit these fragments on the links without violating the increasing-sequence-number rule on any link. Since the process of enqueuing a message for transmission on a link may involve a task switch, it is possible for another network layer entity to attempt to transmit while the first sender is in a suspended state and has not completed fragment queuing. If this happens, it will result in misordered fragments and the loss of both messages. The implementor must either guarantee that no task switch occurs from the time the sequence numbers are first assigned to the fragments until they are safely enqueued on each link, or he must provide a means of detecting this occurrence when the second entity attempts to transmit, and place the second entity's data on a queue for later MP transmission rather than transmitting immediately.

- **Native encapsulation.** Some messages, such as LCP Protocol-Reject, are often sent using native encapsulation (with no MP header) on the link. Others, such as the NCPs, may optionally be sent this way, although they usually are not. Since the NCPs are generally constructed logically "above" the MP layer, except for the per link ECP and CCP options, this means that the implementation must have a means to forward these non-MP messages (such as LCP Protocol-Reject) from any link layer to the bundle and act on them without the normal MP headers as though received as normal MP-encapsulated messages. This generally implies that a flag or switch accompanies the message passed up to indicate whether the source PPP protocol number was MP, so that the headers may be stripped when necessary.

- **Mismatched MRRU.** The RFC states that a system that is joining a link to an existing bundle must use the same MRRU as used for the initial link. Since this negotiation is done at LCP time, before the peer is properly identified, this can pose a problem. What is to be done when a link is identified as part of a bundle after going through authentication, but either this system or the peer has offered a different MRRU from the previous links to that bundle? This can occur if different MRRUs are accidentally configured or if the layer 2 techniques of the following section are used. One possibility is to renegotiate LCP but use the newly discovered "correct" MRRU values as the defaults.

- **Rules of thumb.** Establishing and tearing down calls can be done in a reliable manner without resort to additional protocols. There are three common rules of thumb for doing this. First, either peer may establish a call, but only the peer that established a call may tear it down. This prevents thrashing, since the system that determines that a need for a new link exists also determines when that need has passed.

    a. This rule is modified slightly when MP is used with callback; the initiator of the callback request, not the party doing the callback, is the one that controls tear-down for the subsequent call. Whenever possible, the party ultimately responsible for paying for the call should be the initiator.

    b. Second, if a link is torn down by a peer that was not the initiator of the call, this is an error condition, and another link should not be established until a "damping" time-out occurs. If possible, an operator should also be notified, since this may represent some kind of system failure.

    c. Third, a new link should be established when traffic is heavy in either direction (transmit or receive) for a given period of time. It may come as a surprise, but it is true that both peers have precisely the same information on traffic intensity available for this calculation. Measuring transmit traffic is rather easy, since examining queue depths on the member links gives this information readily. Measuring receive traffic turns out to be also rather easy. To do this, the utilization of the link must be tracked by the receiver. Since, by traditional queuing theory, a utilization that approaches the known bandwidth of the link indicates that the peer's transmit queues are growing without bound, this provides a gauge for establishing a new link.

Establishing a new link for a bundle is very much like establishing the first link. In both cases, if the low-level link fails to establish for any reason, then it is necessary to back off and retry at some later point. It is also necessary to limit the number of consecutive failed attempts, since configuration errors, such as a miskeyed telephone number, could cause pathological behavior.

The rules of thumb serve well in the vast majority of cases. One possible problem with them is that, depending on the usage of reverse-toll lines or callback, it is possible that the initiator of the calls could be the peer that is not paying for them. If this peer is malicious or simply unintelligent, it could cause the payer to pay for unnecessary links. Since the payer did not establish the call, he or she cannot terminate it without risking thrashing and is on the hook for charges he or she cannot control.

Another problem is that if MP is used with callback, then each new link should be established by the peer. These links sometimes cannot be established automatically, since even when callback is used, it is usually the case that the system doing the callback is not actually paying for the call, since the charges are simply tallied and billed to the original caller. This means that establishing additional links requires a separate call and callback pair and, probably, additional charges.

The problem of the malicious or stupid peer can be solved administratively. If your Internet service provider forces you to pay too much for connectivity, find another. Using a bandwidth management protocol could possibly solve the problem, but it is often better simply not to do business with such an outfit. Good implementations measure link utilization and report abnormal conditions, such as continued high usage with no new links and low usage with too many links. If, on the other hand, you own both ends of the link, then it is up to you to find implementations that dial only when necessary and to configure them properly.

The second problem involving callback is not very common but is a good candidate for a simple separate protocol that would allow the original initiator of a callback to request an additional link. (Since this side is also the initiator for termination purposes, it is not necessary to have a special protocol to determine when to tear down the link; the rules of thumb work correctly.) Unfortunately, the proposed bandwidth management protocols are far, far more complex than this trivial problem and attempt to solve problems that do not exist here, as we will see in this next section.

Active Bandwidth Management

Several protocols have been proposed to control establishment and tear-down of MP links. As we found in the previous chapter, these protocols are not at all necessary for proper and efficient operation of a demand-dialed system, but the proponents of these protocols have been able to garner significant market support, and the protocols are advancing in the standards process. Due in part to competition in the marketing rather than technical arena, this area is extremely contentious.

MP+

Ascend Communications has been one of the proponents of active bandwidth management. Its proprietary protocol for bandwidth control, MP+, is described in Informational RFC 1934 (47 pages). This protocol is quite complex and includes a reliable delivery layer (which is part of the protocol; Proposed Standard RFC 1663 reliable delivery is not used) plus extensive remote control and remote management functions (which are otherwise often done with SNMP).

I do not recommend implementing this protocol.

Bandwidth Allocation Control Protocol (BACP)

The Bandwidth Allocation Control Protocol is described in RFC 2125. This protocol defines an additional LCP option (hex 17) called a *Link Discriminator*, plus two PPP control protocols, C02B (BACP) and C02D (BAP).

The LCP option negotiates a two-octet integer that is intended to be a unique identifier for a link within a multilink bundle and is used as a reference for BACP messages. If either end of the connection is using one of the layer-two-forwarding techniques described below, then this number usually cannot be uniquely assigned at LCP time. The only option is to renegotiate LCP after finding that the link is part of an existing bundle.

BACP provides a means to request permission to add a link, request the addition of a dial-back link, and request that a link be dropped. It also provides a way to pass information, such as telephone numbers and link characteristics, between the peers. BACP has a single configuration option that must be negotiated before BAP can be used to send the above requests.

01 Favored-Peer

This option negotiates a four-octet integer that determines the peer that "wins" in cases of a tie, where both peers request the same action. The RFC says that this is to be used when the actions are requested at the same time, which should be interpreted to mean that if after the request is sent and before a reply is received an identical request is received, then the favored peer should send Nak and the unfavored peer should send Ack.

Once BACP has reached Open state, BAP packets are permitted. These messages take the familiar Code-Id-Length format. Responses to BAP messages have an additional single octet after the Length that specifies the status of the message, using 00 for *Ack*, 01 for *Nak* ("maybe later"), 02 for *Reject*, and 03 for *Full-Nak* ("at my limit"). The defined Code values are:

```
01  Call-Request
02  Call-Response
03  Callback-Request
04  Callback-Response
05  Link-Drop-Query-Request
06  Link-Drop-Query-Response
07  Call-Status-Indication
08  Call-Status-Response
```

Following this is a variable-length data field that contains Type-Len-Data fields encoding parameters for the operation. These option types are:

```
01  Link-Type
02  Phone-Delta
03  No-Phone-Number-Needed (boolean)
04  Reason (string)
05  Link-Discriminator
06  Call-Status
```

Should BACP Be Used?

The protocol does appear to have some flaws. For instance, what constitutes a "tie" in negotiation is specified in the draft as only cases where the code number is the same. Consider the exchange in Figure 6.8 between a customer using ISDN BRI and his ISP, both of which have the traffic level triggers set to a default value.

Customer	ISP
Call-Request	Callback-Request
Request-Response (Reject)	Request-Response (Full-Nak)

Figure 6.8: BACP COLLISION

The ISP must send Full-Nak since it must allocate the B channel before sending a callback request, and it therefore has no channels left for this customer. The customer rejects the callback request from the ISP based on configuration, since either the customer doesn't want the ISP telling him when to spend more money or since it has already allocated all its B channels for its call request. This leads to an impasse. The RFC states that no more requests may be made if a Nak is sent until the total bandwidth changes—in other words, until the single link hangs up. The second B channel is not used.

Of the BACP protocol features, the "request to add" (Call-Request) is not useful in most situations, since the rules of thumb generally suffice to handle any call rejection. In fact, it is necessary for all systems, with or without BACP, to be able to handle call rejection gracefully (or misdirection, as detected by failed authentication or an unexpected end-point discriminator), on either the first link or subsequent links. On systems with BACP, the successful Call-Request negotiation provides only the indication that the peer believes that the call might succeed. It may still fail for any number of reasons—for example, switch congestion or low-level negotiation failure (modem training or V.120 SABME). Since such handling is already required and since, at least for commercial services, full servers mean lost customers and servers will thus rarely reject the request, this feature adds little.

A secondary reason offered for use of Call-Request is to receive the telephone number of a line that is more likely to land on a particular system in a multisystem implementation. This reason is less than compelling since (1) the first call in a bundle may land on a busy system, and additional links will then need to be handed out to other systems with the use of layer-two forwarding or tunneling, (2) any system that implements layer-two forwarding does not need to use this option at all, and (3) management of the telephone number deltas themselves is likely to be difficult in nontrivial configurations, which may involve nonlocal call routing during peak periods—precisely the situation in which the feature is needed.

The Callback-Request feature is useful when the initial link was created via callback, and the initiator of that callback wishes to establish additional links without additional calls. Implementation of this option in other circumstances is discouraged, since it permits the nonpaying peer to demand additional links.

The Link-Drop-Query-Request may seem odd at first glance, but it does have a narrow purpose. If both sides of the conversation are actively establishing links, then some links will be under the control of one peer and others under the control of the other. This means that when traffic is light and both peers are configured with the same link-drop thresholds, and a link should be dropped, it is possible that both peers may accidentally elect to drop a link, resulting in too little bandwidth, at least until a new link is established. In extreme cases, it could cause oscillation as both sides establish, then tear down, a single link in each direction. Fortunately, it is very rarely the case that both sides actively establish links, and, in these cases, it is usually quite satisfactory simply to set the link-drop thresholds differently for the two peers. Thus, this option is generally not necessary.

The drop request is suggested also for use when one side of the link is not sufficiently sophisticated to monitor usage. That an implementation will include a complex protocol like BACP but not include simple link utilization monitoring seems rather unlikely.

Another suggested usage of BACP is with metered leased lines. With this type of line, the user pays only when data are sent, but the link is not dialed, so there is no identifiable "caller" or "called" party. However, again, it is true that only one party is ultimately paying for the additional links, and that party must be the one that establishes and tears down links as necessary. If the other party is bringing up links, it is guilty of fraud and should be disabled or replaced.

Still another possible use for BACP, which has been suggested, is to communicate MP usage policy decisions from a central site to dial-up clients. Of course, a central site that wishes to disallow use of MP need only renegotiate LCP and Configure-Reject the MRRU option and also not offer the MRRU option to new sessions that start during the disabled period. Since most current dial-up MP implementations use only one or two links, turning on or off MP, rather than attempting to regulate the number of allowable links, provides exactly as much control as necessary. Again, good implementations can behave gracefully with arbitrary restrictions without using BACP.

Cost Shifting

Callback

Callback is generally used as a form of cost shifting, and occasionally for security, and it allows a dial-up system to disconnect a caller and immediately call back to that caller to establish the PPP session. There are two current means for doing this. The first is documented in RFC 1570 and is a Proposed Standard. The second is a Microsoft proposal used in Windows Dial-Up Networking and described in documents on their ftp site (see Chapter 8 to obtain these documents).

The RFC 1570 standard callback mechanism uses a single LCP option to request the callback. The negotiated value consists of a single-octet operation code and an optional variable-length message field. The operation code is one of the following:

00 Use authenticated name to find phone number
01 Use message as dialing string
02 Use message as keyword to look up phone number
03 Message is a standard E.164 phone number
04 Message is a "distinguished name" (locally defined)

When this form of callback is used, the initial call proceeds through authentication and then is terminated. The callback then occurs, and the callback option is not negotiated on the called-back link.

This form of callback does leave a problem besides the need for the first call to request the callback. The problem is that acceptance of the callback option is done at LCP time when the peer's identity is still unknown. What should be done if callback is not acceptable once the peer is identified? Authentication should not be allowed to complete, since the peer will then expect a callback, which is not going to occur.

Instead, two possibilities exist. First, the system detecting this condition can send LCP Configure-Request again and restart LCP without replying to the PAP Authentication-Request or CHAP Response. This should restart the peer, and then this second time through LCP, callback can be disabled with Configure-Reject. This will allow the call to continue to an established state without the expected dialback. (Of course, an error should also be logged so that an operator can correct this misconfiguration.) Note that the call must not be terminated in anticipation of a callback until the authentication is complete. This means that an extra wait for the Success or Failure message is necessary if CHAP is used.

The second alternative is to send an Authenticate-Nak even though the peer is correctly identified and to include a message saying something like, "Your log-in was valid, but you're not authorized to use callback." This has the advantage of alerting an operator to the condition that should be corrected.

One of these two options should be implemented, though which is implemented depends on whether it is more desirable to allow misconfigured links to operate or to prevent the wrong party from paying for the call.

Callback Control Protocol

The Microsoft Callback Control Protocol (CBCP) is an extension to RFC 1570. It claims that standard callback presents a security hole (despite the fact that initially agreeing to callback during LCP does not require the callback to occur), and it claims that 1570 is not interoperable.

It defines a new operation value 06, which indicates that CBCP should be negotiated after authentication is complete. CBCP (PPP protocol number C029) negotiates a callback before other NCPs are run using three messages. Unfortunately, the data types used are not at all compatible with standard telenetworking equipment or even standard PPP itself. For example, the telephone numbers are specified as ASCIIZ strings (perhaps an MS-DOS concept), when, in contrast, PPP strings are always defined to be counted strings, not null terminated. The telephone numbers also are defined to contain optionally the strange characters *, #, T, P, W, @, and others, which are all defined in the command sets of certain common consumer grade modems but are not at all applicable to standard equipment used at carrier-class installations, and are therefore useless to most service providers.

Implementation of this protocol is not recommended.

Layer-Two Forwarding and Tunneling

Layer-two forwarding is intended to provide "virtual private networking" (VPN) services. A VPN allows a service provider to construct an isolated network on top of an existing network, such as the Internet. Such services are not common now, but telephone companies and some large Internet service providers believe that corporations with commuting employees will use these services to link them to central databases over inexpensive public networks. These services work by extending the link between the HDLC driver and the rest of PPP over a separate network. Since PPP is at layer two (data-link) in the OSI protocol stack, the underlying technology is called *layer-two forwarding* or *tunneling*.

The first proposal for a layer-two technique was Cisco's Layer Two Forwarding Protocol (L2F). The main features of this proposal are that it can carry both SLIP and PPP, it runs over any connectionless network service (the draft mentions use over UDP/IP, but any service would work), it contains an optional message-sequencing mechanism without flow control, and it uses a small management protocol to establish and tear down tunnels.

The second proposal to appear was Microsoft's Point-to-Point Tunneling Protocol (PPTP), a PPP-specific protocol designed to run over a combination of TCP and UDP over IP only. At 62 pages, it is far more complex than L2F but also included important call-setup information, such as link speed and calling number, which were not included in L2F, as well as support for dial-out. It did not, however, include any form of security, other than that provided by PPP itself, which means that its dial-out mechanism was free for use by any hacker.

At the Montreal IETF meeting in June 1996, these two proposals were merged into a single working proposal, Layer Two Tunneling Protocol (L2TP). At 79 pages, draft-ietf-pppext-l2tp-06.txt is extremely complex and includes PPTP's reinvention of the TCP round-trip time estimation and flow control mechanisms for the user data portion of the tunnel. L2TP is an active area of debate and research.

Layer-Two Tunneling and MP

Early in the development of MP, a fundamental problem was discovered with MP implementation. For reliability and scalability, large installations will need to have many physically separate systems to handle PPP calls and will need to use services that automatically distribute incoming calls among those systems. However, standard MP will not work in this environment, since each individual link must terminate on the same system in order for fragment reassembly to function.

To fix this problem, developers have used two routes. One group has proposed mechanisms to steer the additional links to the right individual system. This is the idea behind BACP. The other has proposed means to discover that a new link has landed on the wrong system and to forward the data over local high-speed networks to the right one using layer-two tunneling.

There are several advantages to layer-two techniques. First, the dial-in users do not need to implement any new protocols other than MP, so it is compatible with existing equipment. Second, complete utilization of equipment without arbitrary denial of service is possible. If you use BACP and your first link unfortunately lands on a system that is already busy, then you might not be able to start a second link, even though all the other systems may be idle. With layer-two tunneling, your second connection can land on any system, and the data will be forwarded to the right place.

Vendors may ultimately adopt L2TP for this purpose, but as of this writing, the protocol is too unsettled and too complex to bring interoperable products to market. Several vendors have decided to go ahead with proprietary protocols instead of waiting for the standards to catch up.

Ascend's Multichassis PPP

Ascend's solution, called Stacks, is based on a rather simple protocol that is representative of the solutions to this problem that many manufacturers are creating. To find a possible bundle head when a new link comes up, the Ascend MAX sends out seven request messages within one second. If no response is seen, this link must represent a new bundle. Otherwise, it is joined to the existing bundle indicated in the response.

The messages are sent, by default, to UDP port 5151 with UDP checksumming disabled. The Query messages are sent as Ethernet multicast messages to 01:C0:7B:00:00:01. The first three octets of that Ethernet address are assigned to Ascend. At the IP level, the messages are sent to the local broadcast address (255.255.255.255), perhaps because Ascend has not registered an IP multicast address with the IANA.

The data inside the UDP message have this format:

```
Query:    01 01 LinkID Stack Speed DiscLen Disc
```

```
Response:   01 02 LinkID Stack LinkIDReply MRRU MRU
Data:       01 05 LinkIDReply Length Data
            01 05 LinkID Length Pad Data
Tear-down:  01 06 LinkID/LinkIDReply
```

where the initial 01 appears to be a revision number. The other named fields follow.

- **LinkID:** A four-octet integer assigned sequentially by the system that received the new link. Messages from the bundle head will use this number to contact the link with outbound data.

- **Stack:** A 16-octet ASCII string that names the group of boxes that will be exchanging links. This allows many boxes within a multicast domain to be partitioned into logical groups for administrative reasons.

- **Speed:** A four-octet integer representing the link speed in bits per second.

- **DiscLen:** A four-octet integer representing the length of the end-point discriminator, which follows.

- **Disc:** The variable-length end-point discriminator, with the discriminator class indicated as the initial octet.

- **LinkIDReply:** A four-octet integer assigned by the bundle head to identify the new link. Messages from the link will use this number to contact the bundle head with inbound data.

- **MRRU:** A three-octet (!) integer representing the negotiated peer's MRRU.

- **MRU:** A two-octet integer representing the negotiated peer's MRU.

- **Length:** A four-octet integer representing the data length. It does not include the Pad, if any.

- **Pad:** A ten-octet fill of apparently random data that appears only in outbound messages from the bundle head to the link. Its function is unknown but may serve to avoid situations where one link ends up joining to another link or a bundle head joins to another head due to errors.

- **Data:** The PPP message itself, including address and control fields but not including FCS.

Only the initial Query message is sent as a multicast. All other messages are sent as normal unicast messages directly to the peer.

A start-up and shut-down exchange might look like this:

```
Query:
    01 01 00 00 00 04 48 69 00 00 00 00 00 00 00 00 00 00 00 00
    00 00 00 00 00 FA 00 00 00 00 04 01 14 7E 5B
```

The LinkID is 00000004, the stack name is "Hi," the link speed is 0000FA00 (64Kbps), and the discriminator is locally assigned (type 01) as 147E5B.

```
Response:
  01 02 00 00 00 04 48 69 00 00 00 00 00 00 00 00 00 00 00
  00 00 00 00 00 00 19 00 05 DC 05 F4
```

This is a reply to LinkID 00000004 in stack "Hi." The LinkIDReply value to get back to the bundle is 00000019, the MRRU is 0005DC (1500), and the MRU is 05F4 (1524).

```
Data:
  01 05 00 00 00 19 00 00 00 08 FF 03 C0 21 05 06 00 04
```

This is a message from link to bundle, eight octets long. (LCP Termination Request.)

```
Data:
  01 05 00 00 00 04 00 00 00 08 00 00 00 00 00 00 00 00 00
  00 FF 03 C0 21 06 06 00 04
```

This is a message from bundle to link, eight octets long. (LCP Termination Ack.) Note the padding before the address and control field.

```
Tear-down:
  01 06 00 00 00 04
```

This is a tear-down request from bundle to link. (Sent four times.)

This simple protocol allows a group of Ascend servers to appear to be one large server to dial-up users. The protocol is not yet publicly documented, so compatible implementations are unlikely. Other manufacturers, though, are pursuing the same type of solution.

It is perhaps likely that all of these bandwidth management protocols will become obsolete in the near future. Deregulation of the local telephone service market is granting new providers access to the local loops—the wires from the central office to the home. Some of these providers will undoubtedly want to use these wires for dedicated high-speed access, which would make dial-up obsolete. Other less conventional means of access, such as cable and satellite, have a fair chance to displace dial-up as well.

Chapter

7

Interpreting Traces

Approach

When PPP fails to function properly, a fair bit of detective work is sometimes required to find the source of the problem. In general, the problems users see fall into three categories: communications, negotiation, and networking. Of course, only the negotiation is actually part of PPP, but it is necessary to isolate the problem to one part of the system in order to repair it.

Network Layer Problems

Networking problems are usually the easiest to isolate. If the link comes up, but no data pass or only a few hosts are reachable, a networking problem is likely. A general rule of thumb for establishing that the problem is indeed related to networking is to disable all optional protocols, such as compression, and establish the link. If the problem still appears, networking is suspect.

Debugging networking problems usually requires an intimate knowledge of the routing and forwarding techniques used. Here are some general hints:

- *Check the routing tables.* Examine the network layer routing tables not only on the machine experiencing the problem, but on the peer's side as well, and on any other routers on either side of the link that are in the path to the destination system. It is very common for networking problems, especially those that result in only some hosts being reachable, to be due to misconfiguration of those intermediate routers. Don't forget to check both the path to the destination and the path back; more often than not, the problem is in the return path.

- *Check the available statistics.* Most network layer implementations provide a number of counts, such as packets received and packets forwarded. If the peer system is not too busy, it is often possible to check the statistics, attempt to contact a host, and then reexamine the statistics to find which ones changed. If this does not reveal a problem, then check the same statistics on the next router or the destination host itself.

Negotiation and Communications

The distinction between negotiation problems and communications problems can be difficult to discern sometimes. Some are obvious, such as chat script failures. Some types of communications problems, though, such as a bad ACCM setting, can look like negotiation problems. Here are some of the symptoms of communications errors:

- **Link terminates with "too many Configure-Requests" message.**
  This usually means that one system cannot hear the other. Possible causes include bad cabling, incorrect bit rate settings or flow control, and a chat script failure.

- **Link terminates with "possibly looped-back" message.**
  This is often caused when the peer is not actually running PPP but is left sitting at some kind of command-line prompt due to a chat script error.

- **LCP comes up, but all protocols above that experience strange CRC errors.**
  This is usually caused by an incorrectly set ACCM. Try setting this mask back to the default of FFFFFFFF.

- **LCP comes up, but the link terminates shortly afterward.**
  This can be caused by an incorrect password, depending on how the peer implements the security protocols. In MP systems, this can be caused by a failure to match the expected end-point discriminator on dial-out.

- **IPCP comes up and terminates immediately.**
  This is usually the result of IP address configuration errors.

The PPP debugging Web pages referenced in Chapter 8 can be a big help in isolating these problems for particular implementations.

Example Traces

The following examples show the raw hexadecimal frames sent by each peer, followed by the decoded interpretation of each message. On a particular medium, the actual data captured will differ due to HDLC or AHDLC encapsulation. If you are working with the low-level data, you may want to convert them to raw hexadecimal form first by decoding the HDLC format. For instance, on an asynchronous line, every 7D XX sequence should be replaced with (XX XOR 20) and every 7E marks the end of a frame.

Normal Start-Up with Authentication

Simple IP Example

This simple but complete example shows LCP, PAP authentication, and IPCP negotiation. The options include Address and Control field compression and Protocol field compression in LCP. Peer A is configured to be IP address 10.1.0.1 and peer B is 10.2.0.5.

```
 1A: FF 03 C0 21 01 01 00 0C 03 04 C0 23 07 02 08 02 5A B8
 2B: FF 03 C0 21 01 01 00 0C 03 04 C0 23 07 02 08 02 5A B8
 3B: FF 03 C0 21 02 01 00 0C 03 04 C0 23 07 02 08 02 B4 3F
 4A: FF 03 C0 21 02 01 00 0C 03 04 C0 23 07 02 08 02 B4 3F
 5A: C0 23 01 01 00 12 05 50 65 65 72 41 07 41 53 65 63 72 65
     74 6D CE
 6B: C0 23 01 01 00 12 05 50 65 65 72 42 07 42 53 65 63 72 65
     74 04 B0
 7B: C0 23 02 01 00 16 50 65 72 6d 69 73 73 69 6F 6E 20 67 72
     61 6E 74 65 64 2A 88
 8A: C0 23 02 01 00 04 2F A8
 9A: 80 21 01 01 00 0A 03 06 0A 01 00 01 96 51
10B: 80 21 01 01 00 0A 03 06 0A 02 00 05 D6 F8
11B: 80 21 02 01 00 0A 03 06 0A 01 00 01 FF 25
12A: 80 21 02 01 00 0A 03 06 0A 02 00 05 BF 8C
```

The trace assumes that both peers have reached Req-Sent state at the same time. If one peer reaches Req-Sent state before the other, then its Configure-Request message is usually lost, and the exchange is somewhat easier to read than this example since each side will end up negotiating separately.

Decoded in detail, these messages are:

```
1A:   LCP Configure-Request 1 [03:C023 07 08]
      FF 03 - HDLC Address and Control Field
      C0 21 - PPP Protocol field (LCP)
      01    - Configure Request
      01    - ID 1
      00 0C - Length 12 octets
      03    - Option 3 (Authentication Protocol)
      04    - Length 4 octets
      C0 23 - PAP
      07    - Option 7 (Protocol Field Compression)
      02    - Length 2 octets
      08    - Option 8 (Address and Control Field
              Compression)
      02    - Length 2 octets
      5A B8 - CRC

2B:   FF 03 C0 21 01 01 00 0C 03 04 C0 23 07 02 08 02 5A B8
```

The above Configure-Request messages, which are identical, are sent at nearly the same time in opposite directions on the link, one by peer A and one by peer B. At this point, LCP on both peers is in Req-Sent state. When these messages arrive at the other end of the link, both peers issue Configure-Ack messages and transition to Ack-Sent state, as below:

```
3B: LCP Configure-Ack 1 [03:C023 07 08]
    FF 03 - HDLC Address and Control Field
    C0 21 - PPP Protocol field (LCP)
    02    - Configure Ack
    01    - ID 1
    00 0C - Length 12 octets
    03    - Option 3 (Authentication Protocol)
    04    - Length 4 octets
    C0 23 - PAP
    07    - Option 7 (Protocol Field Compression)
    02    - Length 2 octets
    08    - Option 8 (Address and Control Field
            Compression)
    02    - Length 2 octets
    B4 3F - CRC


4A:  FF 03 C0 21 02 01 00 0C 03 04 C0 23 07 02 08 02 B4 3F
```

These two messages are again identical and pass each other in flight. On reception, both peers transition LCP from Ack-Sent to Open state, and send an Up event to security. The security layer (PAP in this example) on both peers then sends an Authenticate-Request and proceeds to Req-Sent state:

```
5A:  PAP Authenticate-Request 1 ["PeerA" "ASecret"]
     C0 23 - PPP Protocol field (PAP)
     01    - Authenticate Request
     01    - ID 1
     00 12 - Length 18 octets
     05    - Name length is 5 octets
     50 65 65 72 41 - Peer name is "PeerA"
     07    - Password length is 7 octets
     41 53 65 63 72 65 74 - Password is "ASecret"
     6D CE - CRC


6B:  PAP Authenticate-Request 1 ["PeerB" "BSecret"]
     C0 23 - PPP Protocol field (PAP)
     01    - Authenticate Request
     01    - ID 1
     00 12 - Length 18 octets
     05    - Name length is 5 octets
```

```
50 65 65 72 42 - Peer name is "PeerB"
07     - Password length is 7 octets
42 53 65 63 72 65 74 - Password is "BSecret"
04 B0 - CRC
```

On reception of these messages, each peer verifies the identity of the peer, sends an Authenticate-Ack message, and proceeds to Ack-Sent state. Note that peer B chooses to send a friendly "Permission Granted" string, while peer A chooses simply to acknowledge the identity of the peer. These are, of course, equivalent from the point of view of the protocol:

```
7B:  PAP Authenticate-Ack 1 ["Permission Granted"]
     C0 23 - PPP Protocol field (PAP)
     02     - Authenticate Ack
     01     - ID 1
     00 16 - Length 22 octets
     50 65 72 6d 69 73 73 69 6F 6E 20 67 72 61 6E 74 65 64
            - Message "Permission Granted"
     2A 88 - CRC

8A:  PAP Authenticate-Ack 1
     C0 23 - PPP Protocol field (PAP)
     02     - Authenticate Ack
     01     - ID 1
     00 04 - Length 4 octets
     2F A8 - CRC
```

On reception of the above two messages, both peers transition security to the Open state. Note that if only one side is authenticating the other (this is not a recommended configuration, though it is quite common in commercial dial-up systems), then the side that is demanding authentication starts off in Ack-Rcvd state, and the side that is providing its identity (peer name and password) starts off in Ack-Sent state.

Both peers now send Up events to all of the NCP state machines. In this example, only IPCP is being used, so each side transitions IPCP to Req-Sent state and sends an IPCP Configure-Request message:

```
9A:  IPCP Configure-Request 1 [03:10.1.0.1]
     80 21 - PPP Protocol field (IPCP)
     01     - Configure Request
     01     - ID 1
     00 0A - Length 10 octets
     03     - Option 3 (IP Address)
     06     - Length 6 octets
     0A 01 00 01 - Address 10.1.0.1
     96 51 - CRC
```

```
10B: IPCP Configure-Request 1 [03:10.2.0.5]
     80 21 - PPP Protocol field (IPCP)
     01    - Configure Request
     01    - ID 1
     00 0A - Length 10 octets
     03    - Option 3 (IP Address)
     06    - Length 6 octets
     0A 02 00 05 - Address 10.2.0.5
     D6 F8 - CRC
```

On reception of these messages, both peers transition IPCP to Ack-Sent state, and send the following messages:

```
11B: IPCP Configure-Ack 1 [03:10.1.0.1]
     80 21 - PPP Protocol field (IPCP)
     02    - Configure Ack
     01    - ID 1
     00 0A - Length 10 octets
     03    - Option 3 (IP Address)
     06    - Length 6 octets
     0A 01 00 01 - Address 10.1.0.1
     FF 25 - CRC
```

```
12A: IPCP Configure-Ack 1 [03:10.2.0.5]
     80 21 - PPP Protocol field (IPCP)
     02    - Configure Ack
     01    - ID 1
     00 0A - Length 10 octets
     03    - Option 3 (IP Address)
     06    - Length 6 octets
     0A 02 00 05 - Address 10.2.0.5
     BF 8C - CRC
```

On reception of these two messages, IPCP is transitioned to Open state by both peers, and the IP network layer is notified that it can now begin sending data.

Multiple Protocols

With multiple protocols in use, the interleaving of the messages becomes more complex. In this example, peer A supports IP, IPX, and CCP, while peer B supports IP, IPX, AppleTalk, and MP. The authentication is bidirectional using standard CHAP, and parameter negotiation is required due to the configuration:

```
1A: FF 03 C0 21 01 01 00 13 02 06 00 0A 00 00 03 05 C2 23
    05 07 02 08 02 00 18
2B: FF 03 C0 21 01 01 00 1B 01 04 05 F4 03 05 C2 23
    05 05 06 11 26 55 10 07 02 08 02 11 04 05 DC EB AE
3B: FF 03 C0 21 03 01 00 0A 02 06 10 0A 00 00 CD 93
4A: FF 03 C0 21 04 01 00 0E 05 06 11 26 55 10 11 04 05 DC
    90 AD
```

```
 5A: FF 03 C0 21 01 02 00 13 02 06 10 0A 00 00 03 05 C2 23
     05 07 02 08 02 E8 43
 6B: FF 03 C0 21 01 02 00 11 01 04 05 F4 03 05 C2 23 05 07
     02 08 02 66 45
 7B: FF 03 C0 21 02 02 00 13 02 06 10 0A 00 00 03 05 C2 23
     05 07 02 08 02 22 FE
 8A: FF 03 C0 21 02 02 00 11 01 04 05 F4 03 05 C2 23
     05 07 02 08 02 77 75
 9A: C2 23 01 01 00 1A 10 C7 C8 3D BE 83 5F 84 D9 DA 55 29
     61 87 E6 90 1C 50 65 65 72 41 19 FE
10B: C2 23 01 01 00 1A 10 FC 93 B0 B3 81 AD B3 41 63 22 A2
     71 41 F7 8A D3 50 65 65 72 42 C5 A3
11B: C2 23 02 01 00 1A 10 6B ED CC 2D 05 7A DF 6D BC C5 03 F6
     3C 5B 75 DD 50 65 65 72 42 26 CF
12A: C2 23 02 01 00 1A 10 80 3E 61 29 D1 33 F2 CA F3 B0 9A 63
     BA 2E 0C F3 50 65 65 72 41 54 47
13A: C2 23 03 01 00 0B 57 65 6C 63 6F 6D 65 A3 5A
14B: C2 23 03 01 00 09 48 65 6C 6C 6F A4 CA
15B: 80 21 01 01 00 10 02 06 00 2D 0F 01 03 06 84 F5 0B 0A 29
     8E
16B: 80 2B 01 01 00 1A 01 06 00 00 00 33 03 06 00 02 0F 00 05
     08 53 45 52 56 45 52 06 02 9E EF
17B: 80 29 01 01 00 15 01 06 00 17 E8 9B 07 05 6D 61 63 08 06
     00 17 D4 16 D3 B0
18A: 80 21 01 01 00 0A 03 06 00 00 00 00 6D C6
19A: 80 2B 01 01 00 0A 01 06 00 00 00 00 B3 D9
20A: 80 FD 01 01 00 0F 11 05 00 01 04 12 06 00 00 00 01 D9 A9
21A: 80 21 04 01 00 0A 02 06 00 2D 0F 01 F8 30
22A: 80 2B 02 01 00 1A 01 06 00 00 00 33 03 06 00 02 0F 00 05
     08 53 45 52 56 45 52 06 02 7F B0
23A: FF 03 C0 21 08 03 00 1B 80 29 01 01 00 15 01 06 00
     17 E8 9B 07 05 6D 61 63 08 06 00 17 D4 16 94 81
24B: 80 21 03 01 00 0A 03 06 84 F5 0B D1 84 57
25B: 80 2B 03 01 00 0A 01 06 00 00 00 33 E5 82
26B: FF 03 C0 21 08 03 00 15 80 FD 01 01 00 0F 11 05 00 01 04
     12 06 00 00 00 01 9D 81
27B: 80 21 01 02 00 0A 03 06 84 F5 0B 0A 93 B1
28A: 80 21 01 02 00 0A 03 06 84 F5 0B D1 CD D9
29A: 80 2B 01 02 00 0C 01 06 00 00 00 33 06 02 A9 10
30A: 80 21 02 02 00 0A 03 06 84 F5 0B 0A FA C5
31B: 80 21 02 02 00 0A 03 06 84 F5 0B D1 A4 AD
32B: 80 2B 02 02 00 0C 01 06 00 00 00 33 06 02 47 97
```

Unlike the simple IP exchange above, a terser decoding is provided for this example:

```
 1A: LCP Configure-Request 1 [02:000A0000 03:C02305 07 08]
 2B: LCP Configure-Request 1 [01:1524 03:C02305 05:11265510
     07 08 11:1500]
 3B: LCP Configure-Nak 1 [02:100A0000]
 4A: LCP Configure-Reject 1 [05:11265510 11:1500]
 5A: LCP Configure-Request 2 [02:100A0000 03:C02305 07 08]
 6B: LCP Configure-Request 2 [01:1524 03:C02305 07 08]
```

```
 7B: LCP Configure-Ack 2 [02:100A0000 03:C02305 07 08]
 8A: LCP Configure-Ack 2 [01:1524 03:C02305 07 08]
 9A: CHAP Challenge 1 [rand1 "PeerA"]
10B: CHAP Challenge 1 [rand2 "PeerB"]
11B: CHAP Response 1 [MD5(1,secret-ab2,rand1) "PeerB"]
12A: CHAP Response 1 [MD5(1,secret-ba1,rand2) "PeerA"]
13A: CHAP Success 1 ["Welcome"]
14B: CHAP Success 1 ["Hello"]
```

Any well-configured PPP system using CHAP will have at least two secrets if calls can be made in only one direction and will have four if either peer may call the other. In this case, "secret-ab2" is peer B's secret used to authenticate itself to peer A when peer A has initiated the call, and "secret-ba1" is peer A's secret used to authenticate itself to peer B when peer A has initiated the call. The other two secrets for this link, secret-ab1 and secret-ba2, are not used in this example, but would be used if peer B had called peer A.

The function "MD5" above is the MD5 hash of the ID field (the byte 01 in the example above), the secret, and the challenge value (the random number supplied by the peer). This is the standard CHAP response value calculation specified in RFC 1994. Rand1 and rand2, are, of course, random challenge values.

Now that security is complete, both sides send an Up message from the authentication layer to the NCPs chosen for the link. These NCPs then send out Configure-Request messages. The following six messages—three from B and three from A—are likely to be sent nearly simultaneously by both sides. Peer B is requesting use of IP, IPX, and AppleTalk, while peer A is requesting IP, IPX, and CCP. Peer A does not have its network layer addresses configured, so it specifies these as zero to request that peer B supply them, and, for IPXCP, it leaves off the option 6 flag, since it does not want the peer to bring up the link if it would agree to this number. (If peer A could "hear" the Configure-Request from peer B for IPXCP before sending its own Configure-Request, then it should pick up the network number specified in that message rather than sending zero. Since these messages are sent out nearly simultaneously, that does not happen in this case.)

```
15B: IPCP Configure-Request 1 [02:002D0F01 03:132.245.11.10]
16B: IPXCP Configure-Request 1 [01:00000033 03:00020F00
                                05:"SERVER" 06]
17B: ATCP Configure-Request 1 [01:6120.155 07:"mac"
                               08:6100.22]
18A: IPCP Configure-Request 1 [03:0.0.0.0]
19A: IPXCP Configure-Request 1 [01:00000000]
20A: CCP Configure-Request 1 [11:000104 12:00000001]
```

On reception of the above messages, both sides must decide on appropriate replies. In this case, peer A does not want to do VJ header compression (21A) or AppleTalk (23A). It also completely agrees with the parameters sent for IPXCP by peer B. It thus transitions IPXCP to Ack-Sent state and sends a Configure-Ack message, and leaves both IPCP and CCP in Req-Sent state.

Peer B detects the zero addresses in the IPCP and IPXCP messages, so it sends Configure-Nak for each with the appropriate addresses. It does not recognize CCP, so it sends a Protocol-Reject for this. All three NCPs (IPCP, IPXCP, and ATCP) are left in Req-Sent state. (The Protocol-Reject ID numbers are 3, since the last LCP message sent by each—the Configure-Ack—had ID 2.)

```
21A: IPCP Configure-Reject 1 [02:002D0F01]
22A: IPXCP Configure-Ack 1 [01:00000033 03:00020F00
                            05:"SERVER" 06]
23A: LCP Protocol-Reject 3 [8029]
24B: IPCP Configure-Nak 1 [03:132.245.11.209]
25B: IPXCP Configure-Nak 1 [01:00000033]
26B: LCP Protocol-Reject 3 [80FD]
```

When the above messages are received, peer B turns off VJ header compression in IPCP and generates a new Configure-Request. IPXCP is transitioned to Ack-Rcvd state, ATCP is transitioned to Closed state, and IPCP is still in Req-Sent state.

Peer A updates its IP address based on the Configure-Nak message from peer B and resends Configure-Request. IPCP stays in Req-Sent state. IPXCP resends its Configure-Request message based on the network number learned from peer B's Configure-Request (remember: there is only one IPX network number for a given link) and the match received in the Configure-Nak message. IPXCP stays in Ack-Sent state. CCP is transitioned to Closed state.

```
27B: IPCP Configure-Request 2 [03:132.245.11.10]
28A: IPCP Configure-Request 2 [03:132.245.11.209]
29A: IPXCP Configure-Request 2 [01:00000033 06]
```

Peer A agrees to the IP address sent by peer B, so it transitions IPCP to Ack-Sent state and sends Configure-Ack. IPXCP is left in Ack-Sent state. Peer B agrees to the IP address and IPXCP network number sent by peer A, so it transitions IPCP to Ack-Sent state and IPXCP to Open state and sends Configure-Ack messages.

```
30A: IPCP Configure-Ack 2 [03:132.245.11.10]
31B: IPCP Configure-Ack 2 [03:132.245.11.209]
32B: IPXCP Configure-Ack 2 [01:00000033 06]
```

Finally, peer B receives the IPCP Configure-Ack message from peer A, and it transitions IPCP to Open state. Peer A receives the Configure-Ack messages for IPCP and IPXCP and transitions each to Open state.

Negotiation is now complete, with IPCP and IPXCP open and ATCP and CCP closed. Note that although 32 messages have been sent, the above negotiation should happen rapidly on well-designed PPP implementations. In each round, the messages sent are triggered by reception of the peer's message, and not by a time-out, and there are only 11 exchanges of messages. Since the messages are short, the time of transmission is likely for most media to be dominated by the delay across the link for each burst of messages instead of the message size divided by the actual bit rate. Thus, the total negotiation time in this rather complex case is just 11 times the link delay. On a V.34 modem, for instance, this is well under 1 second, which is dwarfed by the typical 2- to 3-second call set-up time through the telephone switches and the 15- to 20-second modem negotiation time.

A technically illegal, though very interesting, optimization is possible here that will reduce this time still further. To do this, it is necessary for each peer to know in advance what the other will send, which is practical for some installations. Each peer precalculates its side of the entire exchange and sends it all as one burst, resulting in only a single link delay for the entire negotiation. The "technically illegal" part of this trick is that a PPP implementation that follows RFC 1661 closely should not be sending Configure-Request for the next layer before the current layer is up. In the best case, this will very quickly establish the link. In the worst case, even if the predicted value of the CHAP challenge is wrong or if the peer won't cooperate with this trick, the extra messages will be silently dropped, and both peers can fall back to an LCP or Authentication layer time-out to continue standard negotiation. See the end of Chapter 3 for a more complete description of this technique.

Network Data

Once the link is up, network layer data will be sent over it. In general, the encapsulation is just 1 or 2 bytes of PPP protocol number followed by the raw network layer information. For example, a complete IP packet from an Ethernet network is shown in Figure 7.1.

That same packet as sent over PPP with both Address and Control field and Protocol field compression enabled is shown in Figure 7.2.

Chapters 4 and 8 contain references to books that cover these upper-level protocols, like IP and ICMP, in detail.

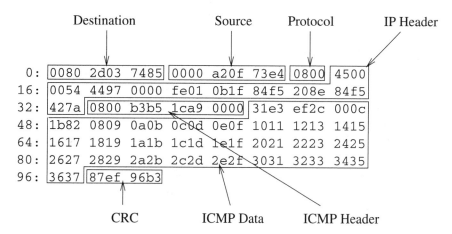

Figure 7.1: IP PACKET FROM ETHERNET

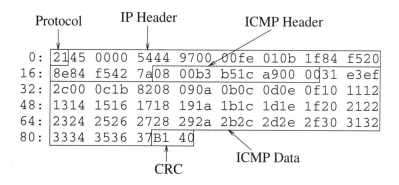

Figure 7.2: IP PACKET SENT OVER PPP

MP, CCP, and ECP

These protocols do not change the basic nature of negotiation as shown in the examples, but they do make it more difficult to follow. In particular, after MP is negotiated by sending MRRU at LCP time and then going through authentication, most implementations will send all messages with MP headers over any of the links. Thus, in order to debug an MP link using external devices, it is necessary to watch all of the data on all of the member links, even during NCP negotiation. Another oddity is that each link has its own LCP and authentication layers, but the bundle has only one set of comment NCPs. Thus, a lost CHAP Success message, for instance, will also cause the loss of any MP fragments on that link and will cause the CHAP Response to be resent after a time-out. This CHAP response is generated by a CHAP state machine local to the link, but the MP fragments seen on the link (and dropped) may contain NCP negotiations, which are global to the MP bundle. And, of course, if LCP renegotiates, then the link leaves the bundle and the LCP negotiation is done with the link's individual copy of LCP.

With CCP and ECP, the decoding of each packet depends on the successful decoding of prior packets and, to a small degree, on knowing which packets may have been lost by the peer. This makes the job of tracing a link using these protocols very difficult. In general, if the trace is taken at an arbitrary point during the life of the link (say, perhaps, at the start of some detected failure condition) instead of at the start of the link, then it usually cannot be decoded. This means that tracing an intermittent failure with these protocols requires either the storage of the entire history of the link or a method to store only the data since the last Reset-Ack message.

Link Failure

Low-Level Communications Hardware

The normal result of a failure in communications hardware is the loss of the link while LCP is in Req-Sent state due to too many Configure-Requests having been sent. This can mean that the peer is not actually running the PPP protocol or that data loss is so high that nothing gets through. On asynchronous lines, a well-implemented PPP system will notice if the data received either always contain the same LCP magic number or if it always has bit 7 set to the same value. Both of these conditions indicate what is termed a *loop-back*. Generally this means that the peer is sitting at some kind of text-mode prompt, probably because of a failure of the start-up script.

If LCP fails while in Ack-Sent state due to too many Configure-Request messages, this usually points to a unidirectional link. The system that fails in this way is able to receive data from the other system, but nothing transmitted is getting through. This can be due to flow control or to character transmission problems, such as parity errors.

If security or an NCP fails in an Ack-Sent state, the problem often is link transparency. When debugging this kind of problem, a good first start is to set the ACCM back to the default of FFFFFFFF. If this fixes the problem, then at least one of the control characters is interfering in data transmission. (On SLIP links, an analogous problem sometimes occurs. If software flow control is accidentally enabled, then

TCP will get through somewhat but may behave poorly. Ping, which is based on ICMP, may work only for "small" packets but not large ones. UDP services, like DNS, will fail completely.)

Authentication

Although all PPP authentication protocols include a means to notify the peer gracefully that the identification was not accepted, it is still necessary to interpret either a hardware-level hang-up (like loss of DCD on a modem) or an LCP Terminate-Request as the failure of authentication if an authentication request has been sent.

NCP Convergence

NCPs normally fail to converge when one side or the other is not configured properly. For instance, IPCP will fail sending Configure-Requests if the peer believes that the address being sent is incorrect, perhaps due to some kind of peer-name-to-address translation table being used on its end or due to an address reuse policy set by an external system, like DHCP. In these cases, both peers become intransigent; one sends Configure-Request repeatedly, and the other sends Configure-Nak. Each side should maintain counters for the number of Configure-Requests, Configure-Rejects, and Configure-Naks sent, and terminate the NCP if the counter passes some configurable threshold (with a suggested default of 10). When done properly, this protects an implementation from lock-up when presented with a misbehaving peer that may not have implemented these counters.

Another possible anomalous behavior is looping. This can still occur even with well-implemented PPP systems that obey the above rules. The usual reason for this failure is that the peer detects something in an NCP negotiation that forces it to drop back to an earlier stage to renegotiate a parameter. For instance, attempted negotiation of BCP (bridging) may cause an implementation to return to LCP in order to request a larger MRU. Since RFC 1661 doesn't specify any maximum number of times that this pattern may repeat, it is possible that it repeats indefinitely due to bugs on either side. To fix this, I suggest implementing a counter that is incremented each time a lower layer reopens and is reset to zero when all layers are open. If this counter passes some preset threshold, then PPP should be terminated.

Common Implementation Errors and Effects

Bad State Machine Transitions

The most common state machine–related problem in implementations seen in the field is a failure to handle Configure-Request messages correctly. This manifests itself as the link cycling LCP up and down several times and then terminating. The problem is that the failing implementation gets its state machine out of synchronization if it is the recipient rather than sender of the first Configure-Request message.

A good implementation should have a configuration option to delay the initial transmission of an LCP Configure-Request message for a single time-out period in order to communicate with the many peers that have this bug. (One of the many systems with this problem is an embedded system intended as an appliance for the general public. Since the problem is incorporated into widely distributed firmware, it is likely that this problem will persist in the field for quite some time.) This problem is often related to the general race condition problem, described below.

LCP to NCP Transition Race Conditions

In order to make the software easier to understand, designers often implement each layer as a separate module and pass messages between them. But in order to satisfy performance constraints, they usually need to handle input data immediately, usually with an asynchronous interrupt mechanism. A common side effect of these two choices is that the first Configure-Request message for the next layer brought up (authentication after LCP or NCP after authentication) is lost because the lower layer has just sent the Up message to the next layer, but it has not yet scheduled the task for that layer to run by the time the message arrives. Since the next higher layer is not yet at least in Req-Sent state, it must ignore it.

This problem also occasionally occurs between the PPP implementation itself and the external network layer entities or between routing or naming daemons. The result is that the NCP goes to Open state, but the external interfaces, routing tables, or name databases have not yet become operational. The result is that the first few user data packets are lost.

Three solutions are possible to fix the problem in PPP:

1. Fix the broken implementation so that it puts negotiation messages at the end of the same queue as is used for the layer-signaling messages, and make sure that the layer-signaling messages are always placed at the front of the queue.

2. Fix the broken implementation so that it disables reception of interrupts for received data when a layer goes to Open state, and reenable when the next layer transitions state.

3. If the broken implementation is unfixable, as is often the case with systems shipped without source code, then the correctly functioning implementation may need to have a short delay added after sending Configure-Ack in each layer. This, of course, should be configurable but can reasonably be automatically enabled when a known broken peer is detected. The LCP Identification message is useful for this purpose.

For the networking and naming problems, the fixes depend strongly on the network protocol being used, but here are some suggestions:

- Use routing protocols and binding services that can quickly and reliably synchronize with the establishment of the PPP NCP, and delay sending the NCP Configure-Ack until the changes have been propagated. Note that these protocols may have to propagate the changes to other systems before synchronization is achieved.
- Use static routing and static name binding instead of dynamic routing protocols and dynamic name binding services.
- Implement a delay of a few seconds after the NCPs go up before data are forwarded.

Parameter Change Race Conditions

This failure mode is more subtle than the previous race condition, but the effects are similar. A well-designed implementation of LCP should, in order to be as liberal as possible, set its receive ACCM when the Configure-Request message from the peer is seen and set its transmit ACCM only after waiting for all output to drain after transitioning LCP to Open state. (Renegotiation is a special case, and the receive ACCM should be left unchanged until Configure-Request is seen, but the transmit ACCM should be immediately set back to the default of FFFFFFFF.)

However, since AHDLC encoding and decoding is a byte-intensive operation, and most routers are optimized to operate better on a packet-by-packet basis, AHDLC handling is often delegated to separate dedicated processors. This means that setting ACCM masks requires a communication between the two CPUs, and this synchronization is an occasional source of failure. The most common failure is that the transmit ACCM is set to the final value either before or even during the transmission of the LCP Configure-Ack message. This causes at least some unescaped characters to be sent, and if the peer is strict in setting its receive ACCM, the packet will be dropped with a corrupt FCS.

Following the rules above in order to make an implementation as liberal as possible in receiving data and as strict as possible in sending them will avoid the problem in most cases.

Renegotiation Failure

Many implementations have trouble with renegotiating at one layer or another. If you do want to renegotiate LCP, you must be prepared for the peer to fall apart completely. Common responses range from immediate termination to negotiation loops (LCP negotiates up, then authentication starts, and LCP restarts). In particular, Shiva engineers have noted that both the ShivaRemote and Windows 95 will immediately terminate the telephone connection if LCP renegotiation is attempted with them.

Compression Failure

When compression fails due to a corrupted dictionary or implementation errors, the most obvious result is strange-looking LCP Protocol Reject messages from the peer. Some of the compression techniques do not detect data corruption well, and the result is a decompressed packet with an illegal protocol number prepended. This causes the receiver to issue the LCP Protocol Reject for this illegal number and to forward the rest of the bad data. This can be confusing because the compressor never appeared to send data that contained this bad protocol number.

Message Fields

Not all implementations validate the various fields of the messages they receive. Some common commercial implementations do not bother to check that the ID field in the Configure-Ack, -Nak, or -Reject matches the last Configure-Request sent. Some do not bother to check the various length fields, and a few will even crash if presented with bad lengths.

The lack of ID field checking can be a nuisance during lengthy authentication requests, since a straightforward implementation will start the authentication with the first message and will queue subsequent messages. If the peer sending the authentication information times out and resends the message, then the first peer will enqueue this new one. When the authentication is complete, it will reply to ID 1, then read the second request from the queue and immediately return a reply for this second message (which may be ID 1 or 2). The broken peer will read and accept the first reply, since it is not looking at the ID number, and may become confused on seeing the second reply. A work-around for this problem is to read in the messages from the queue after completing authentication but before sending the response, and then to send the response using the latest ID number seen.

Strings

Some implementations seem to think that strings should be terminated by an ASCII NUL (00) byte. Of course, with PPP, all strings are bounded by a separate length, so there is no need to terminate the string explicitly with NUL. In order to interoperate with these peers, it is sometimes necessary to discard extra NULs at the end of some messages.

When implementing in languages designed around NUL-terminated strings, like C, be careful in handling PPP strings. It is perfectly legal for strings to contain embedded NUL bytes, so the usual strncpy() and strncmp() functions will not work as expected. Instead, use memcpy() and memcmp(), especially with the AppleTalk zone name.

Missing Reject Messages and Handling

At least one implementation I have seen fails to send LCP Protocol Reject if it recognizes the protocol sent by the peer but does not want to use the protocol (for example, a system that has CCP implemented, but has a configuration option to disable it). This results in the NCP's sending Configure-Request messages until reaching a limit and disabling the NCP. In this case, since other NCPs do establish themselves properly, it can be useful to detect this error and issue an appropriate diagnostic message since the user may believe that the properly functioning implementation is broken since it will log an error indicating that it failed due to having sent too many Configure-Requests.

Incorrect Use of Terminate-Request

The Terminate-Request message will shut down a protocol in Open state; however, it will not shut down a protocol that is still negotiating but rather will push it back to the start of negotiation again. For this reason, Terminate-Request (triggered by a Close event) should not be sent to terminate a misbehaving protocol. Some implementations erroneously attempt to use Terminate-Request instead of Protocol-Reject to shut down a protocol that is failing to negotiate. This behavior appears in the log file as a Configure-Request/Terminate-Request/Terminate-Ack loop. The only available fix is to disable the affected protocol administratively. (Since this is most often seen only with CCP and since the Configure-Request counter should eventually terminate the failing protocol, it should not affect normal PPP operation.)

Appearance of Packets on Various Media

If you are examining PPP data at the lowest level, perhaps using an oscilloscope, you should know that most communications hardware, such as standard synchronous interfaces as well as asynchronous RS-232, will present the bits in backward order, with the least significant bit first. To read this data from the screen, you need to read the bits from right to left and the octets from left to right. Also remember that on asynchronous links, LCP negotiation of the ACCM parameter will alter the escaping of transmitted data when LCP reaches Open state. This problem does not exist on synchronous lines.

If you are examining data from a synchronous hardware interface, it is commonly, though not always, the case that the hardware will verify and remove the CRC automatically and that it will not appear in the data received. This is usually true on PC-based synchronous cards. On most synchronous hardware, this is a selectable feature that can be controlled through configuration registers.

Getting Traces from Common PPP Software

Usually debugging is done by reading logs provided by the PPP software packages or by use of specialized hardware. Here are a few of the more common PPP implementations and the logging information provided by them. This is not intended to be a comprehensive list of PPP implementations available, nor does it show everything that can be done with each implementation. Readers may want to view these logs, though, to get a sense of what to expect when debugging, and implementors in particular may wish to see various techniques for logging in order to choose their favorite.

Some of the examples are long and difficult to read. In the longer traces, the important pieces to examine are given in **boldface** type.

Unix Systems

pppd

pppd is a very high-quality, freely available implementation of PPP for most standard Unix systems. It is the result of the efforts of many people but has been released and maintained by Paul Mackerras at the Australian National University Department of Computer Science. It consists of three parts: a chat utility, a daemon, and a set of kernel extensions. The chat utility is used with scripted log-ins, where you must first dial a modem and then perhaps perform some action on a host (such as logging in) before running PPP. The daemon contains the PPP negotiation state machines. The kernel extensions contain the system-specific drivers that handle the serial I/O and the network layer interfaces.

There are two pieces that users must deal with. First, the chat mechanism brings up the line and then PPP negotiates; both of these can cause trouble. To debug either, you must first properly configure syslogd on your system to log debug-level messages to a file. This is highly system specific but often consists of placing a line like this in /etc/syslog.conf:

```
*.debug          /var/adm/log/debug
```

The chat utility has a "-v" switch on it to enable verbose logging, and the pppd daemon has a "-d" switch to enable the same. Usually it is wise to enable both, as with:

```
pppd -d connect 'chat -vf /users/carlson/.chatrc.local'
```

The chat logs look like this:

```
Aug 11 19:21:52 madison chat[16014]: send (^M)
```

```
Aug 11 19:21:52 madison chat[16014]: send (atdt1-508-555-
     1212^M)
Aug 11 19:21:53 madison chat[16014]: expect (CONNECT)
Aug 11 19:22:19 madison chat[16014]: ^Matdt1-508-555-
     1212^M^M
Aug 11 19:22:19 madison chat[16014]: CONNECT — got it
Aug 11 19:22:19 madison chat[16014]: expect (sername:)
Aug 11 19:22:19 madison chat[16014]: 38400/V32b 14400/V42b^M
```

By examining both the messages presented and the timing, it is usually possible to determine any kind of chatting failure. Typically when chat fails, it is the result of having not received the expected response string from the peer. It will hang for an extended period, then time out at 45 seconds by default. This appears in the logs like this:

```
Apr 26 11:53:00 madison chat[13702]: expect (sername:)
Apr 26 11:53:45 madison chat[13702]: alarm
Apr 26 11:53:45 madison chat[13702]: Failed
Apr 26 11:53:45 madison pppd[17540]: Connect script failed
Apr 26 11:53:45 madison pppd[17540]: Exit.
```

In extreme cases, you may want to use a terminal-mode dial-in program, such as kermit, to verify that log-in on the target system is possible and that PPP will run on that system.

The chat script is sometimes a difficult-to-write piece of the system. I use the following example to dial into my ISP's Annex terminal server:

```
ABORT BUSY
ABORT 'NO CARRIER'
REPORT CONNECT
"" ""
"" "atdt1-508-555-1212"
CONNECT \c
TIMEOUT 3 sername:—sername: carlson
ssword: \qbigsecret
nnex: ppp
```

The \q code in front of the password means that it should not be logged via syslog when debugging is enabled.

If you see something like the following in your log, then the peer is already in PPP mode, but the chat script hasn't terminated correctly. It is likely that the chat script is waiting for some string for which it should not be waiting.

```
Apr 20 16:36:04 madison chat[15420]: ~^?}#@!}!}!} }4}"}&} } } }
```

Once chat has run successfully, pppd then begins negotiating with the peer. This will look something like this:

```
Nov 29 17:05:50 madison pppd[18320]: Serial connection
    established.
Nov 29 17:05:51 madison pppd[18320]: popped stream module:
    tioc
Nov 29 17:05:51 madison pppd[18320]: popped stream module:
    ldterm
Nov 29 17:05:51 madison pppd[18320]: Using interface ppp0
Nov 29 17:05:51 madison pppd[18320]: Connect: ppp0 <—>
    /dev/tty0
Nov 29 17:05:51 madison pppd[18320]: sent [LCP ConfReq
    id=0x1 <mru 296> <asyncmap 0x0> <magic 0xd580242b>
    <pcomp> <accomp>]
Nov 29 17:05:51 madison pppd[18320]: fsm_sdata(LCP): Sent
    code 1, id 1.
Nov 29 17:05:51 madison pppd[18320]: Timeout
    20001848:20004730 in 3 seconds.
Nov 29 17:05:51 madison pppd[18320]: LCP: sending Configure-
    Request, id 1
Nov 29 17:05:51 madison pppd[18320]: rcvd [LCP ConfAck
    id=0x1 <mru 296> <asyncmap 0x0> <magic 0xd580242b>
    <pcomp> <accomp>]
Nov 29 17:05:51 madison pppd[18320]: fsm_rconfack(LCP): Rcvd
    id 1.
**Nov 29 17:05:53 madison pppd[18320]: rcvd [LCP ConfReq
    id=0x2 <asyncmap 0x0> <auth upap> <magic 0xa9119e1b>
    <pcomp> <accomp>]**
Nov 29 17:05:53 madison pppd[18320]: fsm_rconfreq(LCP): Rcvd
    id 2.
Nov 29 17:05:53 madison pppd[18320]: lcp_reqci: rcvd
    ASYNCMAP
Nov 29 17:05:53 madison pppd[18320]: (0)
Nov 29 17:05:53 madison pppd[18320]:  (ACK)
Nov 29 17:05:53 madison pppd[18320]: lcp_reqci: rcvd
    AUTHTYPE
Nov 29 17:05:53 madison pppd[18320]: (c023)
Nov 29 17:05:53 madison pppd[18320]:  (ACK)
Nov 29 17:05:53 madison pppd[18320]: lcp_reqci: rcvd MAGIC-
    NUMBER
Nov 29 17:05:53 madison pppd[18320]: (a9119e1b)
Nov 29 17:05:53 madison pppd[18320]:  (ACK)
Nov 29 17:05:53 madison pppd[18320]: lcp_reqci: rcvd PCOM-
    PRESSION
Nov 29 17:05:53 madison pppd[18320]:  (ACK)
Nov 29 17:05:53 madison pppd[18320]: lcp_reqci: rcvd ACCOM-
    PRESSION
Nov 29 17:05:53 madison pppd[18320]:  (ACK)
Nov 29 17:05:53 madison pppd[18320]: lcp_reqci: returningZ
    CONFACK.
Nov 29 17:05:53 madison pppd[18320]: sent [LCP ConfAck
    id=0x2 <asyncmap 0x0> <auth upap> <magic 0xa9119e1b>
    <pcomp> <accomp>]
```

```
Nov 29 17:05:53 madison pppd[18320]: fsm_sdata(LCP): Sent
    code 2, id 2.
Nov 29 17:05:53 madison pppd[18320]: Untimeout
    20001848:20004730.
```

Note that these logs show all of the negotiation information in a very verbose format. The single LCP Configure-Request above is decoded on 15 separate lines. Later in this same session, we might see the following:

Nov 29 17:05:56 madison pppd[18320]: sent [CCP ConfReq id=0x1 <bsd v1 12>]
```
Nov 29 17:05:56 madison pppd[18320]: fsm_sdata(CCP): Sent
    code 1, id 1.
Nov 29 17:05:56 madison pppd[18320]: Timeout
    20001848:200046b0 in 3 seconds.
Nov 29 17:05:56 madison pppd[18320]: CCP: sending Configure-
    Request, id 1
Nov 29 17:05:56 madison pppd[18320]: rcvd [LCP ProtRej
    id=0x3 80 fd 01 01 00 07 15 03 2c]
Nov 29 17:05:56 madison pppd[18320]: lcp_rprotrej.
```
Nov 29 17:05:56 madison pppd[18320]: lcp_rprotrej: Rcvd Protocol-Reject packet for 80fd!
```
Nov 29 17:05:56 madison pppd[18320]: Untimeout
    20001848:200046b0.
```

This shows that the local system supports the BSD Compress algorithm with CCP. The remote system, though, is rejecting CCP, either because it is unimplemented or because this user is not authorized to use it. Either way, this is not by itself an error; PPP continues running without data compression.

Another series of messages that is likely to appear is this:

```
Nov 29 17:05:59 madison pppd[18320]: rcvd [proto=0x8029] 01
    05 00 2a 01 06 00 18 24 0d 02 04 00 00 06 0d 00 01 0b
    01 00 00 41 6e 6e 65 78 07 09 6d 61 63 69 70 31 00 08
    06 00 17 d4 16
```
Nov 29 17:05:59 madison pppd[18320]: Unknown protocol (0x8029) received
```
Nov 29 17:05:59 madison pppd[18320]: sent [LCP ProtRej
    id=0x2 80 29 01 05 00 2a 01 06 00 18 24 0d 02 04 00 00
    06 0d 00 01 0b 01 00 00 41 6e 6e 65 78 07 09 6d 61 63 69
    70 31 00 08 06 00 17 d4 16]
Nov 29 17:05:59 madison pppd[18320]: fsm_sdata(LCP): Sent
    code 8, id 2.
```

This example shows the peer system offering to run ATCP (AppleTalk Control Protocol). The local system does not implement ATCP (pppd supports only IP as of this writing), so this appears as an "unknown protocol" and is rejected. Again, this is not by itself an error; PPP continues running without AppleTalk.

Yet another common exchange is this one:

```
Nov 29 17:05:59 madison pppd[18320]: sent [IPCP ConfReq
    id=0x1 <addr 0.0.0.0> <compress VJ 0f 01>]
Nov 29 17:05:59 madison pppd[18320]: fsm_sdata(IPCP): Sent
    code 1, id 1.
Nov 29 17:05:59 madison pppd[18320]: Timeout
    20001848:20004048 in 3 seconds.
Nov 29 17:05:59 madison pppd[18320]: IPCP: sending
    Configure-Request, id 1
Nov 29 17:05:59 madison pppd[18320]: rcvd [IPCP ConfNak
    id=0x1 <addr 132.245.11.229>]
Nov 29 17:05:59 madison pppd[18320]: fsm_rconfnakrej(IPCP):
    Rcvd id 1.
Nov 29 17:05:59 madison pppd[18320]: local IP address
    132.245.11.229
Nov 29 17:05:59 madison pppd[18320]: Untimeout
    20001848:20004048.
Nov 29 17:05:59 madison pppd[18320]: sent [IPCP ConfReq
    id=0x2 <addr 132.245.11.229> <compress VJ 0f 01>]
Nov 29 17:05:59 madison pppd[18320]: fsm_sdata(IPCP): Sent
    code 1, id 2.
Nov 29 17:05:59 madison pppd[18320]: Timeout
    20001848:20004048 in 3 seconds.
Nov 29 17:05:59 madison pppd[18320]: IPCP: sending
    Configure-Request, id 2
Nov 29 17:06:00 madison pppd[18320]: rcvd [IPCP ConfAck
    id=0x2 <addr 132.245.11.229> <compress VJ 0f 01>]
Nov 29 17:06:00 madison pppd[18320]: fsm_rconfack(IPCP):
    Rcvd id 2.
Nov 29 17:06:00 madison pppd[18320]: Untimeout
    20001848:20004048.
```

In this case, the local system does not know its own IP address, so it sends 0.0.0.0 to the peer. The peer returns a Configure-Nak message containing the correct address, and the next Configure-Request sent contains the address specified by the peer.

Finally, after IPCP is negotiated, one last message will be issued:

```
Nov 29 17:06:00 madison pppd[18320]: ipcp: up
Nov 29 17:06:00 madison pppd[18320]: local  IP address
    132.245.11.229
Nov 29 17:06:00 madison pppd[18320]: remote IP address
    132.245.11.11
Nov 29 17:06:00 madison pppd[18320]: Setting interface mask
    to 255.255.255.0
```

This message shows the final negotiated end-point IP addresses.

Once the link is up, the pppstats utility can be used to display link statistics:

```
% pppstats
  in    pack   comp uncomp    err  │  out   pack   comp uncomp       ip
 330      17      0      0       0  │    0     15      0      0       15
   0       0      0      0       0  │    0      0      0      0        0
```

An extension to pppd is available that supports MS-CHAP. See the README.mschap80 file in the pppd-2.2.0f distribution or the resources in Chapter 8. If you use this extension to connect to an NT system, remember that your local name entered in the chap-secrets file will actually be the combined NT domain and user name (which must also be specified with the name option) and the remote peer name entered will be the name you assign for that system using the remotename option (this name is arbitrary but must be present, since NT does not identify itself). If you are being called by an NT or 95 system, the reverse is true. For example, put this in chap-secrets to call an NT system that demands MS-CHAP from you:

```
ntdomain\\username remotenamehere userpassword
```

dp

dp is a variant of pppd that supports dial-on-demand links on Solaris and SunOS systems. The extensions that permit dial-on-demand operation have not been ported to other Unix systems as of this writing.

Unix Vendor PPP Implementations

AIX

This PPP system does not support much in the way of debugging syslog messages. The few that are there are fairly rudimentary. Here is an example from AIX 4.1.3:

```
Apr 20 17:33:39 madison pppattachd[18958]: starting attach-
    ment daemon
Apr 20 17:33:39 madison pppattachd[15376]: open /dev/tty0
Apr 20 17:34:36 madison pppattachd[15376]: attachd name
Apr 20 17:34:36 madison pppattachd[15376]: ctl msg badebe08
Apr 20 17:34:36 madison pppattachd[15376]: attachment con-
    nection established
Apr 20 17:34:36 madison pppattachd[15376]: ctl msg badebe07
Apr 20 17:34:38 madison last message repeated 9 times
Apr 20 17:34:39 madison pppattachd[15376]: ctl msg badebe07
Apr 20 17:34:39 madison pppattachd[15376]: ctl msg badebe08
Apr 20 17:34:39 madison /usr/sbin/pppcontrold[19458]: msgid
    badebe01
Apr 20 17:34:39 madison /usr/sbin/pppcontrold[19458]: LOWERUP
    5dc
Apr 20 17:34:39 madison /usr/sbin/pppcontrold[19458]: msgid
    badebe03
Apr 20 17:34:39 madison /usr/sbin/pppcontrold[19458]: msgid
    badebe03
```

```
Apr 20 17:34:39 madison pppattachd[15376]: ctl msg badebe07
Apr 20 17:34:42 madison last message repeated 5 times
Apr 20 17:34:42 madison /usr/sbin/pppcontrold[19458]: msgid
    badebc03
Apr 20 17:34:42 madison /usr/sbin/pppcontrold[19458]:
    /etc/ifconfig pp0 132.245.11.229 132.245.11.106 netmask
    255.255.255.0 >/dev/null 2>&1
Apr 20 17:34:45 madison pppattachd[15376]: ctl msg
    badebe07
```

Here are a few excepted from AIX 4.2. The syslog messages have been improved here but are still not sufficient to debug PPP itself:

```
Jul  1 16:36:49 lacroix /usr/sbin/pppcontrold[11720]: msgid
    badeb101
Jul  1 16:36:49 lacroix /usr/sbin/pppcontrold[11720]: DEMAND
    REQUEST  0 /etc/ppp/dial_out.rhesus
Jul  1 16:36:49 lacroix pppattachd[14690]: Str 0 converted 0
Jul  1 16:36:49 lacroix pppattachd[14690]: starting attach-
    ment daemon
Jul  1 16:36:49 lacroix pppattachd[14690]: open /dev/tty0
Jul  1 16:36:49 lacroix pppdial[12134]: send (at^M)
Jul  1 16:36:49 lacroix pppdial[12134]: expect (OK)
Jul  1 16:36:49 lacroix pppdial[12134]: O CARRIER^M
Jul  1 16:36:50 lacroix pppdial[12134]: at^M^M
Jul  1 16:36:50 lacroix pppdial[12134]: OK — got it
Jul  1 16:36:50 lacroix pppdial[12134]: send
    (atdt9,2364104^M)
Jul  1 16:36:50 lacroix pppdial[12134]: expect (CONNECT)
Jul  1 16:36:50 lacroix pppdial[12134]: ^M
Jul  1 16:36:50 lacroix /usr/sbin/pppcontrold[11720]: msgid
    badeb101
```

AIX does, however have a sophisticated kernel debugging mechanism that can be used to debug PPP connections once the chat file is modified to establish a link correctly (this script is usually /etc/ppp/dial_out.system, which is entered in the Demand Command section of the PPP demand interface configuration menu in smit).

To invoke kernel tracing, run smit trace and enable hooks 2AB, 2AC, 2AD, and 2AE (leave the EVENT GROUPS blank and enter these as ADDITIONAL EVENTS). Stop tracing once the interface has run and failed. Then start with trcrpt -Oids=off -d2AE to produce:

```
ELAPSED_SEC      DELTA_MSEC    APPL    SYSCALL KERNEL   INTERRUPT

25.044231168*                  PPP DATA lcp_send data
                               protocol=C021 Conf-req id=0001
                               01 04 05 DC 02 06 00 00 00 00 0
25.332675712*                  PPP DATA lcp_input data
                               protocol=C021 Conf-req id=0001
                               02 06 00 00 00 00 03 04 C0 23 0
```

```
25.332828160*                          PPP DATA lcp_send data
                                       protocol=C021 Conf-Rej id=0001
                                       13 0B 05 33 31 33 32 33 33 33 3
25.621775744*                          PPP DATA lcp_input data
                                       protocol=C021 Conf-req id=0002
                                       02 06 00 00 00 00 03 04 C0 23 0
25.621921408*                          PPP DATA lcp_send data
                                       protocol=C021 Conf-ACK id=0002
                                       02 06 00 00 00 00 03 04 C0 23 0
28.044558976*                          PPP DATA lcp_send data
                                       protocol=C021 Conf-req id=0001
                                       01 04 05 DC 02 06 00 00 00 00 0
28.358268672*                          PPP DATA lcp_input data
                                       protocol=C021 Conf-ACK id=0001
                                       01 04 05 DC 02 06 00 00 00 00 0
29.341080448*                          PPP DATA ipcp_send data
                                       protocol=8021 Conf-req id=0001
                                       03 06 84 F5 42 79 02 06 00 2D 0
29.436894208*                          PPP DATA lcp_send data
                                       protocol=C021 Protocol-Rej id=02
                                       80 FD 01 03 00 07 15 03 29
29.771947520*                          PPP DATA ipcp_input data
                                       protocol=8021 Conf-req id=0004
                                       03 06 84 F5 42 7C
```

The other trace IDs besides 2AE allow you to capture other events inside the system, such as HDLC errors (2AC), TCP/IP interface events (2AB), and the protocol multiplexing information (2AD).

Solaris

The SunSoft Solaris ppp daemon, called aspppd, writes a log file called /etc/asppp.log. This file contains information about the demand-dialing interface and the PPP negotiation. Before it is configured, you are likely to see logs like this:

```
09:48:09 Link manager (99) started 03/03/97
09:48:09 parse_config_file: no paths defined in
     /etc/asppp.cf
09:48:09 parse_config_file: Errors in configuration file
     /etc/asppp.cf
09:48:09 Link manager (99) exited 03/03/97
```

After inserting a path in the /etc/asppp.cf file, you may see the following, indicating that you need to run the ifconfig utility manually to install the ipdptp0 interface:

```
14:09:13 Link manager (1605) started 04/29/97
14:09:13 parse_config_file: Successful configuration
14:09:13 register_interfaces: IPD_REGISTER failed
```

Following is an example of a fairly common connection failure. In this case, the dialing process is successful, but the remote end is not yet in PPP mode, so aspppd sends LCP Configure-Request, times out, sends it again, and repeats until a counter reaches its maximum value:

```
14:10:43 process_ipd_msg: ipdptp0 needs connection
conn(rhesus)
Trying entry from `/etc/uucp/Systems' - device type ACU.
Device Type ACU wanted
Trying device entry `cua/b' from `/etc/uucp/Devices'.
processdev: calling setdevcfg(ppp, ACU)
fd_mklock: ok
fixline(8, 38400)
gdial(hayes) called
Trying caller script `hayes' from `/etc/uucp/Dialers'.
expect: ("")
got it
sendthem (DELAY
APAUSE
TE1V1X1Q0S2=255S12=255^M<NO CR>)
expect: (OK^M)
ATE1V1X1Q0S2=255S12=255^M^M^JOK^Mgot it
sendthem (ECHO CHECK ON
A^JATTDDTT99,,22336644110044^M^M<NO CR>)
expect: (CONNECT)
^M^JCONNECTgot it
getto ret 8
call cleanup(0)


14:11:12 000001 ipdptp0 SEND PPP ASYNC 23 Octets LCP Config-
     Req  ID=00 LEN=18 MRU=1500 MAG#=117a0953 ProtFCOMP
     AddrCCOMP
14:11:15 000002 ipdptp0 SEND PPP ASYNC 23 Octets LCP Config-
     Req  ID=01 LEN=18 MRU=1500 MAG#=117a0953 ProtFCOMP
     AddrCCOMP
14:11:18 000003 ipdptp0 SEND PPP ASYNC 23 Octets LCP Config-
     Req  ID=02 LEN=18 MRU=1500 MAG#=117a0953 ProtFCOMP
     AddrCCOMP
...
14:11:42 process_ppp_msg: PPP_ERROR_IND Maximum number of
     configure requests exceeded
14:11:43 000011 ipdptp0 PPP DIAG CLOSE
```

After correctly configuring the remote end to answer the call in PPP mode, here is the log of a successful connection. Note that although both CCP and IPX are being rejected here, the trace is somewhat hard to follow because the information in the protocol rejects does not include the actual PPP protocol number being rejected:

```
14:12:46 process_ipd_msg: ipdptp0 needs connection
conn(rhesus)
```

```
Trying entry from `/etc/uucp/Systems' - device type ACU.
Device Type ACU wanted
Trying device entry `cua/b' from `/etc/uucp/Devices'.
processdev: calling setdevcfg(ppp, ACU)
fd_mklock: ok
fixline(10, 38400)
gdial(hayes) called
Trying caller script `hayes' from `/etc/uucp/Dialers'.
expect: ("")
got it
sendthem (DELAY
APAUSE
TE1V1X1Q0S2=255S12=255^M<NO CR>)
expect: (OK^M)
ATE1V1X1Q0S2=255S12=255^M^M^JOK^Mgot it
sendthem (ECHO CHECK ON
A^JATTDDTT99,,22336644110044^M^M<NO CR>)
expect: (CONNECT)
^M^JCONNECTgot it
getto ret 10
call cleanup(0)


14:13:14 000012 ipdptp0 PPP DIAG OPEN
14:13:14 000013 ipdptp0 SEND PPP ASYNC 23 Octets LCP Config-
     Req  ID=0a LEN=18 MRU=1500 MAG#=aeacb38e ProtFCOMP
     AddrCCOMP
14:13:14 000014 ipdptp0 RECEIVE PPP ASYNC 23 Octets LCP
     Config-ACK  ID=0a LEN=18 MRU=1500 MAG#=aeacb38e
     ProtFCOMP AddrCCOMP
14:13:16 000015 ipdptp0 RECEIVE PPP ASYNC 38 Octets LCP
     Config-Req  ID=01 LEN=33 ACCM=00000000 Auth=PAP
     MAG#=a8a89d4f ProtFCOMP AddrCCOMP {Unknown OPTION=13
     l=9}
14:13:16 000016 ipdptp0 SEND PPP ASYNC 18 Octets LCP Config-
     REJ  ID=01 LEN=13 {Unknown OPTION=13 l=9}
14:13:16 000017 ipdptp0 RECEIVE PPP ASYNC 29 Octets LCP
     Config-Req  ID=02 LEN=24 ACCM=00000000 Auth=PAP
     MAG#=a8a89d4f ProtFCOMP AddrCCOMP
14:13:16 000018 ipdptp0 SEND PPP ASYNC 29 Octets LCP Config-
     ACK  ID=02 LEN=24 ACCM=00000000 Auth=PAP MAG#=a8a89d4f
     ProtFCOMP AddrCCOMP
14:13:16 000019 ipdptp0 SEND PPP ASYNC 25 Octets AuthPAP
     Authenticate  ID=01 LEN=20 Peer-ID-Length= 7 Peer-ID:
     63 61 72 6c 73 6f 6e Passwd-Length= 7 Passwd: 6e 6f 74
     6d 69 6e 65
14:13:19 000020 ipdptp0 SEND PPP ASYNC 25 Octets AuthPAP
     Authenticate  ID=02 LEN=20 Peer-ID-Length= 7 Peer-ID:
     63 61 72 6c 73 6f 6e Passwd-Length= 7 Passwd: 6e 6f 74
     6d 69 6e 65
14:13:20 000021 ipdptp0 RECEIVE PPP ASYNC 10 Octets AuthPAP
     Auth ACK  ID=02 LEN=5 Msg-Length= 0
14:13:20 000022 ipdptp0 SEND PPP ASYNC 21 Octets IP_NCP
     Config-Req  ID=0b LEN=16 VJCOMP MAXSID=15 Sid-comp-OK
     IPADDR=132.245.66.121
```

```
14:13:20 000023 ipdptp0 RECEIVE PPP ASYNC 19 Octets
         {Unrecognized protocol: 80fd }
14:13:20 000024 ipdptp0 SEND PPP ASYNC 25 Octets LCP Proto-
         REJ  ID=0c LEN=20 Rej_proto=103 Rej_info: 01 03 00 0e
         01 02 11 05 00 01 03 15 03 2c
14:13:20 000025 ipdptp0 RECEIVE PPP ASYNC 15 Octets IP_NCP
         Config-Req  ID=04 LEN=10 IPADDR=132.245.66.124
14:13:20 000026 ipdptp0 SEND PPP ASYNC 15 Octets IP_NCP
         Config-ACK  ID=04 LEN=10 IPADDR=132.245.66.124
14:13:21 000027 ipdptp0 RECEIVE PPP ASYNC 37 Octets IPX_NCP
14:13:21 000028 ipdptp0 RECEIVE PPP ASYNC 15 Octets IP_NCP
         Config-REJ  ID=0b LEN=10 VJCOMP MAXSID=15 Sid-comp-OK
14:13:21 000029 ipdptp0 SEND PPP ASYNC 43 Octets LCP Proto-
         REJ  ID=0d LEN=38 Rej_proto=105 Rej_info: 01 05 00 20
         01 06 00 00 00 00 02 08 00 80 2d 05 4a bb 04 04 00 02
         05 0a 4c 4d 30 35 34 41 42 42
14:13:21 000030 ipdptp0 SEND PPP ASYNC 19 Octets IP_NCP
         Config-Req  ID=0e LEN=14 OLD_VJCOMP
         IPADDR=132.245.66.121
14:13:21 000031 ipdptp0 RECEIVE PPP ASYNC 13 Octets IP_NCP
         Config-REJ  ID=0e LEN=8 OLD_VJCOMP
14:13:21 000032 ipdptp0 SEND PPP ASYNC 15 Octets IP_NCP
         Config-Req  ID=0f LEN=10 IPADDR=132.245.66.121
14:13:21 000033 ipdptp0 RECEIVE PPP ASYNC 15 Octets IP_NCP
         Config-ACK  ID=0f LEN=10 IPADDR=132.245.66.121
14:13:21 start_ip: IP up on interface ipdptp0, timeout set
         for 120 seconds
14:13:39 000034 ipdptp0 SEND PPP ASYNC 89 Octets IP_PROTO
14:13:39 000035 ipdptp0 RECEIVE PPP ASYNC 89 Octets IP_PROTO
14:13:56 000036 ipdptp0 SEND PPP ASYNC 89 Octets IP_PROTO
14:13:56 000037 ipdptp0 RECEIVE PPP ASYNC 89 Octets IP_PROTO
```

IRIX

Because the ppp program can use the UUCP control files, the best way to install a PPP connection is first to install a simple UUCP connection. So one first creates appropriate entries in the /etc/uucp/Dialers, /etc/uucp/Devices, and /etc/uucp/Systems files, and then "debugs" the connection with cu -d remotesystem. (Do not attempt to debug an ISDN connection with cu.) For example, you might have:

/etc/uucp/Systems

```
rhesus Any ACU 38400 9,2364104
```

/etc/uucp/Devices

```
ACU ttyf2 null 38400 212 x hayes24
```

/etc/ppp.conf

```
rhesus      remotehost=rhesus
            uucp_name=rhesus
            send_username=irix
            send_passwd=irix-test
            debug=4
            -del_route
```

To debug the PPP connection itself, start with -dddd on the command line, or debug=4 in the /etc/ppp.conf file. Start with a configuration like the one above. If dial on demand is desired, add the keyword "quiet" to the ppp.conf file once a nailed-up connection is debugged.

The above configuration was run with ppp -r rhesus. Here is an example of the syslogs generated when the IP address is configured incorrectly (ellipses represent elided material where the negotiation was repeating itself):

```
Jul  2 16:11:21 3D:itra-irix6 ppp[13583]: rhesus: IP activ-
     ity: medium
Jul  2 16:11:21 3D:itra-irix6 ppp[13617]: rhesus: add a line
Jul  2 16:11:21 3D:itra-irix6 ppp[13617]: conn(rhesus)
Jul  2 16:11:21 3D:itra-irix6 ppp[13617]: Device Type ACU
     wanted
Jul  2 16:11:21 3D:itra-irix6 ppp[13617]: Internal caller
     type 212
Jul  2 16:11:21 3D:itra-irix6 ppp[13617]: Use Port
     /dev/ttyf2, acu - /dev/null, Phone Number  x<
Jul  2 16:11:21 3D:itra-irix6 ppp[13617]: /dev/null is open
Jul  2 16:11:21 3D:itra-irix6 ppp[13617]: filelock: ok
Jul  2 16:11:21 3D:itra-irix6 ppp[13617]: filelock: ok
Jul  2 16:11:21 3D:itra-irix6 ppp[13617]: dcf is 9
Jul  2 16:11:21 3D:itra-irix6 ppp[13617]: fixline(9, 38400)
Jul  2 16:11:21 3D:itra-irix6 ppp[13617]: ACU write ok(null)
Jul  2 16:11:21 3D:itra-irix6 ppp[13617]: fixline(9, 38400)
Jul  2 16:11:21 3D:itra-irix6 ppp[13617]: set interface 212
Jul  2 16:11:21 3D:itra-irix6 ppp[13617]: processdev: call-
     ing setdevcfg(, ACU)
Jul  2 16:11:21 3D:itra-irix6 ppp[13617]: gdial(hayes24)
     called
Jul  2 16:11:21 3D:itra-irix6 ppp[13617]: ABORT ON: "BUSY"
Jul  2 16:11:21 3D:itra-irix6 ppp[13617]: ABORT ON: "NO CAR-
     RIER"
Jul  2 16:11:21 3D:itra-irix6 ppp[13617]: ABORT ON: "NO DI-
     ALTONE"
Jul  2 16:11:21 3D:itra-irix6 ppp[13617]: expect: ("")
Jul  2 16:11:21 3D:itra-irix6 ppp[13617]: got it
Jul  2 16:11:23 3D:itra-irix6 ppp[13617]: sendthem
     (<DELAY><NO CR>ATe1q0&d3s2=128L0^M)
Jul  2 16:11:23 3D:itra-irix6 ppp[13617]: expect: (OK)
Jul  2 16:11:23 3D:itra-irix6 ppp[13617]:
     ^A^M^E^SI%^UI5)^?ATe1q0&d3s2=128L0^M^M^JOKgot it
Jul  2 16:11:23 3D:itra-irix6 ppp[13617]: sendthem (<NO
     CR>atdt9,2364104^M)
```

```
Jul   2 16:11:23 3D:itra-irix6 ppp[13617]: timeout=90 expect:
      (CONNECT)
Jul   2 16:11:26 3D:itra-irix6 ppp[13583]: rhesus: IP activ-
      ity: busy
Jul   2 16:11:41 3D:itra-irix6 last message repeated 3 times
Jul   2 16:11:41 3D:itra-irix6 ppp[13617]:
      ^M^Jatdt9,2364104^M^M^JCONNECTgot it
Jul   2 16:11:41 3D:itra-irix6 ppp[13617]: getto ret 9
Jul   2 16:11:41 3D:itra-irix6 ppp[13617]: banner:
      31200/ARQ/V34/LAPM/V42BIS^M^J
Jul   2 16:11:41 3D:itra-irix6 ppp[13617]: rhesus: saving 0
      bytes to salvage
Jul   2 16:11:41 3D:itra-irix6 ppp[13617]: rhesus  LCP: set
      async,acomp=0,pcomp=0,rx_ACCM=0,tx=0xffffffff,pad=0
Jul   2 16:11:41 3D:itra-irix6 ppp[13617]: rhesus: starting
      to use /dev/ttyf2
Jul   2 16:11:41 3D:itra-irix6 ppp[13617]: rhesus  LCP: event
      Open
Jul   2 16:11:41 3D:itra-irix6 ppp[13617]: rhesus  LCP: ac-
      tion TLS
Jul   2 16:11:41 3D:itra-irix6 ppp[13617]: rhesus: entering
      Establish Phase
Jul   2 16:11:41 3D:itra-irix6 ppp[13617]: rhesus  LCP:
      Initial(0)->Starting(1)
Jul   2 16:11:41 3D:itra-irix6 ppp[13617]: rhesus  LCP: event
      Up
Jul   2 16:11:41 3D:itra-irix6 ppp[13617]: rhesus  LCP: send
      Configure-Request ID=0x9b
Jul   2 16:11:41 3D:itra-irix6 ppp[13617]: rhesus  LCP:
      MRU=1505
Jul   2 16:11:41 3D:itra-irix6 ppp[13617]: rhesus  LCP: rx
      ACCM=0
Jul   2 16:11:41 3D:itra-irix6 ppp[13617]: rhesus  LCP:
      magic=0x690a9036
Jul   2 16:11:41 3D:itra-irix6 ppp[13617]: rhesus  LCP: re-
      ceive compressed protocol field
Jul   2 16:11:41 3D:itra-irix6 ppp[13617]: rhesus  LCP: re-
      ceive compressed address field
Jul   2 16:11:41 3D:itra-irix6 ppp[13617]: rhesus  LCP: MP
      MRRU=1500
Jul   2 16:11:41 3D:itra-irix6 ppp[13617]: rhesus  LCP:
      Endpoint Discriminator 8:0:69:a:90:36
Jul   2 16:11:41 3D:itra-irix6 ppp[13617]: rhesus: write 0x25
      bytes: proto=0xc021 01 9b 00 25 01 04 05 e1 02 06 00 00
      00 00 05 06 69 0a 90 36 07 02 08 02 11 04 05 dc 13 09
      03 08 00 69 0a 90 36
Jul   2 16:11:41 3D:itra-irix6 ppp[13617]: rhesus:         raw
      bytes: 7e ff 7d 23 c0 21 7d 21 9b 7d 20 25 7d 21 7d 24
      7d 25 e1 7d 22 7d 26 7d 20 7d 20 7d 20 7d 20 7d 25 7d
      26 69 7d 2a 90 36 7d 27 7d 22 7d 28 7d 22 7d 31 7d
      24 7d 25 dc 7d 33 7d 29 7d 23 7d ...
Jul   2 16:11:41 3D:itra-irix6 ppp[13617]: rhesus  LCP:
      Starting(1)->Req-Sent(6)
```

```
Jul  2 16:11:42 3D:itra-irix6 ppp[13617]: rhesus: read 0x23
     bytes: proto=0xc021 01 01 00 23 02 06 00 00 00 00 03 04
     c0 23 05 06 00 77 96 70 07 02 08 02 13 0b 05 "31323334"
Jul  2 16:11:42 3D:itra-irix6 ppp[13617]: rhesus  LCP: re-
     ceive Configure-Request ID=0x1
Jul  2 16:11:42 3D:itra-irix6 ppp[13617]: rhesus  LCP:
     accept tx ACCM=0
Jul  2 16:11:42 3D:itra-irix6 ppp[13617]: rhesus  LCP:
     note PAP authentication
Jul  2 16:11:42 3D:itra-irix6 ppp[13617]: rhesus  LCP:
     peer's magic=0x779670
Jul  2 16:11:42 3D:itra-irix6 ppp[13617]: rhesus  LCP:
     send compressed protocol field
Jul  2 16:11:42 3D:itra-irix6 ppp[13617]: rhesus  LCP:
     send compressed address field
Jul  2 16:11:42 3D:itra-irix6 ppp[13617]: rhesus  LCP:
     Phone Endpoint Discriminator 5-9-31323334
Jul  2 16:11:42 3D:itra-irix6 ppp[13617]: rhesus  LCP: set
     async,acomp=1,pcomp=1,rx_ACCM=0,tx=0xffffffff,pad=0
Jul  2 16:11:42 3D:itra-irix6 ppp[13617]: rhesus  LCP: event
     RCR+
Jul  2 16:11:42 3D:itra-irix6 ppp[13617]: rhesus  LCP: send
     Configure-ACK ID=0x1
Jul  2 16:11:42 3D:itra-irix6 ppp[13617]: rhesus: write 0x23
     bytes: proto=0xc021 02 01 00 23 02 06 00 00 00 00 03 04
     c0 23 05 06 00 77 96 70 07 02 08 02 13 0b 05 "31323334"
Jul  2 16:11:42 3D:itra-irix6 ppp[13617]: rhesus:        raw
     bytes: 7e ff 7d 23 c0 "!}"}!} #}"}&} } } } }#}$" c0
     "#}%}&} w" 96 "p}'}"}(}"}3}+}%31323334" e8 55 7e
Jul  2 16:11:42 3D:itra-irix6 ppp[13617]: rhesus  LCP: Req-
     Sent(6)->Ack-Sent(8)
Jul  2 16:11:42 3D:itra-irix6 ppp[13617]: rhesus: pass de-
     vice
Jul  2 16:11:42 3D:itra-irix6 ppp[13617]: rhesus: waiting to
     be killed
Jul  2 16:11:42 3D:itra-irix6 ppp[13583]: rhesus 1: took
     /dev/ttyf2 from process 13617
Jul  2 16:11:42 3D:itra-irix6 ppp[13583]: rhesus  LCP1: set
     async,acomp=1,pcomp=1,rx_ACCM=0,tx=0xffffffff,pad=0
Jul  2 16:11:42 3D:itra-irix6 ppp[13617]: rhesus: killed by
     signal 15
Jul  2 16:11:42 3D:itra-irix6 ppp[13583]: rhesus  LCP1:
     event TO+ #1
Jul  2 16:11:42 3D:itra-irix6 ppp[13583]: rhesus  LCP1: send
     Configure-Request ID=0x9c
Jul  2 16:11:42 3D:itra-irix6 ppp[13583]: rhesus  LCP1:
     rx ACCM=0
Jul  2 16:11:42 3D:itra-irix6 ppp[13583]: rhesus  LCP1:
     magic=0x690a9036
Jul  2 16:11:42 3D:itra-irix6 ppp[13583]: rhesus  LCP1:
     receive compressed protocol field
Jul  2 16:11:42 3D:itra-irix6 ppp[13583]: rhesus  LCP1:
     receive compressed address field
```

```
Jul   2 16:11:42 3D:itra-irix6 ppp[13583]: rhesus   LCP1:
      Endpoint Discriminator 8:0:69:a:90:36
Jul   2 16:11:42 3D:itra-irix6 ppp[13583]: rhesus 1: send
      0x1d  bytes: index=25 proto=0xc021 01 9c 00 1d 02 06 00
      00 00 00 05 06 69 0a 90 36 07 02 08 02 13 09 03 08 00
      69 0a 90 36
Jul   2 16:11:42 3D:itra-irix6 ppp[13583]: rhesus   LCP1: Ack-
      Sent(8)->Ack-Sent(8)
Jul   2 16:11:42 3D:itra-irix6 ppp[13583]: rhesus 1: read
      0x1d  bytes: proto=0xc021 02 9c 00 1d 02 06 00 00 00 00
      05 06 69 0a 90 36 07 02 08 02 13 09 03 08 00 69 0a 90
      36
Jul   2 16:11:42 3D:itra-irix6 ppp[13583]: rhesus   LCP1: re-
      ceive Configure-ACK ID=0x9c
Jul   2 16:11:42 3D:itra-irix6 ppp[13583]: rhesus   LCP1:
      event RCA
Jul   2 16:11:42 3D:itra-irix6 ppp[13583]: rhesus   LCP1: ac-
      tion TLU
Jul   2 16:11:42 3D:itra-irix6 ppp[13583]: rhesus   LCP1:
      MTU=1500 MRU=1500 TOS PCOMP ACOMP
Jul   2 16:11:42 3D:itra-irix6 ppp[13583]: rhesus   LCP1: my
      magic=0x690a9036,his=0x779670 rx_ACCM=0 tx=0
Jul   2 16:11:42 3D:itra-irix6 ppp[13583]: rhesus   LCP1: set
      async,acomp=1,pcomp=1,rx_ACCM=0,tx=0,pad=0
Jul   2 16:11:42 3D:itra-irix6 ppp[13583]: rhesus 1: entering
      Authenticate Phase
Jul   2 16:11:42 3D:itra-irix6 ppp[13583]: rhesus AUTH1: will
      send PAP requests but receive no authentication
Jul   2 16:11:42 3D:itra-irix6 ppp[13583]: rhesus AUTH1: send
      PAP request ID=0x7d
Jul   2 16:11:42 3D:itra-irix6 ppp[13583]: rhesus 1: send
      0x14  bytes: index=25 proto=0xc023 01 7d 00 14 04
      "irix" 09                          "irix-test"
Jul   2 16:11:42 3D:itra-irix6 ppp[13583]: rhesus   LCP1: Ack-
      Sent(8)->Opened(9)
Jul   2 16:11:43 3D:itra-irix6 ppp[13583]: rhesus 1: read 0x5
      bytes: proto=0xc023 02 7d 00 05 00
Jul   2 16:11:43 3D:itra-irix6 ppp[13583]: rhesus AUTH1: re-
      ceive PAP Ack ID=0x7d containing ""
Jul   2 16:11:43 3D:itra-irix6 ppp[13583]: rhesus 1: entering
      Network Phase
Jul   2 16:11:43 3D:itra-irix6 ppp[13583]: rhesus   LCP1: set
      async,acomp=1,pcomp=1,rx_ACCM=0,tx=0,pad=0
Jul   2 16:11:43 3D:itra-irix6 ppp[13583]: rhesus IPCP1:
      event Open
Jul   2 16:11:43 3D:itra-irix6 ppp[13583]: rhesus IPCP1: ac-
      tion TLS
Jul   2 16:11:43 3D:itra-irix6 ppp[13583]: rhesus IPCP1:
      Initial(0)->Starting(1)
Jul   2 16:11:43 3D:itra-irix6 ppp[13583]: rhesus IPCP1:
      event Up
Jul   2 16:11:43 3D:itra-irix6 ppp[13583]: rhesus IPCP1: send
      Configure-Request ID=0x28
Jul   2 16:11:43 3D:itra-irix6 ppp[13583]: rhesus IPCP1:
      16 slot VJ compression without compressed slot IDs
```

```
Jul   2 16:11:43 3D:itra-irix6 ppp[13583]: rhesus IPCP1:
      ADDR our address 132.245.33.131
Jul   2 16:11:43 3D:itra-irix6 ppp[13583]: rhesus 1: send 0x10
      bytes: index=25 proto=0x8021 01 28 00 10 02 06 00 2d 0f
      00 03 06 84 f5 21 83
Jul   2 16:11:43 3D:itra-irix6 ppp[13583]: rhesus IPCP1:
      Starting(1)->Req-Sent(6)
Jul   2 16:11:43 3D:itra-irix6 ppp[13583]: rhesus 1: read 0x7
      bytes: proto=0x80fd 01 02 00 07 15 03 29
Jul   2 16:11:43 3D:itra-irix6 ppp[13583]: rhesus  CCP1:
      dropping Configure-Request packet because in Initial(0)
Jul   2 16:11:43 3D:itra-irix6 ppp[13583]: rhesus 1: read 0xa
      bytes: proto=0x8021 01 03 00 0a 03 06 84 f5 42 7c
Jul   2 16:11:43 3D:itra-irix6 ppp[13583]: rhesus IPCP1: re-
      ceive Configure-Request ID=0x3
Jul   2 16:11:43 3D:itra-irix6 ppp[13583]: rhesus IPCP1:
      accept its address 132.245.66.124 from ADDR Request
Jul   2 16:11:43 3D:itra-irix6 ppp[13583]: rhesus IPCP1:
      event RCR+
Jul   2 16:11:43 3D:itra-irix6 ppp[13583]: rhesus IPCP1: send
      Configure-ACK ID=0x3
Jul   2 16:11:43 3D:itra-irix6 ppp[13583]: rhesus 1: send 0xa
      bytes: index=25 proto=0x8021 02 03 00 0a 03 06 84 f5 42
      7c
Jul   2 16:11:43 3D:itra-irix6 ppp[13583]: rhesus IPCP1: Req-
      Sent(6)->Ack-Sent(8)
Jul   2 16:11:44 3D:itra-irix6 ppp[13583]: rhesus 1: read
      0x20 bytes: proto=0x802b 01 04 00 20 01 06 00 00 00 00
      02 08 00 80 2d 05 4a bb 04 04 00 02 05 0a "LM054ABB"
Jul   2 16:11:44 3D:itra-irix6 ppp[13583]: rhesus 1:
      Protocol-Rejecting IPX Protocol
Jul   2 16:11:44 3D:itra-irix6 ppp[13583]: rhesus  LCP1: send
      Protocol-Reject ID=0x9d
Jul   2 16:11:44 3D:itra-irix6 ppp[13583]: rhesus 1: send
      0x26 bytes: index=25 proto=0xc021 08 9d 00 26 80 2b 01
      04 00 20 01 06 00 00 00 00 02 08 00 80 2d 05 4a bb 04
      04 00 02 05 0a "LM054ABB"
Jul   2 16:11:44 3D:itra-irix6 ppp[13583]: rhesus 1: read 0xa
      bytes: proto=0x8021 04 28 00 0a 02 06 00 2d 0f 00
Jul   2 16:11:44 3D:itra-irix6 ppp[13583]: rhesus IPCP1: re-
      ceive Configure-Reject ID=0x28
Jul   2 16:11:44 3D:itra-irix6 ppp[13583]: rhesus IPCP1:
      peer is rejecting header compression
Jul   2 16:11:44 3D:itra-irix6 ppp[13583]: rhesus IPCP1:
      event RCN
Jul   2 16:11:44 3D:itra-irix6 ppp[13583]: rhesus IPCP1: send
      Configure-Request ID=0x29
Jul   2 16:11:44 3D:itra-irix6 ppp[13583]: rhesus IPCP1:
      ADDR our address 132.245.33.131
Jul   2 16:11:44 3D:itra-irix6 ppp[13583]: rhesus 1: send 0xa
      bytes: index=25 proto=0x8021 01 29 00 0a 03 06 84 f5 21
      83
Jul   2 16:11:44 3D:itra-irix6 ppp[13583]: rhesus IPCP1: Ack-
      Sent(8)->Ack-Sent(8)
```

```
Jul  2 16:11:44 3D:itra-irix6 ppp[13583]: rhesus 1: read 0xa
     bytes: proto=0x8021 03 29 00 0a 03 06 84 f5 42 79
```
**Jul 2 16:11:44 3D:itra-irix6 ppp[13583]: rhesus IPCP1: re-
ceive Configure-NAK ID=0x29**
**Jul 2 16:11:44 3D:itra-irix6 ppp[13583]: rhesus IPCP1:
peer says 132.245.66.121 instead of 132.245.33.131 for
our address**
```
Jul  2 16:11:44 3D:itra-irix6 ppp[13583]: rhesus IPCP1:
     event RCN
Jul  2 16:11:44 3D:itra-irix6 ppp[13583]: rhesus IPCP1: send
     Configure-Request ID=0x2a
Jul  2 16:11:44 3D:itra-irix6 ppp[13583]: rhesus IPCP1:
     ADDR our address 132.245.33.131
Jul  2 16:11:44 3D:itra-irix6 ppp[13583]: rhesus 1: send 0xa
     bytes: index=25 proto=0x8021 01 2a 00 0a 03 06 84 f5 21
     83
Jul  2 16:11:44 3D:itra-irix6 ppp[13583]: rhesus IPCP1: Ack-
     Sent(8)->Ack-Sent(8)
Jul  2 16:11:44 3D:itra-irix6 ppp[13583]: rhesus 1: read 0xa
     bytes: proto=0x8021 03 2a 00 0a 03 06 84 f5 42 79
```
**Jul 2 16:11:44 3D:itra-irix6 ppp[13583]: rhesus IPCP1: re-
ceive Configure-NAK ID=0x2a**
**Jul 2 16:11:44 3D:itra-irix6 ppp[13583]: rhesus IPCP1:
peer says 132.245.66.121 instead of 132.245.33.131 for
our address**
```
     [...]
Jul  2 16:11:45 3D:itra-irix6 ppp[13583]: rhesus IPCP1:
     event RCN
Jul  2 16:11:45 3D:itra-irix6 ppp[13583]: rhesus IPCP1: send
     Configure-Request ID=0x32
Jul  2 16:11:45 3D:itra-irix6 ppp[13583]: rhesus IPCP1:
     ADDR our address 132.245.33.131
Jul  2 16:11:45 3D:itra-irix6 ppp[13583]: rhesus 1: send 0xa
     bytes: index=25 proto=0x8021 01 32 00 0a 03 06 84 f5 21
     83
Jul  2 16:11:45 3D:itra-irix6 ppp[13583]: rhesus IPCP1: Ack-
     Sent(8)->Ack-Sent(8)
Jul  2 16:11:45 3D:itra-irix6 ppp[13583]: rhesus 1: read 0xa
     bytes: proto=0x8021 03 32 00 0a 03 06 84 f5 42 79
Jul  2 16:11:45 3D:itra-irix6 ppp[13583]: rhesus IPCP1: re-
     ceive Configure-NAK ID=0x32
Jul  2 16:11:45 3D:itra-irix6 ppp[13583]: rhesus IPCP1:
     peer says 132.245.66.121 instead of 132.245.33.131 for
     our address
```
**Jul 2 16:11:45 3D:itra-irix6 ppp[13583]: rhesus IPCP1: giv-
ing after 11 Configure-NAKs**
**Jul 2 16:11:45 3D:itra-irix6 ppp[13583]: rhesus IPCP1:
event RXJ-**
**Jul 2 16:11:45 3D:itra-irix6 ppp[13583]: rhesus IPCP1: ac-
tion TLF**
**Jul 2 16:11:45 3D:itra-irix6 ppp[13583]: rhesus IPCP1:
event Close**
**Jul 2 16:11:45 3D:itra-irix6 ppp[13583]: rhesus IPCP1:
Stopped(3)->Closed(2)**

```
Jul   2 16:11:45 3D:itra-irix6 ppp[13583]: rhesus   LCP1:
      event Close
Jul   2 16:11:45 3D:itra-irix6 ppp[13583]: rhesus   LCP1: send
      Terminate-Request ID=0x9e
Jul   2 16:11:45 3D:itra-irix6 ppp[13583]: rhesus 1: send 0x4
      bytes: index=25 proto=0xc021 05 9e 00 04
Jul   2 16:11:45 3D:itra-irix6 ppp[13583]: rhesus   LCP1: ac-
      tion TLD
Jul   2 16:11:45 3D:itra-irix6 ppp[13583]: rhesus   LCP1: set
      async,acomp=0,pcomp=0,rx_ACCM=0,tx=0xffffffff,pad=0
Jul   2 16:11:45 3D:itra-irix6 ppp[13583]: rhesus IPCP1:
      event Down
Jul   2 16:11:45 3D:itra-irix6 ppp[13583]: rhesus IPCP1:
      Closed(2)->Initial(0)
Jul   2 16:11:45 3D:itra-irix6 ppp[13583]: rhesus   LCP1:
      Opened(9)->Closing(4)
Jul   2 16:11:45 3D:itra-irix6 ppp[13583]: rhesus 1: entering
      Terminate Phase
Jul   2 16:11:45 3D:itra-irix6 ppp[13583]: rhesus IPCP1: Ack-
      Sent(8)->Initial(0)
Jul   2 16:11:45 3D:itra-irix6 ppp[13583]: rhesus 1: read 0x4
      bytes: proto=0xc021 06 9e 00 04
Jul   2 16:11:45 3D:itra-irix6 ppp[13583]: rhesus   LCP1: re-
      ceive Terminate-Ack: 06 9e 00 04
Jul   2 16:11:45 3D:itra-irix6 ppp[13583]: rhesus   LCP1:
      event RTA
Jul   2 16:11:45 3D:itra-irix6 ppp[13583]: rhesus   LCP1: ac-
      tion TLF
Jul   2 16:11:45 3D:itra-irix6 ppp[13583]: rhesus 1: entering
      Dead Phase
Jul   2 16:11:45 3D:itra-irix6 ppp[13583]: rhesus   LCP1:
      Closing(4)->Closed(2)
Jul   2 16:12:46 3D:itra-irix6 ppp[13583]: rhesus: received
      signal 2
```

Although these logs are quite large, they're also quite easy to read. In particular, the messages for the IPCP Configure-Nak failure give a very clear picture of the problem. This makes the PPP implementation in IRIX quite easy to configure.

The implementation also supports running IP effectively unnumbered. It does not exhibit the point-to-point addressing problems mentioned in Chapter 4. Any available addresses may be negotiated as desired.

Here is an excerpt from a connection that succeeds:

```
Jul   2 16:23:31 3D:itra-irix6 ppp[13689]: rhesus IPCP1:
      event Open
Jul   2 16:23:31 3D:itra-irix6 ppp[13689]: rhesus IPCP1: ac-
      tion TLS
Jul   2 16:23:31 3D:itra-irix6 ppp[13689]: rhesus IPCP1:
      Initial(0)->Starting(1)
Jul   2 16:23:31 3D:itra-irix6 ppp[13689]: rhesus IPCP1:
      event Up
```

```
Jul   2 16:23:31 3D:itra-irix6 ppp[13689]: rhesus IPCP1: send
      Configure-Request ID=0x6b
Jul   2 16:23:31 3D:itra-irix6 ppp[13689]: rhesus IPCP1:
      16 slot VJ compression without compressed slot IDs
Jul   2 16:23:31 3D:itra-irix6 ppp[13689]: rhesus IPCP1:
      ADDR our address 132.245.33.131
Jul   2 16:23:31 3D:itra-irix6 ppp[13689]: rhesus 1: send
      0x10 bytes: index=26 proto=0x8021 01 6b 00 10 02 06 00
      2d 0f 00 03 06 84 f5 21 83
Jul   2 16:23:31 3D:itra-irix6 ppp[13689]: rhesus IPCP1:
      Starting(1)->Req-Sent(6)
Jul   2 16:23:31 3D:itra-irix6 ppp[13689]: rhesus 1: read 0x7
      bytes: proto=0x80fd 01 02 00 07 15 03 29
Jul   2 16:23:31 3D:itra-irix6 ppp[13689]: rhesus  CCP1:
      dropping Configure-Request packet because in Initial(0)
Jul   2 16:23:32 3D:itra-irix6 ppp[13689]: rhesus 1: read 0xa
      bytes: proto=0x8021 01 03 00 0a 03 06 84 f5 42 7c
Jul   2 16:23:32 3D:itra-irix6 ppp[13689]: rhesus IPCP1: re-
      ceive Configure-Request ID=0x3
Jul   2 16:23:32 3D:itra-irix6 ppp[13689]: rhesus IPCP1:
      accept its address 132.245.66.124 from ADDR Request
Jul   2 16:23:32 3D:itra-irix6 ppp[13689]: rhesus IPCP1:
      event RCR+
Jul   2 16:23:32 3D:itra-irix6 ppp[13689]: rhesus IPCP1: send
      Configure-ACK ID=0x3
Jul   2 16:23:32 3D:itra-irix6 ppp[13689]: rhesus 1: send 0xa
      bytes: index=26 proto=0x8021 02 03 00 0a 03 06 84 f5 42
      7c
Jul   2 16:23:32 3D:itra-irix6 ppp[13689]: rhesus IPCP1: Req-
      Sent(6)->Ack-Sent(8)
Jul   2 16:23:32 3D:itra-irix6 ppp[13689]: rhesus 1: read
      0x20  bytes: proto=0x802b 01 04 00 20 01 06 00 00 00 00
      02 08 00 80 2d 05 4a bb 04 04 00 02 05 0a "LM054ABB"
Jul   2 16:23:32 3D:itra-irix6 ppp[13689]: rhesus 1:
      Protocol-Rejecting IPX Protocol
Jul   2 16:23:32 3D:itra-irix6 ppp[13689]: rhesus  LCP1: send
      Protocol-Reject ID=0x8a
Jul   2 16:23:32 3D:itra-irix6 ppp[13689]: rhesus 1: send
      0x26  bytes: index=26 proto=0xc021 08 8a 00 26 80 2b 01
      04 00 20 01 06 00 00 00 00 02 08 00 80 2d 05 4a bb 04
      04 00 02 05 0a "LM054ABB"
Jul   2 16:23:32 3D:itra-irix6 ppp[13689]: rhesus 1: read 0xa
      bytes: proto=0x8021 04 6b 00 0a 02 06 00 2d 0f 00
Jul   2 16:23:32 3D:itra-irix6 ppp[13689]: rhesus IPCP1: re-
      ceive Configure-Reject ID=0x6b
Jul   2 16:23:32 3D:itra-irix6 ppp[13689]: rhesus IPCP1:
      peer is rejecting header compression
Jul   2 16:23:32 3D:itra-irix6 ppp[13689]: rhesus IPCP1:
      event RCN
Jul   2 16:23:32 3D:itra-irix6 ppp[13689]: rhesus IPCP1: send
      Configure-Request ID=0x6c
Jul   2 16:23:32 3D:itra-irix6 ppp[13689]: rhesus IPCP1:
      ADDR our address 132.245.33.131
```

```
Jul  2 16:23:32 3D:itra-irix6 ppp[13689]: rhesus 1: send 0xa
     bytes: index=26 proto=0x8021 01 6c 00 0a 03 06 84 f5 21
     83
Jul  2 16:23:32 3D:itra-irix6 ppp[13689]: rhesus IPCP1: Ack-
     Sent(8)->Ack-Sent(8)
Jul  2 16:23:32 3D:itra-irix6 ppp[13689]: rhesus 1: read 0xa
     bytes: proto=0x8021 02 6c 00 0a 03 06 84 f5 21 83
Jul  2 16:23:32 3D:itra-irix6 ppp[13689]: rhesus IPCP1: re-
     ceive Configure-Ack ID=0x6c
Jul  2 16:23:32 3D:itra-irix6 ppp[13689]: rhesus IPCP1: event
     RCA
Jul  2 16:23:32 3D:itra-irix6 ppp[13689]: rhesus IPCP1: ac-
     tion TLU
Jul  2 16:23:32 3D:itra-irix6 ppp[13689]: rhesus IPCP1: Ack-
     Sent(8)->Opened(9)
Jul  2 16:23:32 3D:itra-irix6 ppp[13689]: rhesus IPCP1:
     ready 132.245.33.131 to 132.245.66.124,
     rx_vj_comp=n,tx=n rx_compslot=n,tx=n rx_slots=16,tx=16
```

Personal Computer Software

Windows 95 Dial-Up Networking (DUN)

To enable PPP tracing on Windows 95, select the Control Panel from the My Computer icon. Select (double-click) Network in the Control Panel, then click once on the Dial-Up Adapter. Press the Properties button and select the Advanced tab. Finally, change the Record a log file property from No to Yes. Now click on OK to exit the Adapter Properties and Network menus.This places a text file called pplog.txt in the \WINDOWS directory. This file contains output similar to this:

```
06-13-1997 10:24:01.01 - Remote access driver log opened.
06-13-1997 10:24:01.01 - Installable CP VxD SPAP is loaded
06-13-1997 10:24:01.01 - Server type is  PPP (Point to Point
     Protocol).
06-13-1997 10:24:01.01 - FSA : Software compression disabled.
06-13-1997 10:24:01.01 - FSA : Adding Control Protocol 803f
     (NBFCP) to control protocol chain.
06-13-1997 10:24:01.01 - FSA : Adding Control Protocol 8021
     (IPCP) to control protocol chain.
06-13-1997 10:24:01.01 - FSA : Adding Control Protocol 802b
     (IPXCP) to control protocol chain.
06-13-1997 10:24:01.01 - FSA : Adding Control Protocol c029
     (CallbackCP) to control protocol chain.
06-13-1997 10:24:01.01 - FSA : Adding Control Protocol c027
     (no description) to control protocol chain.
06-13-1997 10:24:01.01 - FSA : Encrypted Password required.
06-13-1997 10:24:01.01 - FSA : Adding Control Protocol c223
     (CHAP) to control protocol chain.
06-13-1997 10:24:01.01 - FSA : Adding Control Protocol c021
     (LCP) to control protocol chain.
06-13-1997 10:24:01.01 - LCP : Callback negotiation enabled.
```

```
06-13-1997 10:24:01.01 - LCP : Layer started.
06-13-1997 10:24:04.16 - LCP : Received and accepted ACCM
    of 0.
06-13-1997 10:24:04.17 - LCP : NAK authentication protocol
    23c0 with protocol c223 (CHAP).
06-13-1997 10:24:04.17 - LCP : Naking possibly loopback
    magic number.
06-13-1997 10:24:04.17 - LCP : Rejecting unknown option 19.
06-13-1997 10:24:04.30 - LCP : Received and accepted ACCM
    of 0.
06-13-1997 10:24:04.30 - LCP : NAK authentication protocol
    23c0 with protocol c223 (CHAP).
06-13-1997 10:24:04.30 - LCP : Naking possibly loopback
    magic number.
06-13-1997 10:24:04.43 - LCP : Received and accepted ACCM
    of 0.
06-13-1997 10:24:04.43 - LCP : Received and accepted authen-
    tication protocol c223 (CHAP).
06-13-1997 10:24:04.43 - LCP : Received and accepted magic
    number cc9ea55d.
06-13-1997 10:24:04.43 - LCP : Received and accepted proto-
    col field compression option.
06-13-1997 10:24:04.43 - LCP : Received and accepted ad-
    dress+control field compression option.
06-13-1997 10:24:07.14 - LCP : Received configure reject for
    callback control protocol option.
06-13-1997 10:24:07.29 - LCP : Layer up.
06-13-1997 10:24:07.29 - CHAP : Layer started.
```
**06-13-1997 10:24:08.03 - CHAP : Login failed: username, pass
word, or domain was incorrect.**
```
06-13-1997 10:24:08.03 - LCP : Received terminate request.
06-13-1997 10:24:08.03 - LCP : Layer down.
06-13-1997 10:24:11.04 - LCP : Layer finished.
06-13-1997 10:32:37.92 - Remote access driver is shutting
    down.
06-13-1997 10:32:37.92 - CRC Errors                0
06-13-1997 10:32:37.92 - Timeout Errors            0
06-13-1997 10:32:37.92 - Alignment Errors          0
06-13-1997 10:32:37.92 - Overrun Errors            0
06-13-1997 10:32:37.92 - Framing Errors            0
06-13-1997 10:32:37.92 - Buffer Overrun Errors     0
06-13-1997 10:32:37.92 - Incomplete Packets        0
06-13-1997 10:32:37.92 - Bytes Received            310
06-13-1997 10:32:37.92 - Bytes Transmittted        380
06-13-1997 10:32:37.92 - Frames Received           8
06-13-1997 10:32:37.92 - Frames Transmitted        9
06-13-1997 10:32:37.92 - LCP : Layer started.
06-13-1997 10:32:37.92 - Remote access driver log closed.
06-13-1997 10:32:57.65 - Remote access driver log opened.
```

Of course, in the example, the user's password is incorrect. Note that "CHAP" in these logs is actually MS-CHAP. Windows 95 supports standard CHAP only with a patch available from Microsoft.

This next example shows an interface establishing itself normally. This system does not have the ISDN Accelerator Pack installed that implements RFC 1990 standard MP (over modems as well as over ISDN, despite the moniker), so option decimal 19 (hex 13), the Multi-link Endpoint Discriminator is rejected. Also note that the IP addresses are displayed as 32-bit hexadecimal numbers rather than as the more familiar decimal dotted quads:

```
06-13-1997 10:34:46.07 - Installable CP VxD SPAP is loaded
06-13-1997 10:34:46.07 - Server type is  PPP (Point to Point
    Protocol).
06-13-1997 10:34:46.07 - FSA : Software compression disabled.
06-13-1997 10:34:46.07 - FSA : Adding Control Protocol 803f
    (NBFCP) to control protocol chain.
06-13-1997 10:34:46.07 - FSA : Adding Control Protocol 8021
    (IPCP) to control protocol chain.
06-13-1997 10:34:46.07 - FSA : Adding Control Protocol 802b
    (IPXCP) to control protocol chain.
06-13-1997 10:34:46.07 - FSA : Adding Control Protocol c029
    (CallbackCP) to control protocol chain.
06-13-1997 10:34:46.07 - FSA : Adding Control Protocol c027
    (no description) to control protocol chain.
06-13-1997 10:34:46.07 - FSA : Adding Control Protocol c023
    (PAP) to control protocol chain.
06-13-1997 10:34:46.07 - FSA : Adding Control Protocol c223
    (CHAP) to control protocol chain.
06-13-1997 10:34:46.07 - FSA : Adding Control Protocol c021
    (LCP) to control protocol chain.
06-13-1997 10:34:46.07 - LCP : Callback negotiation enabled.
06-13-1997 10:34:46.07 - LCP : Layer started.
06-13-1997 10:34:49.22 - LCP : Received and accepted ACCM
    of 0.
06-13-1997 10:34:49.22 - LCP : Received and accepted authen-
    tication protocol c023 (PAP).
06-13-1997 10:34:49.22 - LCP : Received and accepted magic
    number 4849ece6.
06-13-1997 10:34:49.22 - LCP : Received and accepted proto-
    col field compression option.
06-13-1997 10:34:49.22 - LCP : Received and accepted ad-
    dress+control field compression option.
06-13-1997 10:34:49.22 - LCP : Rejecting unknown option 19.
06-13-1997 10:34:49.34 - LCP : Received and accepted ACCM
    of 0.
06-13-1997 10:34:49.34 - LCP : Received and accepted authen-
    tication protocol c023 (PAP).
06-13-1997 10:34:49.34 - LCP : Received and accepted magic
    number 4849ece6.
06-13-1997 10:34:49.34 - LCP : Received and accepted proto-
    col field compression option.
06-13-1997 10:34:49.34 - LCP : Received and accepted ad-
    dress+control field compression option.
06-13-1997 10:34:52.20 - LCP : Received configure reject for
    callback control protocol option.
06-13-1997 10:34:52.33 - LCP : Layer up.
```

```
06-13-1997 10:34:52.33 - PAP : Layer started.
06-13-1997 10:34:53.72 - PAP : Login was successful.
06-13-1997 10:34:53.72 - PAP : Layer up.
06-13-1997 10:34:53.72 - IPXCP : Layer started.
06-13-1997 10:34:53.72 - IPCP : Layer started.
06-13-1997 10:34:53.72 - IPCP : IP address is 0.
06-13-1997 10:34:53.72 - NBFCP : Layer started.
06-13-1997 10:34:53.83 - FSA : Sending protocol reject for
    control protocol 80fd.
06-13-1997 10:34:54.38 - IPCP : Received and accepted IP ad
    dress of 84f5427c.
06-13-1997 10:34:54.38 - IPCP : Turning off IP header com-
    pression.
06-13-1997 10:34:54.94 - IPXCP : Accepted matching net num-
    ber 0.
06-13-1997 10:34:54.94 - IPXCP : Received and accepted peer
    node number 0 80 2d 5 4a bb.
06-13-1997 10:34:54.99 - FSA : Received protocol reject for
    control protocol 803f.
06-13-1997 10:34:54.99 - NBFCP : Layer finished.
06-13-1997 10:34:55.07 - IPXCP : Accepted matching net num-
    ber 0.
06-13-1997 10:34:55.07 - IPXCP : Received and accepted peer
    node number 0 80 2d 5 4a bb.
06-13-1997 10:34:55.07 - IPXCP : Received and accepted rout-
    ing protocol 0.
06-13-1997 10:34:55.07 - IPXCP : Received and accepted
    router name LM054ABB.
06-13-1997 10:34:55.07 - IPXCP : Layer up.
06-13-1997 10:34:56.95 - IPCP : Changing IP address from 0
    to 84f54279.
06-13-1997 10:34:57.06 - IPCP : Layer up.
06-13-1997 10:34:57.07 - FSA : Last control protocol is up.
```

Communications Servers

Xyplex

Xyplex servers log PPP state transitions in syslog:

```
IPCP Event: DOWN State: OPEN => STARTING
IPXCP Event: DOWN State: INITIAL => INITIAL
LCP Event: DOWN State: OPEN => STARTING
IPCP Event: DOWN State: STARTING => STARTING
IPXCP Event: DOWN State: INITIAL => INITIAL
```

Bay Networks Xylogics Annex

Annex servers log state transitions, significant events, and a summary of the state in case of failure to syslog:

```
May  8 17:42:48 guenevere ppp[2559]: Port-
    Begin:asy42:PPP:::[local]
```

```
May   8 17:42:48 guenevere ppp[2559]: ppp:asy42:ADM Start LCP
May   8 17:42:48 guenevere line_adm[1298]: started mp on mp126
      as PID 2573
May   8 17:42:48 guenevere system[0]: ppp:asy42:detach link
      from bundle mp126
May   8 17:42:48 guenevere mp[2573]: ppp:mp126:terminating:
      errno: Success
May   8 17:42:51 guenevere ppp[2559]: ppp:asy42:LCP Started
      LCP
May   8 17:42:52 guenevere ppp[2559]: ppp:asy42:Security
      Started PAP
May   8 17:42:55 guenevere ppp[2559]: ppp:asy42:ipxcp started
May   8 17:42:55 guenevere ppp[2559]: ppp:asy42:rejecting un-
      known protocol 803F
May   8 17:42:55 guenevere ppp[2559]: ppp:asy42:send protocol
      reject for 803F
May   8 17:42:55 guenevere ppp[2559]: ppp:asy42:LCP:received
      protocol reject for 8029 (ATCP)
May   8 17:42:55 guenevere ppp[2559]: ppp:asy42:NCP Closed
      ATCP
May   8 17:42:55 guenevere ppp[2559]: ppp:asy42:NCP Started
      IPCP
May   8 17:42:55 guenevere ppp[2559]: ifconfig asy42 local
      132.245.11.10 remote 132.245.11.92 mask 255.255.255.255
      metric 1
```

The summary is printed if no NCPs go to open state. It appears like this:

```
Apr 18 08:09:55 annex ppp[20817]: ppp:asy2: *** LCP SYSLOG
    HISTORY ***
Apr 18 08:09:55 annex ppp[20817]: ppp:asy2:Rcv cfg req: Send
    cfg req with MRU: 1500
Apr 18 08:09:55 annex ppp[20817]: ppp:asy2:Rcv cfg req:
    Sending ACCM of: a0000
Apr 18 08:09:55 annex ppp[20817]: ppp:asy2:Rcv cfg req:
    Requesting CHAP security
Apr 18 08:09:55 annex ppp[20817]: ppp:asy2:Rcv cfg req:
    Request for ACFC
Apr 18 08:09:55 annex ppp[20817]: ppp:asy2:Rcv cfg req:
    Sending random magic number
Apr 18 08:09:55 annex ppp[20817]: ppp:asy2:Rcv cfg req:
    Request PFC
Apr 18 08:09:55 annex ppp[20817]: ppp:asy2: *** END LCP HIS-
    TORY ***
```

Livingston Portmaster

From a command prompt, the administrator can enable debug mode 0x51, which displays the raw PPP data (minus the AHDLC address and control field, and the PPP protocol field) plus notes on the state transitions (such as the LCP Open message below):

```
> set console
> set debug 0x51
Setting debug value to 0x51
Sending LCP_CONFIGURE_REQUEST to port S2 of 24 bytes con-
    taining:
01 02 00 18 01 04 03 ee 02 06 00 00 00 00 05 06
83 59 4b 5e 07 02 08 02
Received LCP_CONFIGURE_ACK on port S2 of 20 bytes contain-
    ing:
02 02 00 18 01 04 03 ee 02 06 00 00 00 00 05 06
83 59 4b 5e 07 02 08 02
S2: LCP Open
```

These logs can be decoded into more readable text by copying them into a "decoder ring" Web page set up by Livingston technical support at http://www.livingston.com/Tech/Support/dring.shtml. This perl script will decode each option as a separate line of text with a verbose expansion of the option values.

The PortMaster also logs PPP conditions to any syslog host.

```
Mar 1 18:01:23 pma dialnet: port S2 ppp_sync failed dest
1.2.3.4
```

Ascend MAX

From a terminal-mode command line, the Ascend devices allow the administrator to enable various levels of PPP debug messages. Shown below are the pppfsm (finite state machine) and pppif (interface) levels of debug. Note that the actual data are not shown and that the messages include internal software implementation notes.

```
> pppfsm
PPPFSM state display is ON
> pppif
PPPIF debug is ON
> PPPIF: open: routeid 372, incoming YES
PPPIF-105: vj comp on
PPPIF-105: _initAuthentication, mpID=0
PPPIF-105: auth mode 3
PPPIF-105: PAP/CHAP/MS-CHAP auth, incoming
PPPFSM-105: Layer 0   State INITIAL       Event OPEN...
PPPFSM-105: ...New State STARTING
PPPFSM-105: Layer 0   State STARTING      Event UP...
PPPFSM-105: ...New State REQSENT
PPPIF-105: Link Is up.
PPPFSM-105: Layer 1   State INITIAL       Event UP...
PPPFSM-105: ...New State CLOSED
PPPFSM-105: Layer 2   State INITIAL       Event UP...
PPPFSM-105: ...New State CLOSED
```

Analyzers

Dedicated analyzers provide a good bit more detail than the debug logs from most implementations, are usually easier to use, and are very useful when the implementation under test may be failing in a way that is not recorded in the standard logs. They range in price from free to a few hundred dollars for software-only implementations, and as much as $20,000 for dedicated hardware. For the extra money, dedicated systems are usually more reliable, decode more protocols, offer specialized test modes, and can run at much higher speeds than the software-only systems. If you are working only with asynchronous PPP on RS-232 lines, the software versions are quite capable. If you are working with high-speed telecommunications lines, then the dedicated systems are worth investigation.

A very important feature of analyzers is that they are much more objective than the log file from a PPP implementation. They will show what is on the wire, and only what is on the wire. Occasionally, when the bug being investigated is inside the HDLC driver, the PPP log files may show things that simply did not take place. An analyzer is the best way to settle the matter.

Using analyzers sometimes requires a bit more practice than reading the debug logs. Since most parts of PPP have shared state between the peers (such as the negotiation state machines, the negotiated parameters themselves, and the CCP compression history), it is sometimes difficult for a third party observing the communication to determine the meaning of the data correctly. This results in occasional misleading data in the verbose decode sections of the output, so the user often must read the hexadecimal data itself to interpret the frame.

LANPharaoh

This PC-based analyzer from Azure Technologies can monitor data on BRI (Basic Rate ISDN) links using an external module that attaches to the S/T interface between the NT1 and the unit under test.

```
Seconds     Bytes    Ad    Ctl    PID    PPP Protocol         Type    Description
18:07:53    19       ff    03     003d   Multilink (Seq=253)  PPP     Multilink PPP

                            Point-to-Point Protocol Layer
        Time Stamp: 18:07:53.294109 Inter-frame Gap(uSecs):    >65535
        Frame Source: DTE    PPP Header: x'FF03'
        Protocol Identifier: x'003D'        (PPP Multilink)
                                    Multilink PPP

        Fragment indicator: x'C0'
          1... .... Beginning of fragment
          .1.. .... End of fragment
          ..00 0000 Reserved
        Sequence number: 253
                                Hexadecimal Frame
    0000 ff 03 00 3d c0 5c 00 fd 04 d5 7f f9 80 70 00       ...=@\.}.U.y.p.
```

SerialView and ISDNView

These are PC-based analyzers produced by Klos Technologies, Inc. The asynchronous version uses two standard serial ports on an IBM PC-compatible system to monitor data passing in each direction. It can correctly handle in-band flow control (XON/XOFF), and standard AHDLC escaping, which makes reading the PPP frames much less tedious. This example shows a portion of an LCP exchange:

```
===============================================================
PPP:
    From Port B to Port A            Size: 0035         Number:          8
                                                        Time:        31.025

MAC DATA:
0000   FF 7D 23 C0 21 7D 21 7D-20 7D 20 7D 39 7D 22 7D     .}#@!}!} } }9}"}
0010   26 7D 20 7D 20 7D 20 7D-20 7D 23 7D 25 C2 23 80     &} } } } }#}%B#.
0020   7D 25 7D 26 7D 20 7D 20-62 3C 7D 27 7D 22 7D 28     }%}&} } b<}'}"}(
0030   7D 22 7D 33 BB                                      }"}3;

+++++++++++++++++++++++++++++++++++++++++++++++++++++++++++++++
PPP:
    From Port B to Port A            Size: 0019         Number:          8
                                     Type: C021         Time:        31.025

LCP:
    Code: Configure-Request (1)
    Identifier: 0        Length: 0019

Option 2 - Async-Control-Character-Map
    Length = 6
    ACCM = 00000000
Option 3 - Authentication-Protocol
    Length = 5
    Protocol = C223 (CHAP)
    Data = 80 (Microsoft)
Option 5 - Magic-Number
    Length = 6
    Magic Number = 0000623C
Option 7 - Protocol-Field-Compression
    Length = 2
Option 8 - Address-and-Control-Field-Compression
    Length = 2

===============================================================
PPP:
    From Port A to Port B            Size: 0034         Number:          9
                                                        Time:        31.035

MAC DATA:
0000   FF 7D 23 C0 21 7D 22 7D-20 7D 20 7D 39 7D 22 7D     .}#@!}"} } }9}"}
0010   26 7D 20 7D 20 7D 20 7D-20 7D 23 7D 25 C2 23 80     &} } } } }#}%B#.
```

```
0020  7D 25 7D 26 7D 20 7D 20-62 3C 7D 27 7D 22 7D 28      }%}&} } b<}'}"}(
0030  7D 22 9E B7                                          }".7
```

++

```
PPP:
     From Port A to Port B            Size: 0019        Number:           9
                                      Type: C021        Time:        31.035

LCP:
     Code: Configure-Ack (2)
     Identifier: 0        Length: 0019

Option 2 - Async-Control-Character-Map
   Length = 6
   ACCM = 00000000
Option 3 - Authentication-Protocol
   Length = 5
   Protocol = C223 (CHAP)
   Data = 80 (Microsoft)
Option 5 - Magic-Number
   Length = 6
   Magic Number = 0000623C
Option 7 - Protocol-Field-Compression
   Length = 2
Option 8 - Address-and-Control-Field-Compression
   Length = 2
```

==

Summary

Most PPP packages can be coaxed into providing debugging information that can help isolate and identify commonly encountered problems, although the information given is often incomplete. If you support a large number of PPP users or are developing a PPP implementation, I highly recommend the use of stand-alone analyzers.

Chapter

8

Resources

IN THIS CHAPTER

Any list of resources for an actively evolving technology like PPP will almost immediately be outdated. In addition to the various sources listed below, I encourage you to seek out the latest information from your local library, Internet search services, and bookstores that specialize in technical publications.

Related Books and Other Publications

W. Richard Stevens, *TCP/IP Illustrated*, vol. 1, Addison–Wesley, ISBN 0-201-63346-9.
This book, part of a series on networking, does a superb job of describing the IP network layer and the transport and application layers above it. If you implement or use IPCP over PPP, this will help you design and debug your system once PPP is running.

Douglas E. Comer, *Internetworking with TCP/IP: Principles, Protocols and Architecture*, vols. 1 and 2, Prentice-Hall, ISBN 0-13-216987-8 and 0-13-125527-4.
This is another good series of books on the TCP/IP suite of protocols. It is referred to often enough in the Internet world that most people simply call it "Comer."

Marshall Kirk McKusick et al., *The Design and Implementation of the 4.4 BSD Operating System*, Addison–Wesley, ISBN 0-201-54979-4.
4.4 BSD is a reference version of Unix produced by the University of California at Berkeley. It contains a number of networking-related mechanisms that are typical of high-performance implementations of TCP/IP and PPP. If you need more information about how to design a networking system from scratch, this is a good place to start.

Ian Wade, *NOSintro: TCP/IP over Packet Radio: An Introduction to the KA9Q Network Operating System*, Dowermain.
This is a book specifically about the KA9Q networking system, which includes PPP drivers, and many common TCP/IP applications.

G. Sidhu, R. Andrews, A. Oppenheimer, *Inside AppleTalk*, 2d ed., Addison–Wesley, ISBN 0201550210.
This is the standard reference for the AppleTalk networking protocols.

Local Area Network Technical Reference, IBM, SC30-3383-2.
This is the standard reference for NetBEUI/NetBIOS.

Internet Transport Protocols, Xerox, XNSS 029101.
This is the standard reference for XNS.

DNA Routing Layer Functional Specification, Digital Equipment Corporation, AA-X436A-TK.
This is the standard reference for DECNet.

Media Access Control (MAC) Bridges, ISO/IEC 15802-3:1993, ANSI/IEEE Std 802.1D, July 1993; *Draft Standard 802.1G: Remote MAC Bridging*, IEEE P802.1G/D7, December 30, 1992; *Token-Ring Network Architecture Reference*, 3d ed., September 1989.
These three books cover the standard spanning tree protocols used in bridging applications.

Programming Windows 95 Unleashed, Sams Development Group. ISBN 0-672-30602-6; Karen Hazzah, *Writing Windows VxDs and Device Drivers*, Miller Freeman Books. ISBN 0-87930-438-3; Jim Kelsey, *Programming Plug and Play*, Sams. ISBN 0672307030.
These are three reference books that PC programmers might find useful. There are a very large number of similar books on the market today.

Getting RFCs, Internet Drafts, and Other Documents

There are a large number of repositories of the standards-related documents (RFCs, STDs, Internet Drafts, and IENs). The primary FTP repositories are:

```
DS.INTERNIC.NET        SRC.DOC.IC.AC.UK
NIS.NSF.NET            FTP.NCREN.NET
NISC.JVNC.NET          FTP.SESQUI.NET
FTP.ISI.EDU            NIS.GARR.IT
WUARCHIVE.WUSTL.EDU
```

These are also retrievable via email to `mailserv@ds.internic.net`. Simply put the word "help" in the body of your message to retrieve full instructions for both email and ftp access.

To start, the reader should use anonymous FTP to connect to `ds.internic.net`, then retrieve the following files from the "rfc" directory:

```
rfc1661.txt     rfc1661.txt
rfc1334.txt     rfc1332.txt
rfc-index.txt
```

These may also be retrieved from the Web site `http://ds.internic.net/`.

UUNET maintains a secondary archive with an extensive collection of documents. The list of these is in a file called `/archive/inet/ls-lR.Z` on `ftp.uu.net`.

Current Internet Draft documents are available from FTP site `nnsc.nsf.net` in directory internet-drafts.

The Microsoft proprietary PPP extensions are available from their FTP site, `ftp.microsoft.com`, in directory `/developr/rfc/`.

There are also companies that reproduce RFCs in convenient formats, such as CD-ROM. See the "Other Resources" section at the end of this chapter.

The International Telecommunication Union (ITU) has some of its documentation on-line at `http://www.itu.ch`. This organization does not allow unlimited access, and most of the documents are available for a fee only.

The American National Standards Institute is reachable through `http://www.ansi.org`. ANSI documents are not free.

The Electronic Industries Association (EIA) is the source of many communications standards. They are reachable through `http://www.eia.org/`. These documents are not free.

All of the above documents can be conveniently ordered from Global Engineering Documents, 15 Inverness Way, Englewood, CO 80112-5704. Call (303) 397-7956 or, in the U.S. or Canada, (800) 854-7179. The Web site is at `http://www.ihs.com/`.

Mailing Lists, Web Sites, and Usenet News Groups

Before posting or emailing a question anywhere, read the list of frequently asked questions (FAQ) for PPP and for the group. Many of the folks on the Internet can be quite abrupt if the question you are asking has already been answered many times. The FAQ for PPP can be found at `http://cs.uni-bonn.de/ppp/faq.html`. The FAQ lists for most USENET groups are archived at MIT. The FTP server is `ftp://rtfm.mit.edu/pub/usenet-by-group/`. In this directory you will find a single subdirectory for each USENET group; a copy of the FAQ list for each is kept in those subdirectories.

comp.protocols.ppp

This is the main PPP news group. If you have questions about PPP in general, this is the place to turn. This is not the right place to ask specific questions about a particular implementation or about application programs, so if your email package is not working correctly over PPP, look for a different group.

A Web version of the FAQ for this group is kept at `http://www.faqs.org/faqs/ppp-faq/part1/index.html`.

comp.protocols.tcp-ip

This is the main TCP/IP discussion group. Of course, PPP supports a lot more protocols than just TCP/IP, but this is an important enough use that many people debugging PPP problems end up here.

comp.dcom.servers

This is the group for discussing data communications servers. If you have a problem with your IPX file server, this is not the right place to post your question. If you are using terminal servers or communications servers, this is the right place.

comp.dcom.frame-relay

comp.dcom.isdn

comp.dcom.modems

comp.dcom.xdsl

These groups are all related to link-layer technologies that can and do use PPP.

comp.os.linux.networking

This group is dedicated to the Linux operating system networking features. Linux is a free Unix implementation available at many FTP sites and runs on a number of platforms, including IBM PC compatibles, DEC ALPHA RISC, and Apple PowerPC systems.

comp.os.ms-windows.networking.ras

This group discusses the Remote Access Services for Microsoft Windows. This should be the first place to turn if you have problems with the PPP implementation that comes with Windows.

comp.os.ms-windows.nt.admin.networking

This is for administrators of Windows-NT networks. Administrators of sites using the NT PPP implementation should follow this group.

comp.os.os2.networking.misc

This is the IBM OS/2 networking group.

comp.unix.*

For most Unix systems, the vendor's news group is the right place to ask questions about the vendor's implementation of PPP. For instance, IBM's AIX is covered by `comp.unix.aix`.

ietf-ppp

This is the official mailing list of the Internet Engineering Task Force (IETF) PPP extensions working group. It is the official list for discussing issues related to the PPP protocol for developers. If you are developing a PPP implementation or want to listen in on the discussions that go on to develop new protocols, send your subscription request to `ietf-ppp-request@merit.edu`.

Do not post inappropriate questions to this list, such as those that relate to a specific implementation (for example, questions about the Windows Plug-and-Play mechanism) or about user-level interfaces (for example, the MacPPP menu system). This is not the purpose of this mailing list, and the responses you get will likely be much less helpful than you would imagine.

Livingston PPP "Decoder Ring"

`http://www.livingston.com/Tech/Support/dring.shtml`

PPP Debugging Tips

`http://reality.sgi.com/employees/scotth/dialup-support.html`

PPP on Linux Answers to Frequently Asked Questions (FAQ)

`http://www.xws.com/linux/PPP-FAQ.html`

TCP/IP Resources Reference

This is an extensive list put together by Raz Uri and others of other reference sites:

`http://www.qnx.com/~mphunter/tcpip_resources.html`

    http://www.faqs.org/faqs/internet/tcp-ip/resource-
        list/index.html

    ftp://rtfm.mit.edu/pub/usenet-by-
        group/news.answers/internet/tcp-ip/resource-list

    ftp://rtfm.mit.edu/pub/usenet-by-hierarchy/comp/protocols/tcp-
        ip/TCP_IP_Resources_List

Publicly Available Source Code and Executables

Pppd is a PPP implementation that runs on a wide variety of Unix systems. It is available from ftp://cs.anu.edu.au/pub/software/ppp/.

Dp, which runs only SunOS and Solaris systems, is a demand-dialing version of pppd. It is available from ftp://ftp.acn.purdue.edu/dp/.

Another freely-available implementation is "iij-ppp", which runs only on HP-UX systems. More information is available from http://www.verinet.com/~barthold/ppp.html.

SGI has made working Predictor-1 source code available on its ftp site in ftp://ftp.sgi.com/other/ppp-comp/predictor1.c.

A DES library (called libdes-3.06) for implementing MS-CHAP is available from ftp://ftp.psy.uq.oz.au/pub/Crypto/DES/.

Phil Karn wrote an IBM PC-based PPP implementation called ka9q (after his ham radio call sign). It has been ported to other small computers, such as the Atari, by many volunteers. You can fetch the original from http://people.qualcomm.com/karn/tcpip.html.

The packet drivers written at Clarkson University in New York for various network interfaces on IBM PC systems are maintained by Crynwr Software. These are available from ftp://ftp.crynwr.com/drivers/.

Another free PPP implementation for PCs is available from the SIMTEL archives ftp://ftp.simtel.net/pub/simtelnet/msdos/pktdrvr/dosppp05.zip. Still another free implementation of PPP for PCs is available from Klos Technologies. http://www.klos.com/.

A replacement Windows 95 PPP driver is available from http://www.vt.edu:10021/K/kewells/net/index.html.

FreePPP for MacIntosh computers based on MacPPP 2.0.3 from Merit is available from Rockstar Studios (which also sells a development kit for PPP experimenters): http://www.rockstar.com/.

Meetings and Groups

Internet Engineering Task Force

The IETF holds week-long meetings approximately every four months. The meetings are open to anyone interested in the standards process, though a registration fee is required. To be notified of upcoming IETF events, send a subscription request to `ietf-announce-request@IETF.org`.

No fee is charged for participating in the group itself through the various email lists. The work of the IETF is conducted on the mailing lists, not at the IETF meetings, so it is not necessary to attend these meetings to be part of the standards-setting process. Many people who are very active in the standards process by way of the mailing lists have never been to an IETF meeting.

Bake-Offs

These are informal get-togethers of the implementors of the IETF protocols. They are organized and announced on the mailing lists for the various working groups. In a bake-off, preproduction code for new protocols is tested between the participating implementors in order to shake out compatibility problems and specification errors. These meetings are generally not as open as the IETF meetings and are intended for active developers only.

One frequently-organized bake-off is primarily for ISDN-based implementations of PPP, which include MP and BACP. This is sponsored by PacBell in California.

Networld/Interop

Networld/Interop is a major networking trade show run about twice a year. This is a marketing and sales show; most of the attendees are the people who will buy the products. Demonstrations of new products are done at Interop, but these are not testing events for developers.

Other Resources

InfoMagic (11950 North Highway 89, Flagstaff, AZ 86004, USA) publishes CD-ROMs containing useful public domain source code as well as RFCs, IENs, and CCITT/ITU documents. Phone: +1 (520) 526-9565. Web site: `http://www.infomagic.com`.

Klos Technologies, Inc. (604 Daniel Webster Highway, Merrimack, NH 03054, USA) makes PPP drivers for IBM-compatible PCs and PC-based asynchronous and ISDN PPP analyzers, and can license PPP implementations for use in other systems. Phone: +1 (603) 424-8300. Email: `klos@klos.com`. Web site: `http://www.klos.com`.

Azure Technologies (63 South Street, Hopkinton, MA 01748, USA) makes analyzers for most network types, including ISDN and PPP. Phone: +1 (508) 435-3800. Fax: +1 (508) 435-0448. Email: `sales@azure-tech.com`. Web site: `http://www.azure-tech.com`.

Morningstar PPP is a well-known commercial implementation of PPP for most Unix systems. Phone: +1 (614) 326-4600. Web site: `http://www.progressive-systems.com/`.

The ANVL test suite from Midnight Networks (200 Fifth Avenue, Waltham, MA 02154, USA) is helpful for doing automated testing of a PPP implementation. Contact them through `http://www.midnight.com`. Phone: +1 (617) 890-1001. Fax: +1 (617) 890-0028. Email: `midnight@midnight.com`.

Bruce Schneier's web site, `http://www.counterpane.com/`, contains information on his book, *Applied Cryptography,* and a highly recommended essay on why cryptography is harder than it looks.

STAC Electronics, Inc. (12636 High Bluff Drive/San Diego, CA 92130-2093/USA) makes PPP compression hardware and software. Phone: +1 (619) 794-3741. Fax: +1 (619) 794-4575. Web site: http://www.stac.com.

The "Calgary Corpus" is a body of text files that are standard benchmarks for compression performance. If you are implementing or testing CCP, you will probably want to have these for reference. They are available from FTP site `ftp.cpsc.ucalgary.ca` in directory `/pub/projects/text.compression.corpus/`.

The League for Programming Freedom (1 Kendall Square #143, PO Box 9171, Cambridge, MA 02139, USA) helps protect the rights of individual programmers versus the power of corporate software patenting and other issues. Phone: +1 (617) 243-4091. Web site: `http://www.lpf.org`. Email: `lpf@lpf.org`.

The Free Software Foundation (59 Temple Place, Suite 330, Boston, MA 02111, USA) coordinates the production and distribution of Gnu and other free software. Phone: +1 (617) 542-5942. Web site: `http://www.fsf.org`. Email: `gnu@prep.ai.mit.edu`.

I am registered with the Internic as handle JC6738. My current email and mailing addresses are available by running `whois \!JC6738`. Due to the volume of mail, not all questions can be answered directly.

Appendix
A

AHDLC Implementation

The following code implements a simple AHDLC interface for a PPP system. It supports escaping of arbitrary characters, 16- and 32-bit CRCs, and hardware with FIFOs. A copy of this code is available from my Web site:

```
http://id.wing.net/People/carlson/ppp
```

```
/*
 * This code shows a simple AHDLC interface.  It assumes that some
 * kind of serial hardware with FIFOs is in use and that interrupts
 * from this hardware and from the PPP system above can be disabled
 * and that the CPU uses 8 bit bytes and 32 bit longs.
 *
 * It is also assumed that packets sent and received pass through
 * queues and are simple buffers.  Generic "queue_append" and
 * "queue_fetch" functions are used for access, and buffers are
 * acquired through "buffer_fetch" and released back to the system by
 * a "buffer_release" function.  The ACCM mechanism supports escaping
 * of all characters.
 *
 * A synchronization mechanism based on the standard BSD kernel
 * sleep/wakeup mechanism is also provided.
 *
 * This code may be used for any purpose as long as the author's
 * copyright is cited in any source code distributed.  This code
 * is also available electronically from the author's web site.
 */

#include <stdlib.h>

/* Interface to networking portion of operating system. */
struct queue;
extern void queue_append(struct queue *que, char *buffer, int size);
extern void queue_fetch(struct queue *que, char **bufferp, int *sizep);
extern char *buffer_fetch(int size);
extern void buffer_release(char *buffer);
extern void interrupts_off(void);
extern void interrupts_on(void);
extern void wakeup(void *event);
extern void sleep(void *event, int level);

typedef unsigned char octet;
typedef unsigned short uint16;
typedef unsigned long uint32;

#define MAXIMUM_MRU 2048

/* Standard CRC tables from RFC 1662. */
static uint16 fcstab_16[256] = {
    0x0000, 0x1189, 0x2312, 0x329b, 0x4624, 0x57ad, 0x6536, 0x74bf,
    0x8c48, 0x9dc1, 0xaf5a, 0xbed3, 0xca6c, 0xdbe5, 0xe97e, 0xf8f7,
    0x1081, 0x0108, 0x3393, 0x221a, 0x56a5, 0x472c, 0x75b7, 0x643e,
    0x9cc9, 0x8d40, 0xbfdb, 0xae52, 0xdaed, 0xcb64, 0xf9ff, 0xe876,
    0x2102, 0x308b, 0x0210, 0x1399, 0x6726, 0x76af, 0x4434, 0x55bd,
    0xad4a, 0xbcc3, 0x8e58, 0x9fd1, 0xeb6e, 0xfae7, 0xc87c, 0xd9f5,
    0x3183, 0x200a, 0x1291, 0x0318, 0x77a7, 0x662e, 0x54b5, 0x453c,
    0xbdcb, 0xac42, 0x9ed9, 0x8f50, 0xfbef, 0xea66, 0xd8fd, 0xc974,
    0x4204, 0x538d, 0x6116, 0x709f, 0x0420, 0x15a9, 0x2732, 0x36bb,
    0xce4c, 0xdfc5, 0xed5e, 0xfcd7, 0x8868, 0x99e1, 0xab7a, 0xbaf3,
    0x5285, 0x430c, 0x7197, 0x601e, 0x14a1, 0x0528, 0x37b3, 0x263a,
    0xdecd, 0xcf44, 0xfddf, 0xec56, 0x98e9, 0x8960, 0xbbfb, 0xaa72,
    0x6306, 0x728f, 0x4014, 0x519d, 0x2522, 0x34ab, 0x0630, 0x17b9,
    0xef4e, 0xfec7, 0xcc5c, 0xddd5, 0xa96a, 0xb8e3, 0x8a78, 0x9bf1,
    0x7387, 0x620e, 0x5095, 0x411c, 0x35a3, 0x242a, 0x16b1, 0x0738,
    0xffcf, 0xee46, 0xdcdd, 0xcd54, 0xb9eb, 0xa862, 0x9af9, 0x8b70,
    0x8408, 0x9581, 0xa71a, 0xb693, 0xc22c, 0xd3a5, 0xe13e, 0xf0b7,
    0x0840, 0x19c9, 0x2b52, 0x3adb, 0x4e64, 0x5fed, 0x6d76, 0x7cff,
    0x9489, 0x8500, 0xb79b, 0xa612, 0xd2ad, 0xc324, 0xf1bf, 0xe036,
    0x18c1, 0x0948, 0x3bd3, 0x2a5a, 0x5ee5, 0x4f6c, 0x7df7, 0x6c7e,
    0xa50a, 0xb483, 0x8618, 0x9791, 0xe32e, 0xf2a7, 0xc03c, 0xd1b5,
    0x2942, 0x38cb, 0x0a50, 0x1bd9, 0x6f66, 0x7eef, 0x4c74, 0x5dfd,
    0xb58b, 0xa402, 0x9699, 0x8710, 0xf3af, 0xe226, 0xd0bd, 0xc134,
    0x39c3, 0x284a, 0x1ad1, 0x0b58, 0x7fe7, 0x6e6e, 0x5cf5, 0x4d7c,
    0xc60c, 0xd785, 0xe51e, 0xf497, 0x8028, 0x91a1, 0xa33a, 0xb2b3,
    0x4a44, 0x5bcd, 0x6956, 0x78df, 0x0c60, 0x1de9, 0x2f72, 0x3efb,
    0xd68d, 0xc704, 0xf59f, 0xe416, 0x90a9, 0x8120, 0xb3bb, 0xa232,
```

```
      0x5ac5, 0x4b4c, 0x79d7, 0x685e, 0x1ce1, 0x0d68, 0x3ff3, 0x2e7a,
      0xe70e, 0xf687, 0xc41c, 0xd595, 0xa12a, 0xb0a3, 0x8238, 0x93b1,
      0x6b46, 0x7acf, 0x4854, 0x59dd, 0x2d62, 0x3ceb, 0x0e70, 0x1ff9,
      0xf78f, 0xe606, 0xd49d, 0xc514, 0xb1ab, 0xa022, 0x92b9, 0x8330,
      0x7bc7, 0x6a4e, 0x58d5, 0x495c, 0x3de3, 0x2c6a, 0x1ef1, 0x0f78
};

static uint32 fcstab_32[256] = {
      0x00000000, 0x77073096, 0xee0e612c, 0x990951ba,
      0x076dc419, 0x706af48f, 0xe963a535, 0x9e6495a3,
      0x0edb8832, 0x79dcb8a4, 0xe0d5e91e, 0x97d2d988,
      0x09b64c2b, 0x7eb17cbd, 0xe7b82d07, 0x90bf1d91,
      0x1db71064, 0x6ab020f2, 0xf3b97148, 0x84be41de,
      0x1adad47d, 0x6ddde4eb, 0xf4d4b551, 0x83d385c7,
      0x136c9856, 0x646ba8c0, 0xfd62f97a, 0x8a65c9ec,
      0x14015c4f, 0x63066cd9, 0xfa0f3d63, 0x8d080df5,
      0x3b6e20c8, 0x4c69105e, 0xd56041e4, 0xa2677172,
      0x3c03e4d1, 0x4b04d447, 0xd20d85fd, 0xa50ab56b,
      0x35b5a8fa, 0x42b2986c, 0xdbbbc9d6, 0xacbcf940,
      0x32d86ce3, 0x45df5c75, 0xdcd60dcf, 0xabd13d59,
      0x26d930ac, 0x51de003a, 0xc8d75180, 0xbfd06116,
      0x21b4f4b5, 0x56b3c423, 0xcfba9599, 0xb8bda50f,
      0x2802b89e, 0x5f058808, 0xc60cd9b2, 0xb10be924,
      0x2f6f7c87, 0x58684c11, 0xc1611dab, 0xb6662d3d,
      0x76dc4190, 0x01db7106, 0x98d220bc, 0xefd5102a,
      0x71b18589, 0x06b6b51f, 0x9fbfe4a5, 0xe8b8d433,
      0x7807c9a2, 0x0f00f934, 0x9609a88e, 0xe10e9818,
      0x7f6a0dbb, 0x086d3d2d, 0x91646c97, 0xe6635c01,
      0x6b6b51f4, 0x1c6c6162, 0x856530d8, 0xf262004e,
      0x6c0695ed, 0x1b01a57b, 0x8208f4c1, 0xf50fc457,
      0x65b0d9c6, 0x12b7e950, 0x8bbeb8ea, 0xfcb9887c,
      0x62dd1ddf, 0x15da2d49, 0x8cd37cf3, 0xfbd44c65,
      0x4db26158, 0x3ab551ce, 0xa3bc0074, 0xd4bb30e2,
      0x4adfa541, 0x3dd895d7, 0xa4d1c46d, 0xd3d6f4fb,
      0x4369e96a, 0x346ed9fc, 0xad678846, 0xda60b8d0,
      0x44042d73, 0x33031de5, 0xaa0a4c5f, 0xdd0d7cc9,
      0x5005713c, 0x270241aa, 0xbe0b1010, 0xc90c2086,
      0x5768b525, 0x206f85b3, 0xb966d409, 0xce61e49f,
      0x5edef90e, 0x29d9c998, 0xb0d09822, 0xc7d7a8b4,
      0x59b33d17, 0x2eb40d81, 0xb7bd5c3b, 0xc0ba6cad,
      0xedb88320, 0x9abfb3b6, 0x03b6e20c, 0x74b1d29a,
      0xead54739, 0x9dd277af, 0x04db2615, 0x73dc1683,
      0xe3630b12, 0x94643b84, 0x0d6d6a3e, 0x7a6a5aa8,
      0xe40ecf0b, 0x9309ff9d, 0x0a00ae27, 0x7d079eb1,
      0xf00f9344, 0x8708a3d2, 0x1e01f268, 0x6906c2fe,
      0xf762575d, 0x806567cb, 0x196c3671, 0x6e6b06e7,
      0xfed41b76, 0x89d32be0, 0x10da7a5a, 0x67dd4acc,
      0xf9b9df6f, 0x8ebeeff9, 0x17b7be43, 0x60b08ed5,
      0xd6d6a3e8, 0xa1d1937e, 0x38d8c2c4, 0x4fdff252,
      0xd1bb67f1, 0xa6bc5767, 0x3fb506dd, 0x48b2364b,
      0xd80d2bda, 0xaf0a1b4c, 0x36034af6, 0x41047a60,
      0xdf60efc3, 0xa867df55, 0x316e8eef, 0x4669be79,
      0xcb61b38c, 0xbc66831a, 0x256fd2a0, 0x5268e236,
      0xcc0c7795, 0xbb0b4703, 0x220216b9, 0x5505262f,
      0xc5ba3bbe, 0xb2bd0b28, 0x2bb45a92, 0x5cb36a04,
      0xc2d7ffa7, 0xb5d0cf31, 0x2cd99e8b, 0x5bdeae1d,
      0x9b64c2b0, 0xec63f226, 0x756aa39c, 0x026d930a,
      0x9c0906a9, 0xeb0e363f, 0x72076785, 0x05005713,
      0x95bf4a82, 0xe2b87a14, 0x7bb12bae, 0x0cb61b38,
      0x92d28e9b, 0xe5d5be0d, 0x7cdcefb7, 0x0bdbdf21,
      0x86d3d2d4, 0xf1d4e242, 0x68ddb3f8, 0x1fda836e,
      0x81be16cd, 0xf6b9265b, 0x6fb077e1, 0x18b74777,
      0x88085ae6, 0xff0f6a70, 0x66063bca, 0x11010b5c,
      0x8f659eff, 0xf862ae69, 0x616bffd3, 0x166ccf45,
      0xa00ae278, 0xd70dd2ee, 0x4e048354, 0x3903b3c2,
      0xa7672661, 0xd06016f7, 0x4969474d, 0x3e6e77db,
      0xaed16a4a, 0xd9d65adc, 0x40df0b66, 0x37d83bf0,
      0xa9bcae53, 0xdebb9ec5, 0x47b2cf7f, 0x30b5ffe9,
      0xbdbdf21c, 0xcabac28a, 0x53b39330, 0x24b4a3a6,
```

```
    0xbad03605, 0xcdd70693, 0x54de5729, 0x23d967bf,
    0xb3667a2e, 0xc4614ab8, 0x5d681b02, 0x2a6f2b94,
    0xb40bbe37, 0xc30c8ea1, 0x5a05df1b, 0x2d02ef8d
};

#define PPPINITFCS16 0xFFFF
#define PPPINITFCS32 0xFFFFFFFF
#define PPPGOODFCS16 0xF0B8
#define PPPGOODFCS32 0xDEBB20E3

#define PPP_FRAME 0x7E
#define PPP_ESCAPE 0x7D
#define PPP_ESCAPE_BIT 0x20

struct ahdlc_state {
  /* User controlled variables. */
  octet tx_accm[32],rx_accm[32];
  char usecrc32;

  /* Internal state data. */
  struct queue *tx_queue,*rx_queue;
  char *rx_buffer,*rx_bufp;
  char *tx_buffer,*tx_bufp;
  int rx_octets,tx_octets;
  uint16 rx_crc,tx_crc;
  uint32 rx_crcl,tx_crcl;
  char escaped,escaping;
  char outputsync;
  char needstart;
  char localfcs[4];
};

/*
 * This function allocates a state structure for AHDLC.  This
 * structure is used to hold all of the variables necessary for AHDLC
 * operation across multiple invocations from the serial interrupt
 * handlers.
 *
 * The 'tosend' argument is a pointer to a system queue where packets
 * waiting to be sent are held.  It is the responsibility of the
 * caller to detect that the tosend queue is empty and to start the
 * transmission process by calling the output routine once.  As long
 * as the queue still has data, the output routine will send packets.
 *
 * The "fromreceive" argument is also a pointer to a system queue.
 * Packets received from the serial interface will be placed there.
 * The caller is responsible for removing packets from this queue.
 * This could be triggered by the "queue_append" routine, depending on
 * system implementation.
 */
void *
ahdlc_create(struct queue *tosend, struct queue *fromreceive)
{
  struct ahdlc_state *as;
  int i;

  as = (struct ahdlc_state *)malloc(sizeof(*as));
  if (as != NULL) {
    memset(as,'\0',sizeof(*as));
    as->tx_queue = tosend;
    as->rx_queue = fromreceive;
    for (i = 0; i < 4; i++) {
      as->tx_accm[i] = 0xFF;
      as->rx_accm[i] = 0xFF;
    }
    as->tx_accm[PPP_FRAME/8] |= 1<<(PPP_FRAME&7);
    as->tx_accm[PPP_ESCAPE/8] |= 1<<(PPP_ESCAPE&7);
    as->rx_bufp = as->rx_buffer = buffer_fetch(MAXIMUM_MRU);
    as->rx_crc = PPPINITFCS16;
```

```
      as->rx_crcl = PPPINITFCS32;
      as->needstart = 1;
  }
  return (void *)as;
}

/*
 * This function removes storage associated with an AHDLC link.  I/O
 * on the link itself should have be stopped before this function is
 * called.
 */
void
ahdlc_destroy(void *statep)
{
  struct ahdlc_state *as = (struct ahdlc_state *)statep;

  if (as != NULL) {
    buffer_release(as->rx_buffer);
    if (as->tx_buffer != NULL)
      buffer_release(as->tx_buffer);
    free(statep);
  }
}

/*
 * This routine handles a block of data received from the serial
 * interface.  The serial driver must keep track of the AHDLC state
 * pointer associated with that interface and deliver it to this
 * routine.  When packets are correctly received, this routine will
 * place them on the PPP input queue.
 */
void
ahdlc_receive(void *statep, char *buffer, int count)
{
  struct ahdlc_state *as = (struct ahdlc_state *)statep;
  octet chr;

  while (--count >= 0) {
    chr = 0xFF&(int)*buffer++;

    /*
     * If ACCM bit is set, then this shouldn't be seen.  Drop it.
     * This isn't an error, though.  The receiver may be transparent
     * to control characters which are used for purposes other than
     * PPP.
     */
    if (as->rx_accm[chr/8] & (1 << (chr&7)))
      continue;

    if (as->escaped) {
      /* Handle the escape mechanism. */
      as->escaped = 0;
      if (chr == PPP_FRAME)
        goto reset_buffer;
      chr ^= PPP_ESCAPE_BIT;
    } else if (chr == PPP_FRAME) {
      /* End of frame. */
      if ((as->usecrc32 && as->rx_crcl == PPPGOODFCS32) ||
          (!as->usecrc32 && as->rx_crc == PPPGOODFCS16)) {
        queue_append(as->rx_queue,as->rx_buffer,
                     as->rx_octets - (as->usecrc32 ? 4 : 2));
        as->rx_buffer = buffer_fetch(MAXIMUM_MRU);
      } else if (as->rx_octets > 3)
        goto notify_error;
      goto reset_buffer;
    } else if (chr == PPP_ESCAPE) {
      as->escaped = 1;
      continue;
    }
```

```
    /* If we're here, then we have an input data octet. */
    if (as->rx_octets >= MAXIMUM_MRU) {
    notify_error:
      /*
       * Notify PPP of receive error here!  Some protocols, like VJ
       * compressed TCP/IP, work much better when receive errors are
       * caught and reported by the driver.
       */
    reset_buffer:
      as->rx_bufp = as->rx_buffer;
      as->rx_crc = PPPINITFCS16;
      as->rx_crcl = PPPINITFCS32;
      as->rx_octets = 0;
    } else {
      /*
       * On most systems, it's faster to just calculate both of these
       * than to attempt to conditionally calculate one based on the
       * type of CRC negotiated.
       */
      as->rx_crc = (as->rx_crc >> 8) ^ fcstab_16[(as->rx_crc ^ chr) & 0xFF];
      as->rx_crcl = (as->rx_crcl >> 8)^fcstab_32[(as->rx_crcl^ chr) & 0xFF];
      *as->rx_bufp++ = (char)chr;
      as->rx_octets++;
    }
  }
}


/*
 * This routine will place up to 'maxcount' characters for
 * transmission on the serial link in the given buffer.  It should be
 * called by a FIFO-empty interrupt on the serial link.  It returns a
 * count of the actual number of characters written to the buffer,
 * which may be less than the maximum given if no more data from PPP
 * is ready to be sent.
 *
 * When PPP places a message on the output queue, it must determine if
 * the queue was empty when it did this.  If so, then the PPP output
 * routine should arrange to have the serial driver call this routine
 * once to get the ball rolling.
 */
int
ahdlc_transmit(void *statep, char *buffer, int maxcount)
{
  struct ahdlc_state *as = (struct ahdlc_state *)statep;
  int omaxcount = maxcount;
  octet chr;

  while (--maxcount >= 0) {

    /* If we need a new buffer to transmit, then go get one from PPP. */
    if (as->tx_buffer == NULL) {
      /* If the user is trying to synchronize, then break out here. */
      if (as->outputsync)
        break;
      queue_fetch(as->tx_queue,&as->tx_buffer,&as->tx_octets);
      if (as->tx_buffer == NULL || as->tx_octets == 0) {
        /* Nothing left in queue; will need PPP frame marker next time. */
        as->needstart = 1;
        break;
      }
      as->tx_bufp = as->tx_buffer;
      as->tx_crc = PPPINITFCS16;
      as->tx_crcl = PPPINITFCS32;
      /* If we need a frame marker at the beginning, then insert it now. */
      if (as->needstart) {
        as->needstart = 0;
        *buffer++ = (char)PPP_FRAME;
        continue;
      }
```

```
    }

    if (as->tx_octets == 0) {
      /* If no more octets of data left, then set up to send the CRC. */
      if (as->usecrc32) {
        as->tx_crcl = ~as->tx_crcl;
        as->localfcs[0] = as->tx_crcl & 0xFF;
        as->localfcs[1] = (as->tx_crcl >> 8) & 0xFF;
        as->localfcs[2] = (as->tx_crcl >> 16) & 0xFF;
        as->localfcs[3] = (as->tx_crcl >> 24) & 0xFF;
      } else {
        as->tx_crc = ~as->tx_crc;
        as->localfcs[0] = as->tx_crc & 0xFF;
        as->localfcs[1] = (as->tx_crc >> 8) & 0xFF;
        as->tx_octets = -2;
      }
      /*
       * Note that the CRC is sent as though it were data -- we have
       * to escape characters in the CRC also!  Neglecting this is a
       * common AHDLC implementation bug.
       */
      as->tx_bufp = as->localfcs;
    } else if (as->tx_octets == -4) {
      /* All out of CRC octets; give back the buffer and end the frame. */
      buffer_release(as->tx_buffer);
      as->tx_buffer = NULL;
      *buffer++ = (char)PPP_FRAME;
      continue;
    }

    if (as->escaping) {
      as->escaping = 0;
      *buffer++ = *as->tx_bufp++ ^ PPP_ESCAPE_BIT;
      as->tx_octets--;
    } else {
      chr = 0xFF&(int)*as->tx_bufp;
      as->tx_crc = (as->tx_crc >> 8) ^ fcstab_16[(as->tx_crc ^ chr) & 0xFF];
      as->tx_crcl = (as->tx_crcl >> 8)^fcstab_32[(as->tx_crcl^ chr) & 0xFF];
      if (as->tx_accm[chr/8] & (1 << (chr&7))) {
        *buffer++ = (char)PPP_ESCAPE;
        as->escaping = 1;
      } else {
        *buffer++ = (char)chr;
        as->tx_bufp++;
        as->tx_octets--;
      }
    }
  }
}

/*
 * This block is only here to support the optional synchronization
 * routine below.  It is not necessary for proper operation.  It
 * relies on the BSD kernel sleep/wakeup() mechanism to operate.
 */
if (as->tx_buffer == NULL && as->outputsync) {
  as->needstart = 1;
  as->outputsync = 0;
  wakeup(as);
}

/* Calculate number of bytes in buffer and return. */
return omaxcount-maxcount-1;
}

/*
 * This is an optional routine which achieves synchronization with the
 * output function.  This can be necessary to change some variables,
 * such as the ACCM.  It relies on the BSD kernel sleep()/wakeup()
 * mechanism.  If you are programming at the normal user level, these
```

```
 * functions do not exist.
 */
void
ahdlc_sync_wait(void *statep)
{
  struct ahdlc_state *as = (struct ahdlc_state *)statep;

  as->outputsync = 1;
  while (as->outputsync)
    sleep(as,0);
}

/*
 * This routine sets the standard PPP receive and transmit ACCM.  It
 * should be called by LCP.  Again, like the sync routine above, it
 * assumes a number of BSD kernel functions.
 */
void
ahdlc_set_accm(void *statep, uint32 rx_accm, uint32 tx_accm)
{
  struct ahdlc_state *as = (struct ahdlc_state *)statep;

  interrupts_off();
  ahdlc_sync_wait(statep);
  as->rx_accm[0] = rx_accm & 0xFF;
  as->rx_accm[1] = (rx_accm >> 8) & 0xFF;
  as->rx_accm[2] = (rx_accm >> 16) & 0xFF;
  as->rx_accm[3] = (rx_accm >> 24) & 0xFF;
  as->tx_accm[0] = tx_accm & 0xFF;
  as->tx_accm[1] = (tx_accm >> 8) & 0xFF;
  as->tx_accm[2] = (tx_accm >> 16) & 0xFF;
  as->tx_accm[3] = (tx_accm >> 24) & 0xFF;
  interrupts_on();
}

/*
 * This is an example of a wrapper routine to change the CRC mode
 * flag.  Note that because both CRCs are always calculated, no
 * synchronization is necessary.
 */
void
ahdlc_set_crc_mode(void *statep, int mode)
{
  struct ahdlc_state *as = (struct ahdlc_state *)statep;

  as->usecrc32 = mode;
}
```

Appendix

B

MP Fragmentation

The following code implements a simple MP fragment assembler/disassembler for a PPP system. A copy of this code is available from my Web site:

```
http://id.wing.net/People/carlson/ppp
```

```
/*
 * Multilink PPP example code.
 *
 * Assumptions:
 *
 *        Input data is in linear buffers, which probably
 *        isn't the case for many implementations, and input
 *        buffers have sufficient leading and trailing padding
 *        to allow for any expansion necessary.
 *
 *        Strict adherence to RFC 1661 is desired, which may not
 *        necessarily be the case for the protocol field.
 *
 *        Underlying machine has 8-bit bytes and a fairly modern
 *        architecture.
 */

#include <stdlib.h>
#include <syslog.h>

typedef unsigned char octet;
typedef unsigned short uint16;
typedef unsigned long uint32;
typedef int BOOLEAN;

/* Contains information for a single fragment awaiting reassembly. */
struct mp_fragment {
  struct mp_fragment *next;
  int length;
  uint32 seq;
  octet flags;
  octet data[1];
};

/* State data needed for MP level between bundle and links */
struct mp_state {
  struct mp_state *next;
  struct ppp_link *lptr,*links,*in_on,*next_out_link;
  int numlinks;
  BOOLEAN snd_short_seq,rcv_short_seq;
  uint32 send_seq;
  struct mp_fragment *frags;
};

/* Individual PPP link or bundle level */
struct ppp_link {
  struct ppp_link *next;         /* Next link when using MP */
  struct xcp_state *xcp_list;       /* Pointer to list of protocols */
  int frame_drops;               /* Illegal frames discarded */
  void *handle;
  void (*link_output)(struct ppp_link *link, octet *outdata, int outlen,
                  uint16 proto);
  void (*user_output)(void *handle, octet *outdata, int outlen);
  BOOLEAN acfc_in, acfc_out;
  BOOLEAN pfc_in, pfc_out;
  struct mp_state *mp;
  BOOLEAN ecp_in_use,ccp_in_use;
  int mtu;
  uint32 seq;
  char *peername;                /* Authenticated peer name, if any */
  char *endpoint;                /* Peer's reported endpoint discriminator */
  int ep_size,pn_size;
};

/* LCP or NCP state */
struct xcp_state {
  struct xcp_state *next;
  struct ppp_link *link;
  enum { Initial, Starting, Closed, Stopped, Closing, Stopping,
```

```
          ReqSent, AckRcvd, AckSent, Opened } state;
    octet id_number;
    octet conf_req_id;
    uint16 proto;
    void (*handler)(struct xcp_state *xcp, octet *indata, int inlen);
    void (*send_data)(struct xcp_state *xcp, octet *outdata, int outlen);
};

/* External entry points.  See code below for usage. */
extern char *ecp_decrypt(struct xcp_state *xcp, char *indata, int *inlen);
extern char *ccp_uncompress(struct xcp_state *xcp, char *indata, int *inlen);
extern void ccp_uncompressed(struct xcp_state *xcp, uint16 proto,
                             char *indata, int inlen);
extern void lcp_handler(struct xcp_state *xcp, octet *indata, int inlen);

/* Forward declarations. */
void destroy_ppp_link(void *link);
void *create_ppp_link(void *handle,void (*outhandler)());
void *add_xcp(struct ppp_link *lptr, uint16 proto, void (*handler)(),
              void (*sender)());
void destroy_xcp(struct xcp_state *xcp);

struct mp_state *global_mp_list = NULL;

#define PPP_PROTO_MP            0x003D
#define PPP_PROTO_EP            0x0053
#define PPP_PROTO_EP_LINK       0x0055
#define PPP_PROTO_CP_LINK       0x00FB
#define PPP_PROTO_CP            0x00FD
#define PPP_PROTO_ECP           0x8053
#define PPP_PROTO_ECP_LINK      0x8055
#define PPP_PROTO_CCP_LINK      0x80FB
#define PPP_PROTO_CCP           0x80FD
#define PPP_PROTO_LCP           0xC021
#define PPP_PROTO_PAP           0xC023
#define PPP_PROTO_CHAP          0xC223
#define PROTO_REJ        8
#define MIN_FRAG_SIZE          200
#define MP_BEGIN 0x80
#define MP_END 0x40
#define MAX_MRRU         2048

/*
 * Locate a given NCP handler by PPP protocol ID.
 */
static struct xcp_state *
find_xcp(struct ppp_link *lptr, uint16 proto)
{
  struct xcp_state *xcp;

  for (xcp = lptr->xcp_list; xcp != NULL; xcp = xcp->next)
    if (xcp->proto == proto)
      break;
  return xcp;
}

/*
 * Send an LCP reject for an unknown protocol.
 */
static void
send_lcp_protocol_reject(struct ppp_link *lptr, uint16 proto,
                         octet *indata, int inlen)
{
  struct xcp_state *xcp;

  xcp = find_xcp(lptr,PPP_PROTO_LCP);
  if (xcp == NULL || xcp->state != Opened)
    return;
  syslog(LOG_DEBUG,"Unknown protocol %04X; rejecting.",proto);
```

```
    /* Add LCP protocol reject header */
    indata -= 6;
    indata[0] = PROTO_REJ;
    indata[1] = ++xcp->id_number;
    indata[2] = inlen >> 8;
    indata[3] = inlen & 0xFF;
    indata[4] = proto >> 8;
    indata[5] = proto & 0xFF;
    inlen += 6;
    (*xcp->send_data)(xcp,indata,inlen);
}

/*
 * Next level handler above HDLC or AHDLC.  Assumes that CRC has been
 * verified and removed, and that all escaping (transparency)
 * characters have been handled.  The PPP processing continues here by
 * decoding the address and control fields, then by demultiplexing
 * based on the PPP protocol number.
 */
void
link_receive(struct ppp_link *lptr, octet *indata, int inlen)
{
  uint16 proto;
  struct xcp_state *xcp;

  if (inlen < 2)
    return;

  /* Handle address and control field compression */
  if (lptr->acfc_in) {
    if (indata[0] == 0xFF && indata[1] == 0x03) {
      indata += 2;
      inlen -= 2;
    }
  } else {
    if (indata[0] != 0xFF || indata[1] != 0x03) {
      lptr->frame_drops++;
      return;
    }
    indata += 2;
    inlen -= 2;
  }

  /* Handle protocol field compression */
  if (lptr->pfc_in) {
    if (inlen < 1)
      return;
    proto = *indata++;
    inlen--;
    if (!(proto & 1)) {
      if (inlen < 1)
        return;
      proto = (proto << 8) | *indata++;
      inlen--;
    }
  } else {
    if (inlen < 2)
      return;
    proto = (indata[0] << 8) | indata[1];
    inlen -= 2;
    indata += 2;
  }

  /* Discard frames with illegal protocol fields. */
  if ((proto & 0x101) != 1) {
    lptr->frame_drops++;
    return;
  }
```

```
/*
 * If per-link ECP is used, then we have to do this first.  This
 * must be done here because demultiplexing when MP is in use is
 * done at the MP bundle level, not at the link level.
 *
 * For better security, it may be desirable to discard any non-LCP,
 * non-ECP packets when ECP is in open state.  This provides some
 * protection against attackers who are able to insert data on the
 * line.
 */
if (lptr->ecp_in_use && proto == PPP_PROTO_EP_LINK) {
  xcp = find_xcp(lptr,proto);
  indata = ecp_decrypt(xcp,indata,&inlen);
  if (indata == NULL)
    return;
  if (inlen < 1)
    return;
  proto = *indata++;
  inlen—;
  if (!(proto & 1)) {
    if (inlen < 1)
      return;
    proto = (proto << 8) | *indata++;
    inlen—;
  }
}


/*
 * If we're doing per-link CCP, then we have to do it before normal
 * demultiplexing because CCP usually needs to inspect all data and
 * because demultiplexing on an MP system is done at the bundle
 * level.
 */
if (lptr->ccp_in_use) {
  xcp = find_xcp(lptr,PPP_PROTO_CP_LINK);
  if (proto == PPP_PROTO_CP_LINK) {
    indata = ccp_uncompress(xcp,indata,&inlen);
    if (indata == NULL)
      return;
    if (inlen < 1)
      return;
    proto = *indata++;
    inlen—;
    if (!(proto & 1)) {
      if (inlen < 1)
        return;
      proto = (proto << 8) | *indata++;
      inlen—;
    }
  } else
    ccp_uncompressed(xcp,proto,indata,inlen);
}


/*
 * If we're a link in an MP bundle, then send to NCP at bundle level
 * when necessary.  Most LCP messages should be handled at the link
 * level.  Protocol-Reject (code 8), though, should go to the bundle
 * level, since it is used to shut down NCPs.  One might consider
 * sending the Time-Remaining message to the bundle level as well,
 * depending on system architecture.
 *
 * Note that LCP should disconnect this link from the bundle if it
 * leaves the Open state.
 */
if (lptr->mp != NULL &&
    (proto != PPP_PROTO_LCP || indata[0] == 8)) {
  lptr->mp->in_on = lptr;
  xcp = find_xcp(lptr->mp->lptr,proto);
```

```
    } else
      xcp = find_xcp(lptr,proto);

    /* Dispatch to appropriate handler now. */
    if (xcp != NULL)
      (*xcp->handler)(xcp,indata,inlen);
    else
      /* No handler for this protocol, log it and reject it. */
      send_lcp_protocol_reject(lptr,proto,indata,inlen);
}

/*
 * Add address, control, and protocol fields.
 */
static int
add_acf_and_pf(struct ppp_link *lptr, octet *outdata, uint16 proto)
{
  octet *ood = outdata;

  if (lptr->pfc_out && (proto & 0xFF00) == 0)
    *--outdata = proto & 0xFF;
  else {
    *--outdata = proto & 0xFF;
    *--outdata = proto >> 8;
  }

  if (!lptr->acfc_out && proto != PPP_PROTO_LCP) {
    *--outdata = 0x03;
    *--outdata = 0xFF;
  }

  return ood-outdata;
}

/*
 * Standard (non-MP) PPP output routine.
 */
static void
normal_output(struct ppp_link *link, octet *outdata, int outlen, uint16 proto)
{
  int i;

  i = add_acf_and_pf(link,outdata,proto);
  outdata -= i;
  outlen += i;
  (*link->user_output)(link->handle,outdata,outlen);
}

/*
 * This routine replaces the normal link_output routine for the bundle
 * level PPP link.
 */
static void
mp_output(struct ppp_link *lptr, octet *outdata, int outlen, uint16 proto)
{
  struct mp_state *mp = lptr->mp;
  struct ppp_link *ind_lptr;
  int fragsize,len,hdrsize;
  octet flags;

  if (proto <= 0xFF) {
    *--outdata = proto;
    outlen++;
  } else {
    *--outdata = proto & 0xFF;
    *--outdata = proto >> 8;
    outlen += 2;
  }
  if (outlen < MIN_FRAG_SIZE)
```

```
      fragsize = outlen;
    else
      fragsize = (outlen+mp->numlinks-1)/mp->numlinks;
  if (mp->snd_short_seq)
    hdrsize = 2;
  else
    hdrsize = 4;
  flags = MP_BEGIN;
  ind_lptr = mp->next_out_link;
  while (outlen > 0) {
    if (ind_lptr == NULL) {
      ind_lptr = mp->links;
      if (ind_lptr == NULL)
        break;
    }
    len = outlen;
    if (len > fragsize)
      len = fragsize;
    if (len > ind_lptr->mtu-hdrsize)
      len = ind_lptr->mtu-hdrsize;
    if ((outlen -= len) == 0)
      flags |= MP_END;
    *—outdata = mp->send_seq & 0xFF;
    if (mp->snd_short_seq)
      *—outdata = ((mp->send_seq>>8) & 0xF) | flags;
    else {
      *—outdata = (mp->send_seq>>8) & 0xFF;
      *—outdata = (mp->send_seq>>16) & 0xFF;
      *—outdata = flags;
      len += 2;
    }
    len += 2;
    (*ind_lptr->link_output)(ind_lptr,outdata,len,PPP_PROTO_MP);
    flags = 0;
    outdata += len;
    mp->send_seq++;
    ind_lptr = ind_lptr->next;
  }
  mp->next_out_link = ind_lptr;
}

/*
 * MP input handler.  Does reassembly and demultiplexing.
 *
 * The modular arithmetic tests done are a little tricky, so they're
 * commented with the equivalent regular arithmetic test.
 *
 * Comments indicating where the PPP system can be notified of lost
 * packets are also included, as are notes identifying peer
 * misbehavior.
 *
 * "link" is bundle level state pointer.  "lptr" is link level for
 * received data.
 */
static void
mp_handler(struct xcp_state *mpxcp, octet *indata, int inlen)
{
  struct ppp_link *lptr,*link = mpxcp->link, *ltmp;
  struct mp_state *mp = link->mp;
  struct mp_fragment *frag,*newfrag,*start,*nextf;
  int flags;
  uint32 newseq,thisseq,sbit,smask,minseq;
  static char buffer[MAX_MRRU];
  char *bp;
  uint16 proto;
  struct xcp_state *xcp;

  /* Get pointer to link on which this message came in. */
  lptr = mp->in_on;
```

```
/* Decode MP flags and sequence number. */
flags = indata[0];
if (mp->rcv_short_seq) {
  if (inlen < 2 || (indata[0] & 0x30) != 0) {
    syslog(LOG_NOTICE,"corrupted MP header");
    return;
  }
  newseq = ((indata[0] & 0xF) << 8) | indata[1];
  indata += 2;
  inlen -= 2;
  sbit = 0x800;
} else {
  if (inlen < 4 || (indata[0] & 0x3F) != 0) {
    syslog(LOG_NOTICE,"corrupted MP header");
    return;
  }
  newseq = (indata[1] << 16) | (indata[2] << 8) | indata[3];
  indata += 4;
  inlen -= 4;
  sbit = 0x800000;
}
smask = (sbit << 1) - 1;

/* Find minimum sequence number over all links and save at bundle level.
 */
minseq = lptr->seq = newseq;
for (ltmp = mp->links; ltmp != NULL; ltmp = ltmp->next)
  /* if ltmp->seq < minseq */
  if (((ltmp->seq-minseq) & sbit) != 0)
    minseq = ltmp->seq;
link->seq = minseq;

/* Create fragment record for this new message. */
newfrag = (struct mp_fragment *)malloc(sizeof(*newfrag)+inlen);
if (newfrag == NULL) {
  syslog(LOG_ERR,"MP storage allocation failure; fragment dropped.");
  if (flags & MP_END)
    /* Packet has been dropped. */
    link->frame_drops++;
  return;
}
newfrag->flags = flags;
newfrag->seq = newseq;
newfrag->length = inlen;
memcpy(newfrag->data,indata,inlen);

/* If this new fragment is before the first one, then enqueue it now. */
if ((frag = mp->frags) == NULL ||
    /* newseq < frag->seq */
    ((newseq-frag->seq) & sbit) != 0) {
  newfrag->next = frag;
  mp->frags = newfrag;
  newfrag = NULL;
}

start = NULL;
frag = mp->frags;
if (frag->flags & MP_BEGIN)
  start = frag;
mp->frags = NULL;
while (start != NULL || newfrag != NULL) {

  thisseq = frag->seq;
  nextf = frag->next;

  /* Drop any duplicate fragments */
  if (newfrag != NULL && thisseq == newseq) {
    free(newfrag);
```

```
      newfrag = NULL;
}

/* Insert new fragment before next element if possible. */
if (newfrag != NULL &&
    (nextf == NULL ||
     /* newseq < nextf->seq */
     ((newseq-nextf->seq) & sbit) != 0)) {
  newfrag->next = nextf;
  frag->next = nextf = newfrag;
  newfrag = NULL;
}

/* Check for start */
if (start != NULL) {
  if (start != frag && (frag->flags & MP_BEGIN)) {
    syslog(LOG_NOTICE,"new BEGIN flag with no prior END");
    while (start != frag) {
      nextf = start->next;
      free(start);
      start = nextf;
    }
    nextf = frag->next;
    /* Packet has been dropped. */
    link->frame_drops++;
  }
  /* If thisseq <= minseq */
} else if (((minseq-thisseq) & sbit) == 0)
  if (frag->flags & MP_BEGIN)
    start = frag;
  else {
    if (frag->flags & MP_END)
      /* Packet has been dropped. */
      link->frame_drops++;
    free(frag);
    frag = nextf;
    continue;
  }

if (start != NULL && (frag->flags & MP_END)) {
  /*
   * This next statement is not actually necessary, but can be
   * helpful in multitasking systems where delivery of a packet
   * may cause a task switch.
   */
  mp->frags = nextf;

  /* Reassemble packet into local buffer */
  bp = buffer;
  minseq = link->seq = (thisseq+1)&smask;
  while (start != nextf) {
    frag = start->next;
    if (bp != NULL && (bp-buffer)+start->length <= MAX_MRRU) {
      if (start->length > 0) {
        memcpy(bp,start->data,start->length);
        bp += start->length;
      }
    } else
      bp = NULL;
    free(start);
    start = frag;
  }
  start = NULL;
  frag = NULL;

  /* "bp" is used as a flag — it's set to NULL when packet is dropped.*/
  /* At this point, it's null if the packet was dropped due to MRRU. */

  /* All reassembled and unfragmented data gets dispatched. */
```

```
if (bp != NULL && bp > buffer+1) {
  inlen = bp-buffer;
  bp = buffer;
  proto = *bp++;
  inlen--;
  if (!(proto & 1)) {
    proto = (proto << 8) | *bp++;
    inlen--;
  }

  /* Discard frames with illegal protocol fields or missing data. */
  if (inlen <= 0 || (proto & 0x101) != 1)
    bp = NULL;

  /*
   * If we're doing bundle level ECP, then we process it first.
   * This is done to make the ECP code symmetric with respect to
   * the link level handling.
   */
  if (bp != NULL && link->ecp_in_use && proto == PPP_PROTO_EP) {
    xcp = find_xcp(link,PPP_PROTO_EP);
    bp = ecp_decrypt(xcp,bp,&inlen);
    if (inlen < 1)
      bp = NULL;
    if (bp != NULL) {
      proto = *bp++;
      inlen--;
      if (!(proto & 1)) {
        if (inlen < 1)
          bp = NULL;
        else {
          proto = (proto << 8) | *bp++;
          inlen--;
        }
      }
    }
  }

  /*
   * If we're doing bundle level CCP, then we have to do it
   * before demultiplexing because CCP usually needs to inspect
   * all data.
   */
  if (bp != NULL && link->ccp_in_use) {
    xcp = find_xcp(link,PPP_PROTO_CP);
    if (proto == PPP_PROTO_CP) {
      bp = ccp_uncompress(xcp,bp,&inlen);
      if (inlen < 1)
        bp = NULL;
      if (bp != NULL) {
        proto = *bp++;
        inlen--;
        if (!(proto & 1)) {
          if (inlen < 1)
            bp = NULL;
          else {
            proto = (proto << 8) | *bp++;
            inlen--;
          }
        }
      }
    } else
      ccp_uncompressed(xcp,proto,bp,inlen);
  }

  if (bp != NULL) {
    /* Dispatch to appropriate handler now. */
    xcp = find_xcp(link,proto);
    if (xcp != NULL)
```

```
                (*xcp->handler)(xcp,bp,inlen);
            else
                /* No handler for this protocol, log it and reject it. */
                send_lcp_protocol_reject(lptr,proto,bp,inlen);
          }
      }
      if (bp == NULL)
        link->frame_drops++;
      mp->frags = NULL;
    }

    /*
     * If the next one is not contiguous then we don't have a complete
     * packet.
     */
    if (nextf == NULL || ((thisseq+1)&smask) != nextf->seq) {
      /* if thisseq < minseq */
      if (((thisseq-minseq) & sbit) != 0) {
        /* Packet has been dropped. */
        link->frame_drops++;
        if (start != NULL)
          while (start != nextf) {
            frag = start->next;
            free(start);
            start = frag;
          }
        frag = NULL;
      } else if (mp->frags == NULL)
        mp->frags = start;
      start = NULL;
    } else
      /* If we just reassembled and the next one is here, then do it. */
      if (frag == NULL)
        if (nextf->flags & MP_BEGIN)
          start = nextf;
        else
          syslog(LOG_NOTICE,"END flag with no following BEGIN");
    if (start == NULL && frag != NULL && mp->frags == NULL)
      mp->frags = frag;
    frag = nextf;
  }
  if (mp->frags == NULL)
    mp->frags = frag;
}


/*
 * This is called after a link goes through LCP and authentication,
 * but before any NCPs begin running.  If the link is part of a bundle,
 * then it is joined, otherwise a new bundle is created.  Assumes that
 * PPP MRRU has been negotiated.
 *
 * Returns pointer to link for bundle head.
 */
struct ppp_link *
find_bundle_head(struct ppp_link *newlink)
{
  struct mp_state *mp;
  struct xcp_state *xcp,*xcpp,*xcpn;

  /* Search for matching bundle based on peer name and ED. */
  for (mp = global_mp_list; mp != NULL; mp = mp->next)
    if (((newlink->peername == NULL && mp->links->peername == NULL) ||
         (newlink->peername != NULL && mp->links->peername != NULL &&
          newlink->pn_size == mp->links->pn_size &&
          memcmp(newlink->peername,mp->links->peername,newlink->pn_size)
            == 0)) &&
        ((newlink->endpoint == NULL && mp->links->endpoint == NULL) ||
         (newlink->endpoint != NULL && mp->links->endpoint != NULL &&
          newlink->ep_size == mp->links->ep_size &&
```

```
                    memcmp(newlink->endpoint,mp->links->endpoint,newlink->ep_size)
                        == 0)))
            break;

      /* If no such bundle exists, then create it now. */
      if (mp == NULL) {
        struct ppp_link *lptr;

        mp = malloc(sizeof(*mp));
        if (mp == NULL)
          return NULL;
        memset(mp,'\0',sizeof(*mp));
        mp->links = NULL;
        mp->frags = NULL;
        mp->next = global_mp_list;
        global_mp_list = mp;
        lptr = mp->lptr = create_ppp_link(NULL,NULL);
        /* Everything but LCP and authentication moves to bundle level. */
        xcpp = NULL;
        for (xcp = newlink->xcp_list; xcp != NULL; xcpp = xcp, xcp = xcpn) {
          xcpn = xcp->next;
          if (xcp->proto < 0xC000 && xcp->proto != PPP_PROTO_ECP_LINK &&
              xcp->proto != PPP_PROTO_CCP_LINK) {
            if (xcpp != NULL)
              xcpp->next = xcp->next;
            else
              newlink->xcp_list = xcp->next;
            xcp->next = lptr->xcp_list;
            lptr->xcp_list = xcp;
            xcp->link = lptr;
            xcp = xcpp;
          }
        }
        lptr->mp = mp;
        /*
         * The MP defragmenter actually lives at the bundle level, since
         * all links actually demultiplex at the bundle level.
         */
        lptr->handle = add_xcp(lptr,PPP_PROTO_MP,mp_handler,NULL);
        lptr->link_output = mp_output;
      } else {
        /* Remove unwanted XCPs */
        for (xcp = newlink->xcp_list; xcp != NULL; xcp = xcpn) {
          xcpn = xcp->next;
          if (xcp->proto < 0xC000 && xcp->proto != PPP_PROTO_ECP_LINK &&
              xcp->proto != PPP_PROTO_CCP_LINK)
            destroy_xcp(xcp);
        }
      }
      newlink->seq = mp->lptr->seq;
      newlink->next = mp->links;
      mp->links = mp->next_out_link = newlink;
      mp->numlinks++;
      newlink->mp = mp;
      return mp->lptr;
}

/*
 * Add an XCP to a PPP link.
 */
void *
add_xcp(struct ppp_link *lptr, uint16 proto, void (*handler)(),
        void (*sender)())
{
  struct xcp_state *xcp;

  xcp = (struct xcp_state *)malloc(sizeof(*xcp));
  if (xcp == NULL)
    return NULL;
```

```c
  memset(xcp,'\0',sizeof(*xcp));
  xcp->state = Initial;
  xcp->proto = proto;
  xcp->handler = handler;
  xcp->send_data = sender;
  xcp->link = lptr;
  xcp->next = lptr->xcp_list;
  lptr->xcp_list = xcp;
  return (void *)xcp;
}

/*
 * Normal data sender for most NCP protocols.
 */
void
generic_sender(struct xcp_state *xcp, octet *outdata, int outlen)
{
  struct ppp_link *lptr = xcp->link;

  (*lptr->link_output)(lptr,outdata,outlen,xcp->proto);
}

/*
 * This function creates a new PPP state structure for a single PPP
 * link.  The outhandler function will be called with the user's handle
 * (a blind pointer), a pointer to the data to send, and the length
 * of the data.
 */
void *
create_ppp_link(void *handle, void (*outhandler)())
{
  struct ppp_link *lptr;

  lptr = (struct ppp_link *)malloc(sizeof(*lptr));
  if (lptr == NULL)
    return NULL;
  memset(lptr,'\0',sizeof(*lptr));
  lptr->xcp_list = NULL;
  lptr->handle = handle;
  lptr->link_output = normal_output;
  lptr->user_output = outhandler;
  lptr->mtu = 1500;
  lptr->mp = NULL;
  if (add_xcp(lptr,PPP_PROTO_LCP,lcp_handler,generic_sender) == NULL) {
    destroy_ppp_link((void *)lptr);
    return NULL;
  }
  /* Other NCPs may be initialized here with add_xcp or added later. */
  return (void *)lptr;
}

/*
 * Remove storage associated with an XCP.
 */
void
destroy_xcp(struct xcp_state *xcp)
{
  struct ppp_link *lptr = xcp->link;
  struct xcp_state *xcprev;

  if (xcp == lptr->xcp_list)
    lptr->xcp_list = xcp->next;
  else {
    for (xcprev = lptr->xcp_list; xcprev != NULL; xcprev =
           xcprev->next)
      if (xcprev->next == xcp) {
        xcprev->next = xcp->next;
        break;
      }
```

```
    }
    free(xcp);
}


/*
 * Delete an MP session.
 */
static void
destroy_mp(struct mp_state *mp)
{
    struct mp_state *mlp;
    struct mp_fragment *frag,*fragn;

    if (global_mp_list == mp)
        global_mp_list = mp->next;
    else {
        for (mlp = global_mp_list; mlp != NULL; mlp = mlp->next)
            if (mlp->next == mp) {
                mlp->next = mp->next;
                break;
            }
    }
    fragn = mp->frags;
    while ((frag = fragn) != NULL) {
        fragn = frag->next;
        free(frag);
    }
    free(mp);
}

/*
 * Detach a link from an MP bundle and tear down the bundle if no
 * more links are active.
 */
static void
mp_detach(struct ppp_link *link)
{
    struct mp_state *mp = link->mp;
    struct ppp_link *lp;

    link->mp = NULL;
    if (--mp->numlinks <= 0) {
        destroy_mp(mp);
        return;
    }
    if (mp->links == link)
        mp->links = link->next;
    else {
        for (lp = mp->links; lp != NULL; lp = lp->next)
            if (lp->next == link) {
                lp->next = link->next;
                break;
            }
    }
    if (mp->next_out_link == link)
        mp->next_out_link = NULL;
}

/*
 * Tear down a PPP link.
 */
void
destroy_ppp_link(void *link)
{
    struct ppp_link *lptr = (struct ppp_link *)link;
    struct xcp_state *xcp;

    if (lptr->mp != NULL)
        mp_detach(lptr);
```

```
  while ((xcp = lptr->xcp_list) != NULL)
    destroy_xcp(xcp);
  free(lptr);
}

/* Only for testing purposes. */
void
set_link_mtu(void *handle, int mtu)
{
  struct ppp_link *lptr = (struct ppp_link *)handle;

  lptr->mtu = mtu;
}
```

Appendix

C

PPP RFCs

This is a list of PPP-related RFCs that are current as of August 1997.

In Numeric Order

1332	Internet Protocol (IPCP). Older version is 1172.
1377	OSI (OISNLCP).
1378	AppleTalk (ATCP).
1552	IPX (IPXCP).
1553	IPX header compression (CIPX).
1570	LCP extensions; includes dial-back, identification, self-describing-padding, and other options. Older version is 1548.
1598	PPP on X.25.
1618	PPP on ISDN.
1619	PPP on SONET/SDH.
1634	IPXWAN. Older versions are 1551 and 1362.
1638	Bridging (BCP). Older version is 1220.
1661	The base document for PPP; contains the state machine and LCP options. Older versions are 1548, 1331, 1171, and 1134.
1662	PPP over HDLC-type framing; transmission of PPP over various media. Older version is 1549.
1663	Numbered mode (reliable transmission).
1762	DECNet Phase IV (DNCP). Older version is 1376.
1763	Banyan Vines (BVCP).
1764	XNS (XNSCP).
1841	LAN extension.
1877	Name server addresses with IPCP.
1915	Allows patented techniques for CCP/ECP.
1962	Data compression (CCP).
1963	Serial data transport (SDTP).
1967	LZS-DCP compression.
1968	Encryption (ECP).
1969	DES encryption (DESE).

1973	PPP on FrameRelay.
1974	STAC compression.
1975	Magnalink compression.
1976	DCE compression.
1977	BSD compression.
1978	Predictor compression.
1979	Deflate compression.
1989	Link Quality Monitoring (LQM). Older version is 1333.
1990	Multilink (MP). Older version is 1717.
1993	FZA compression.
1994	Authentication (CHAP). Older version is 1334 and includes PAP.
2023	IP version 6 (IPV6CP).
2043	SNA (SNACP).
2097	NetBIOS (NBFCP).
2125	Bandwidth allocation (BACP).
2153	Vendor extensions.

Grouped by Function

Basic PPP

1661	The base document for PPP; contains the state machine and LCP options. Older versions are 1548, 1331, 1171, and 1134.
1662	PPP over HDLC-type framing; transmission of PPP over various media. Older version is 1549.

LCP Options and Authentication

1570	LCP extensions; includes dial-back, identification, self-describing-padding, and other options. Older version is 1548.
1663	Numbered mode (reliable transmission).
1989	Link Quality Monitoring (LQM). Older version is 1333.
1994	Authentication (CHAP). Older version is 1334 and includes PAP.
2153	Vendor extensions.

Network Protocols

1332	Internet Protocol (IPCP). Older version is 1172.
1377	OSI (OISNLCP).
1378	AppleTalk (ATCP).
1552	IPX (IPXCP).
1553	IPX header compression (CIPX).
1634	IPXWAN. Older versions are 1551 and 1362.

1638	Bridging (BCP). Older version is 1220.
1762	DECNet Phase IV (DNCP). Older version is 1376.
1763	Banyan Vines (BVCP).
1764	XNS (XNSCP).
1841	LAN extension.
1877	Name server addresses with IPCP.
2023	IP version 6 (IPV6CP).
2043	SNA (SNACP).
2097	NetBIOS (NBFCP).

Media

1598	PPP on X.25.
1618	PPP on ISDN.
1619	PPP on SONET/SDH.

Compression/Encryption

1915	Allows patented techniques for CCP/ECP.
1962	Data compression (CCP).
1963	Serial data transport (SDTP).
1967	LZS-DCP compression.
1968	Encryption (ECP).
1969	DES encryption (DESE).
1973	PPP on FrameRelay.
1974	STAC compression.
1975	Magnalink compression.
1976	DCE compression.
1977	BSD compression.
1978	Predictor compression.
1979	Deflate compression.
1993	FZA compression.

Multilink

1990	Multilink (MP). Older version is 1717.
2125	Bandwidth allocation (BACP).

Appendix

D

Decimal, Hexadecimal, Octal, and Standard Characters

Dec	Hex	Oct	ASCII		Dec	Hex	Oct	ASCII		Dec	Hex	Oct	ASCII
0	00	000	NUL		30	1E	036	RS		60	3C	074	<
1	01	001	SOH		31	1F	037	US		61	3D	075	=
2	02	002	STX		32	20	040	SP		62	3E	076	>
3	03	003	ETX		33	21	041	!		63	3F	077	?
4	04	004	EOT		34	22	042	"		64	40	100	@
5	05	005	ENQ		35	23	043	#		65	41	101	A
6	06	006	ACK		36	24	044	$		66	42	102	B
7	07	007	BEL		37	25	045	%		67	43	103	C
8	08	010	BS		38	26	046	&		68	44	104	D
9	09	011	HT		39	27	047	'		69	45	105	E
10	0A	012	LF		40	28	050	(		70	46	106	F
11	0B	013	VT		41	29	051	)		71	47	107	G
12	0C	014	FF		42	2A	052	*		72	48	110	H
13	0D	015	CR		43	2B	053	+		73	49	111	I
14	0E	016	SO		44	2C	054	,		74	4A	112	J
15	0F	017	SI		45	2D	055	-		75	4B	113	K
16	10	020	DLE		46	2E	056	.		76	4C	114	L
17	11	021	DC1		47	2F	057	/		77	4D	115	M
18	12	022	DC2		48	30	060	0		78	4E	116	N
19	13	023	DC3		49	31	061	1		79	4F	117	O
20	14	024	DC4		50	32	062	2		80	50	120	P
21	15	025	NAK		51	33	063	3		81	51	121	Q
22	16	026	SYN		52	34	064	4		82	52	122	R
23	17	027	ETB		53	35	065	5		83	53	123	S
24	18	030	CAN		54	36	066	6		84	54	124	T
25	19	031	EM		55	37	067	7		85	55	125	U
26	1A	032	SUB		56	38	070	8		86	56	126	V
27	1B	033	ESC		57	39	071	9		87	57	127	W
28	1C	034	FS		58	3A	072	:		88	58	130	X
29	1D	035	GS		59	3B	073	;		89	59	131	Y

Dec	Hex	Oct	ASCII
90	5A	132	Z
91	5B	133	[
92	5C	134	\
93	5D	135	]
94	5E	136	^
95	5F	137	_
96	60	140	`
97	61	141	a
98	62	142	b
99	63	143	c
100	64	144	d
101	65	145	e
102	66	146	f
103	67	147	g
104	68	150	h
105	69	151	i
106	6A	152	j
107	6B	153	k
108	6C	154	l
109	6D	155	m
110	6E	156	n
111	6F	157	o
112	70	160	p
113	71	161	q
114	72	162	r
115	73	163	s
116	74	164	t
117	75	165	u
118	76	166	v
119	77	167	w
120	78	170	x
121	79	171	y
122	7A	172	z
123	7B	173	{
124	7C	174		
125	7D	175	}
126	7E	176	~
127	7F	177	DEL

Dec	Hex	Oct	ANSI/ISO 8859-1.2
128	80	200	PAD
129	81	201	HOP
130	82	202	BPH
131	83	203	NBH
132	84	204	IND
133	85	205	NEL
134	86	206	SSA
135	87	207	ESA
136	88	210	HTS
137	89	211	HTJ
138	8A	212	VTS
139	8B	213	PLD
140	8C	214	PLU
141	8D	215	RI
142	8E	216	SS2
143	8F	217	SS3
144	90	220	DCS
145	91	221	PU1
146	92	222	PU2
147	93	223	STS
148	94	224	CCH
149	95	225	MW
150	96	226	SPA
151	97	227	EPA
152	98	230	SOS
153	99	231	SGCI
154	9A	232	SCI
155	9B	233	CSI
156	9C	234	ST
157	9D	235	OSC
158	9E	236	PM
159	9F	237	APC
160	A0	240	NBS
161	A1	241	invert !
162	A2	242	cent
163	A3	243	Pound
164	A4	244	currency

Dec	Hex	Oct	ANSI/ISO 8859-1.2
165	A5	245	Yen
166	A6	246	vert bar
167	A7	247	section
168	A8	250	diaeresis
169	A9	251	copyright
170	AA	252	fem. ordinal
171	AB	253	<<
172	AC	254	not
173	AD	255	—
174	AE	256	registered
175	AF	257	macron/overbar
176	B0	260	degree
177	B1	261	+-
178	B2	262	super 2
179	B3	263	super 3
180	B4	264	acute
181	B5	265	micro
182	B6	266	para./pilcro
183	B7	267	middle dot
184	B8	270	cedilla
185	B9	271	super 1
186	BA	272	masc. ordinal
187	BB	273	>>
188	BC	274	1/4
189	BD	275	1/2
190	BE	276	3/4
191	BF	277	invert ?
192	C0	300	A grave
193	C1	301	A acute
194	C2	302	A circum
195	C3	303	A tilde
196	C4	304	A umlaut
197	C5	305	A ring
236	EC	354	i grave
237	ED	355	i acute
238	EE	356	i circum
239	EF	357	i umlaut

Dec	Hex	Oct	ANSI/ISO 8859-1.2
198	C6	306	AE
199	C7	307	C cedilla
200	C8	310	E grave
201	C9	311	E acute
202	CA	312	E circum
203	CB	313	E umlaut
204	CC	314	I grave
205	CD	315	I acute
206	CE	316	I circum
207	CF	317	I umlaut
208	D0	320	Eth
209	D1	321	N tilde
210	D2	322	O grave
211	D3	323	O acute
212	D4	324	O circum
213	D5	325	O tilde
214	D6	326	O umlaut
215	D7	327	multiply
216	D8	330	O slash
217	D9	331	U grave
218	DA	332	U acute
219	DB	333	U circum
220	DC	334	U umlaut
221	DD	335	Y acute
222	DE	336	Thorn
223	DF	337	Ess-tzet
224	E0	340	a grave
225	E1	341	a acute
226	E2	342	a circum
227	E3	343	a tilde
228	E4	344	a umlaut
229	E5	345	a ring
230	E6	346	ae
231	E7	347	c cedilla
232	E8	350	e grave
233	E9	351	e acute
234	EA	352	e circum
235	EB	353	e umlaut

Dec	Hex	Oct	ANSI/ISO 8859-1.2
240	F0	360	eth
241	F1	361	n tilde
242	F2	362	o grave
243	F3	363	o acute
244	F4	364	o circum
245	F5	365	o tilde
246	F6	366	o umlaut
247	F7	367	divide
248	F8	370	o slash
249	F9	371	u grave
250	FA	372	u acute
251	FB	373	u circum
252	FC	374	u umlaut
253	FD	375	y acute
254	FE	376	thorn
255	FF	377	y umlaut

Index

AAL-5, 9
ACCM (Asynchronous Control Character
    Map), 14, 15, 16, 47–48, 136, 149
ACFC (Address and Control Field
    Compression), 50–51
ACP (Access Control Protocol), 5
active bandwidth management, 111,
    125–129
Address and Control Field Compression
    (ACFC) option (LCP), 50–51
address field, HDLC, 10
Address Resolution Protocol (ARP), 7,
    74–75
aggregation of multiple links, 111,
    113–125
AHDLC (asynchronous HDLC), 12–16,
    25–26
AIX, 157–159
Align NPDU option (OSINLCP), 85
analyzers, 177
Annex, 175
AppleTalk (ATCP), 2, 182
    description of, 82–84
    multiple protocols example with,
    140–144
    Address option (ATCP), 83
    Compression Protocol option (ATCP), 84
APPN-HPR (Advanced Peer-to-Peer
    Networking High Performance
    Routing), 85
ARAP (AppleTalk Remote Access
    Protocol), 20, 21, 22, 84
ARP (Address Resolution Protocol), 7
Ascend Communications, 125, 131,
    176–177
asynchronous auto-detect, 20–22
asynchronous HDLC (AHDLC), 12–16,
    24–26
asynchronous line hardware, 7–8
ATM (Asynchronous Transfer Mode),
    18–19, 26, 112, 113
Authentication Protocol option (LCP), 48

authentication
    examples of traces, 137–144
    problems with, 147
    protocols, 55–65
auto-detecting, 20–24
    asynchronous, 20–22
    synchronous, 22–24
Azure Technologies, 188

BACP (Bandwidth Allocation Control
    Procedure), 55, 126
    options with, 126–127
    reasons for using, 127–129
    switched circuit integration and, 30
bake-offs, 187
bandwidth management, 111–133
Banyan, 86–87
BCP (bridging), 20, 87–91
BCVP (Banyan Vines), 86–87
Beginning-of-fragment (B bit) option
    (MP), 119
bit-synchronous HDLC, 16–18
BLAST (Blocked Asynchronous
    Transmission), 2
bonding, 111, 113
BOOTP, 76, 78
Bridge Identification option (BCP), 88
bridging (BCP), 20, 87–91
Bridging Authorization Protocol, 65
BRI (Basic-Rate ISDN), 111, 177
BRI S/T, 9
British Telecom, 106
BSD LZW compress option (CCP), 99, 106

Calgary Corpus, 188
callback, 125, 129–130
Call-back Control Protocol (CBCP), 53,
    130
Call-Back option (LCP), 52–53
Call-Request (BACP), 127–128

221